The LOAVES and FISHES COOKBOOK

By Anna Pump

with Gen LeRoy

Illustrated by Philippe Weisbecker

THE LOAVES *and* FISHES PRESS

Für meine Mutter
von der ich gelernt habe
mit Freude zu kochen,
Neues zu entdecken
und zu geniessen

For further information, contact the publisher:
THE LOAVES *and* FISHES PRESS
Box 318
Sagaponack, NY 11962

Library of Congress Cataloging-in-Publication Data
Pump, Anna.
The loaves and fishes cookbook.

Includes index.
1. Cookery. I. LeRoy, Gen. II. Title.
[TX715.P957 1987] 641.5 86-24435

Printed in the United States of America

ACKNOWLEDGMENTS

This book belongs as much to Gen and Sybille as it does to me. Gen sorted out my ramblings, organized my thoughts and has written this book the way I would have liked to have done. Sybille, my daughter, who is also Chef at Loaves and Fishes, helped test and retest all the recipes, never once complaining. I want to thank Detlef, my husband and my best friend for his untiring support. Also Alison Bond, my friend and agent, for believing in me, Arlene Friedman and Andrea Raab, our editors, for guiding us along the way, and Wendy Palitz and Philippe Weisbecker, for their creative talents. And to Harm Pump, my son, for having a great appetite and astonishing patience while trying at one and the same meal Curried Chicken Salad, Oriental Chicken Salad, and Mexican Chicken Salad. Dennis Holland was part of the team, commenting enthusiastically and astutely as he typed the manuscript for us. Bridget LeRoy and Bernadette Penotti made research seem like so much fun, thank you. And a special thanks to Tim Higgins, Michael Fengler, my son-in-law, and Alex Werner for keeping things running smoothly at Loaves and Fishes while this book was being compiled. And, finally, many thanks to all my friends and customers for their encouragement, and discriminating palates.

A.P.

CONTENTS

INTRODUCTION

The pleasant hours of our life are all connected, by a more or less intangible link, with some memory of the table.
—Charles Monselet

y daughter, Sybille, turned to me one day at Loaves and Fishes and asked, "When did you decide to become a cook? When did you *know* this is what you wanted to do?" I thought about it for a moment and realized my decision hadn't sprung from any conscious effort on my part. I had always loved cooking. It simply was a way of life, something I had enjoyed doing from the time I was tall enough to reach the stove and old enough to measure out ingredients for a cake. I honestly couldn't think of another profession that would give me the same kind of pleasure.

I was born on a seventy-acre farm, in a small town named Tarp in northern Germany, about ten kilometers from the Danish border. Our farmhouse had about ten rooms and was sturdy enough to withstand the relentless, driving winds that sweep across the thin peninsula of land that separates the frigid North Sea from the shores of the Baltic. I find it an interesting coincidence that after so many years and so many miles I have finally settled in an area so similar to the one where I was raised. Loaves and Fishes, on Sagg Main Street, in Sagaponack, Long Island, sits about two miles from the Atlantic Ocean on one side, and about seven miles on the other from Long Island Sound. Another coincidence is that potato fields spread out all around the store. My father farmed potatoes, as well as crops of wheat, carrots, peas, rutabagas, and other vegetables and herbs. We also raised cattle, pigs, chickens, ducks, and geese. Ours was a working farm, and by that I mean that every single square inch of those precious seventy acres yielded produce at harvest time.

We made our own sausages, slaughtered and smoked our own meats, salted fresh fish which was delivered every morning by the fish man, who rolled into our yard on a three-wheeled wagon. We had fresh milk from our cows from which we made creams, cheeses, and butters, and fruit trees from which we made pies, cakes, sauces, and preserves.

After harvesting, the farm closed down in preparation for the long, cold winter. Carrots, potatoes, and rutabagas were stored in our basement, giving off a warm, musty fragrance throughout the cold months. Sealed jars of plums, apples, cherries, and pears filled wooden shelves. Wheels of cheeses sat atop another shelf, while milk and butter were stored in yet another part of the room.

Winter in Scandinavian countries is notoriously gloomy. The fog rolls in off the sea and hangs over the rooftops and bare trees until spring. It's a wet, bitter

cold that permeates your clothes and lodges inside the marrow of your bones. Yet, to me, winter was when all the fun began. The opera season opened in Flensburg and our parents went all the time, bringing loads of friends home with them afterwards.

Wintertime was for elegant entertainment. We never entertained less than fifteen people for dinner. Usually it was fifty. I suppose that is where I had my most immediate and practical training for catering parties. The holidays were a swirl of activity. My mother excelled at desserts. Every year her ingenuity reached new peaks. It was a warm, happy, exciting, busy atmosphere, filled with love and fun, and that's the feeling I carry with me when I think about cooking.

I never had second thoughts about entering cooking school. I wanted to continue learning so that I could improve at what I enjoyed doing the most. Soon after I graduated, I was married and we started a family. (Our son, Harm, lives in New Jersey, where we moved when we first came to the United States. Sybille, who with her husband, Michael, works at Loaves and Fishes, lives in Sag Harbor, which is a stone's throw from Noyac, where we have an old farmhouse of our own.)

I missed cooking on a grand scale. For a while I offered my services planning and cooking for private parties. In America there were new vegetables, fruits, nuts, herbs, and meats to experiment with. It was an altogether exciting time for me when we first moved here. A new world of culinary possibilities inspired me even more. I couldn't get enough of a day to do all I wanted to do.

My husband, Detlef, and I made yearly trips abroad, and I began taking notes at every restaurant, country inn, or sidewalk cafe where we stopped. We

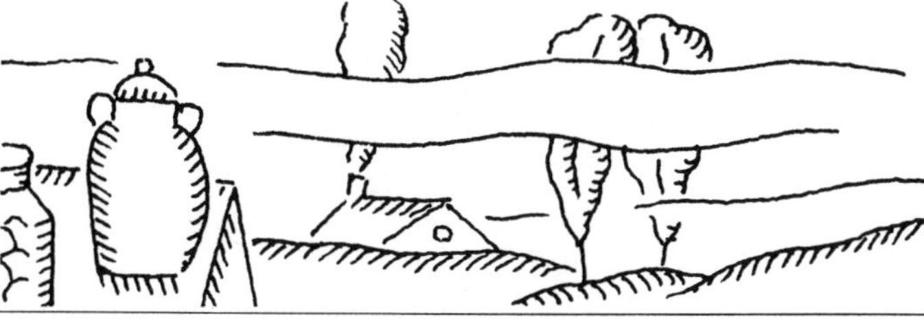

traveled through Mexico and came back infatuated with the food of that country. After spending winters in Italy, France, and Holland, my notebooks were crammed with so many ideas that they practically sprang from the pages as soon as we returned home. I read everything I could. I experimented and tested as often as I could. I was always open to new recipe ideas. I studied with James Beard, Maurice Moore-Betty, and Annemarie Huste. The more I learned, the more I wanted to do. But still I felt I had only a limited area into which I could channel all my energies and enthusiasm.

I took a job as a professional chef and caterer with a wonderful food store in Westhampton Beach on Long Island. It still wasn't enough. I gave classes to a group of professional people who had sophisticated palates, loved to cook, yet didn't have the time to spend in the kitchen. Creating quick dinners without losing quality or taste was a wonderful challenge.

Soon after that, I heard that a local food store very close to where we lived was for sale. All of my family and friends urged me to buy it. I was both excited and terrified at the prospect. I wanted to retain a certain integrity in my cooking. I didn't in any way want to become a "food factory" or dispel the intimacy gained by long associations with friends for whom I had catered privately. I never wanted there to be even a hint of complacency in anything I did.

I drove over myself. The kitchen had all the facilities I would need to cater on a grand scale. It was a small, cozy building surrounded by lush greenery and with enough space in the back to start my own garden, from which I would be able to gather the freshest produce to use in my cooking. I walked through the store and looked into every corner. I ran a finger over a

dusty window ledge. I sighed deeply and started towards a door, which opened onto a large room, where all the food would be displayed. I thought back to the excitement of my youth—the best times—the days when the house would be filled with friends, when my mother would constantly be baking fresh breads, muffins, tarts, and cakes, and cooking savory stuffed roasts and poultry. I remembered the beauty of our table set for twenty-four, the porcelain tureens gracing its center, filled with steaming, robust stew and spiked with the very best red wine. I thought back to the summers, and the steady hum of the bees outside our windows as we sat around sharing funny stories while sipping cool cucumber soup sprinkled with fresh dill. I put down my briefcase and took off my coat. At that precise moment I knew the store would be mine.

I love simple foods as well as grand. Dinners that take a half hour from skillet to plate are as important as a five-course dinner. A meal that can materialize in an hour and be presented with care, love, and pride is something every busy person longs to be able to do. You can; the recipes in this book will show you how. Some are more complicated, but basically I feel that if you have planned ahead, you can prepare any of the recipes in this book with ease. It has been written with you in mind, by someone who shares your love of a good, home-cooked meal.

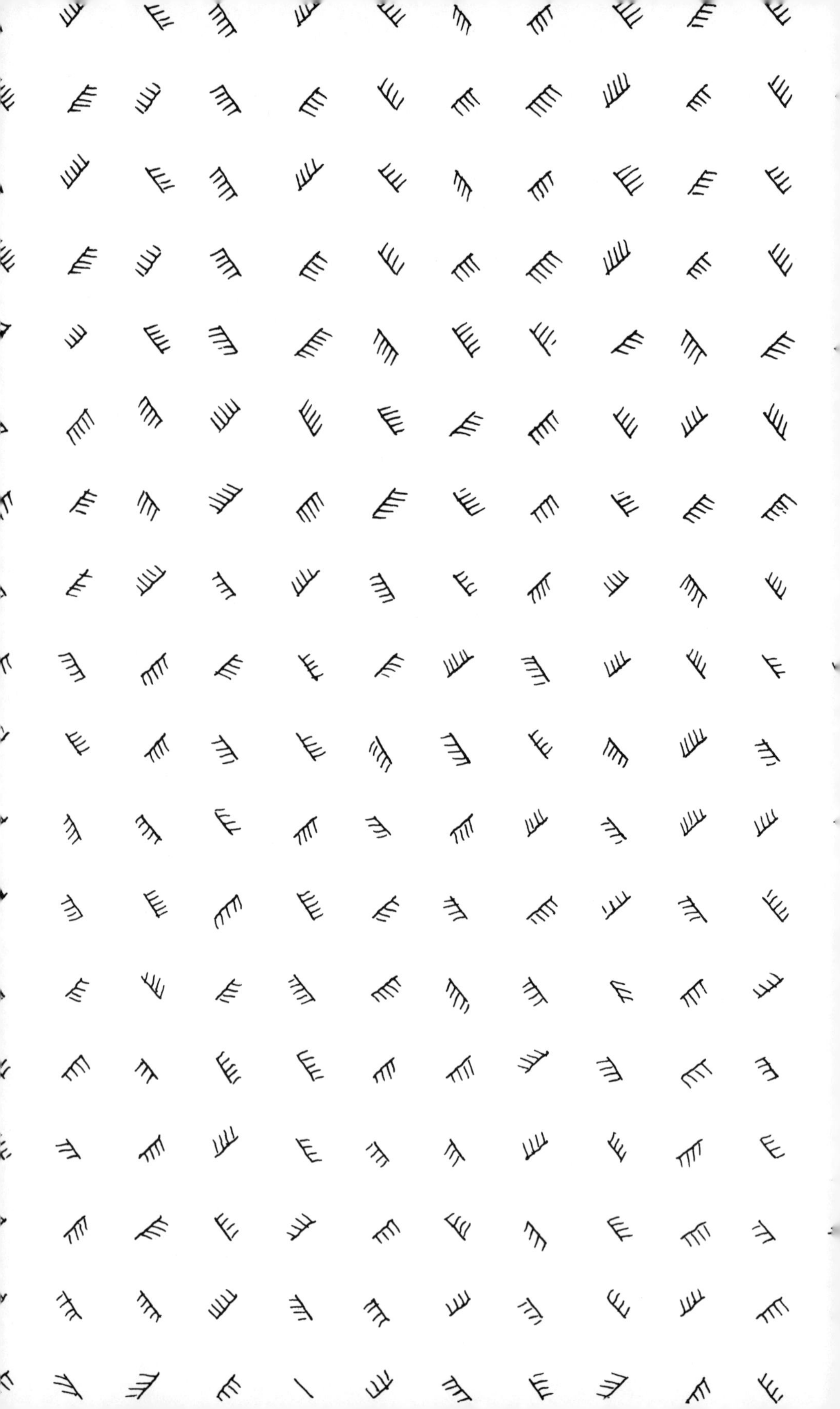

THE ESSENTIAL KITCHEN

The reward of a thing well done is to have done it.
—Ralph Waldo Emerson

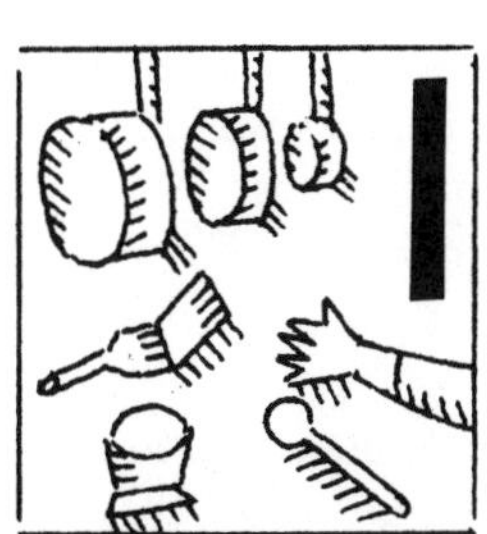

It makes no sense to scrimp on kitchen equipment. As the saying goes, a worker is only as good as his tools, and that is never truer than in the kitchen. Buy the best you can afford. You'll end up saving money in the long run. When you shop for pans, choose ones that are solid and heavy with tight-fitting lids. I personally prefer heavy aluminum pans lined with stainless steel. Thin pans will cause sauces to burn. They corrode much faster and can dent, distorting their shape—two additional hazards when you need even cooking. Make sure you have *good saucepans*, varying in size from a *1-quart* saucepan, used for simple jobs such as clarifying butter, to an *8-quart* saucepan, for making soups. All of them should have *lids.* A *10-quart* saucepan is necessary for making stock. It could be plain aluminum, since you never need to cook stock using such acidic products as lemon juice, wine, or egg yolks.

I am not recommending that you hurry out now and buy every piece of equipment I've just mentioned. But I do suggest that you get to know your kitchen well. Be sure you have all the right sized pans ready for you when you need them. There's nothing more frustrating than having a dinner half started and discovering you've misplaced or broken the lid of the pan you need to cover. Also, if you do decide to invest in additional equipment, just remember that pots and pans don't go out of style. If treated properly, they can last for years.

Another prerequisite would be *three skillets* of varying size, with *lids*. Topping the list would be a *12-inch* skillet, essential for browning meats, fish, and poultry. The smallest of these could be a *6-inch* skillet, ideal for making omelettes or crepes, especially if it's been treated with a special nonstick coating. *Straight-sided sauté pans,* with *covers,* in the *9-* to *12-inch* range, should also be a chief priority, as well as a *22-inch fish poacher.* A smaller size would be impractical: You can always poach a small fish in a large poacher.

There's nothing that dulls a sharp knife faster than slicing bread. Bread should be cut with a *serrated knife*. All the other knives you own should be top-quality instruments, with good balance, good handles, and good blades, and they should be stored in a *knife block*. With a *good set of knives* you will also need a *sharpening steel.* I used to tell my classes that it isn't necessary to do anything more to a knife than rinse it off, wipe it clean, and keep it sharp. You will also need a good *cleaver* for chopping meats and poultry. A *poultry scissors* is good only after the poultry has been cooked. It wasn't designed to cut raw meat, which brings me to another kitchen essential: *cutting boards*. I have a couple, one of which is set aside for onions and garlic.

For roasting I use an *8-quart oven pan* with a *lid.* I also find I need an *18-by-12-inch roasting pan,* as well as a *9-by-13-inch roasting pan* with *lid.* You should make certain you have *two* or *three* various sized *casserole* and *soufflé dishes*. These can be glass, china, pottery, or copper, as long as they're ovenproof.

When it comes to baking needs, I suggest using heavy-duty aluminum. You should have at least *two baking sheets,* one that should be approximately *12 by 18 inches.* You'll also need *one or two springform pans, several baking pans,* a *glass quiche pan,* and a couple of *9-by-5-inch loaf pans.* And don't forget a nice clean brick for weighing down your terrines, and a cooling rack. I have a recipe that calls for a *tube pan,* which is essential to have on hand for pound cakes. And of course, a couple of *muffin tins.*

The smaller tools necessary to stock a well-equipped kitchen are *a couple of metal spatulas* for lifting fish, omelettes, or frittatas from pan to plate and *a couple of rubber spatulas* for stirring, folding, and mixing. *Ladles, a meat pounder,* and *a pair of tongs* are musts. I use tongs all the time when turning meat in a skillet or transferring food from one receptacle to another. *Cheesecloth* is important for straining soups and stocks, also a *rolling pin*, some *cotton string* for tying rolled meats filled with stuffing or for stuffed roasts and poultry, a *trussing needle*, a few *pastry brushes*, a *kitchen scale*, and some *parchment paper*. Also *three good wire whisks* are needed: one with a *large balloon* for attaining the maximum volume when beating eggs, a *medium-sized whisk* for general use in beating and mixing, and a *small whisk* for omelettes. Peelers, colanders, measuring spoons and cups, mixing bowls, timers, salad spinners, wooden spoons, slotted spoons, zester, and graters are, I'm sure, already part of your kitchen.

Appliances are another priority for me. *A heavy-duty mixer* makes life so much easier. I use a KitchenAid, which I swear by. I also use my *Cuisinart* food processor to do a lot of work. That doesn't make my *blender* redundant; blenders are still essential for pureeing, chopping, and grating. Add to this list an *electric juicer* and an *electric coffee grinder*.

I store peppercorns in an extra coffee grinder so I can make freshly ground pepper whenever I need to.

I suppose I would have to rate hands as perhaps the most essential of all kitchen tools. I show my students how simple it is to separate eggs by moving the raw egg from palm to palm, easing the whites into a bowl and ending up with a perfect, unbroken yolk. Your hands are sensitive to temperature, consistency, and texture. They are gentle tools. You can toss a salad (and I urge you to do so only with your hands) without disturbing the fragility of tomato slices or mashing delicate wedges of avocado. Your hands know when the salad has been sufficiently coated. I mix with my hands, knead, whip, fold, blend, and stir. Your hands are the most important tools you own, and it's extremely fortunate that we can't misplace them or wear them out.

If you own good kitchen tools, excellent equipment, and reliable appliances, your kitchen will allow you to work wonders. You will become a cook who spends only quality time in the kitchen, turning out meals appreciated by everyone, yet simple to produce. The more planning ahead you do, the more competent a cook you will become. It's a wonderful feeling to walk into the kitchen and feel assured that everything you can possibly need is right there, within your reach.

THE ESSENTIAL PANTRY

Aside from the proper kitchen tools, equipment, and appliances, there is the Essential Pantry to consider: all the spices, herbs, oils, grains, and basics we usually need in one way or another. I mention them because they will all be needed for recipes in this book. It is always helpful to know what to store, how to store it, and the length of its shelf life.

If you keep hazelnuts, almonds, pecans, or walnuts for any length of time, they should be stored in the freezer; bread crumbs, too. If you plan to keep raisins, dried apricots, or prunes for more than three weeks, store them in the freezer, as well as shredded coconut. Yellow cornmeal, unbleached flour, and whole wheat flour could be stored in a dry place for six to eight weeks, but after that it ought to be placed in the freezer, where it can last for up to a year.

For shelf storage, I recommend keeping cans of Italian plum tomatoes, crushed tomatoes, tomato paste, flat anchovies, artichoke hearts, and water chestnuts.

Also for shelf storage would be a supply of baking powder, baking soda, unsweetened baking chocolate, chocolate chips, and cocoa powder. These store a long time at room temperature.

Cornstarch, oatmeal, orzo, granulated sugar, confectioners' sugar, and light and dark brown sugars, as well as the ever-important packets of yeast, should all be stored in a dry place.

Dry pastas, brown rice, converted rice, and Italian rice could all be stored in your pantry, as could safflower oil, peanut oil, and olive oil. I buy imported olive oil from Tuscany, a high-quality, deep, fruity, extra-virgin olive oil that has a lot of body to it. Also you'll need red, white, and sherry vinegars. Spend money on these products, since the better the ingredients, the better your food. Capers, tarragon leaves in vinegar, black peppercorns, hot red pepper flakes, ground sesame seed (tahini), and oyster sauce all last a long time, as does soy sauce, Tabasco, Dijon mustard, and mango chutney. I know that some people think the last two products need to be stored in the refrigerator, but they don't.

You will need a good bottle each of French

Most cans have a recommended shelf life printed somewhere on the label or can, but if they don't, I wouldn't keep them longer than six to eight months.

The discoloration that affects chocolate, its whitish "bloom," comes not from spoilage but from improper storage temperature: It was either too hot or too cold. The chocolate, however, is perfectly usable.

Orzo, a rice-shaped Greek pasta, can be purchased in most grocery stores.

Whenever a recipe calls for wine, I always mean good-quality wine. If it's not good enough to drink, it's not good enough to cook with. All the spirits used in cooking recipes should be the best. They last a long time, since most of the recipes only require a tablespoonful of this or that.

Buy an inexpensive nutmeg grater and use whole nutmegs only.

In the Planning Ahead section I will give you a recipe for making your own vanilla essence, which lasts nearly forever.

brandy and cognac, dark rum, Framboise, Calvados, Kahlua, Madeira, port wine, dry white wine, red wine, and sherry.

As far as spices, herbs, and condiments are concerned, I have made sure that in all the recipes that require the use of a fresh herb, I have given alternative measures for dried herbs. That's to help you if the fresh herbs simply are not available. I advise you not to buy these in quantity, because dried herbs shouldn't be kept more than six months; that's usually the term of their effectiveness. This includes: bay leaves, thyme, tarragon, rosemary, fennel, cayenne pepper, caraway seeds, ground white pepper, oregano, basil, sage, coriander, turmeric, saffron, and coarse salt. In the Planning Ahead section I will suggest ways to store fresh herbs in oil so they will last for at least four months in the refrigerator. This is yet another alternative to using dried herbs.

When you shop for curry powder, examine the label. It should be the best, and the best is a blend of many spices, including coriander, turmeric, fenugreek, cumin, cayenne pepper, ginger, allspice, and nutmeg. Buy the best cinnamon, allspice, cardamom, cumin seeds, cloves, ground black pepper, and whole peppercorns. Also keep some almond extract on the shelves and some pure vanilla extract.

Buy a large chunk of Parmesan, grate it, and keep it in the refrigerator inside a sealed plastic container. Always have some blue cheese on hand, and some Swiss or Gruyère, since these are the cheeses you will need in preparing many of the following recipes.

Don't save pennies on your pantry stores, because all the effort in the world will yield only mediocre results. To me, the best is just good enough.

PLANNING AHEAD

The theme of this book deals with the flexibility and ease that come from having all the necessary basics on hand *before* you start to cook. I've written about the Essential Kitchen tools, equipment, and appliances, and all the items that help make up the Essential Pantry. In this section I want to talk about another important element that will help make cooking more enjoyable by cutting down on the time it takes to prepare a meal. It's called Planning Ahead.

In my very first class I impressed my students with the idea of using only the freshest produce that could be found in the marketplace. You simply cannot fake quality, no matter how simple or grand and complicated the meal gets. Every single component part eventually makes up the whole, which means that everything you use in the recipe ought to be the best you can possibly provide. For example, we talked about stock, a fundamental ingredient found in so many recipes. Within ten minutes the students had two stock pots started, one with leftover beef bones I provided, the other with a bag of frozen leftover chicken parts. Why should anyone go out and buy cans of stock when homemade stock is more economical, tastier, healthier, and very easy to make?

In the Breads section you will have to use your discretion about when to preheat your oven. Many of the recipes require rising time, and I want to make a blanket rule that you preheat the oven on the last rising.

We talked next about bread. Again I felt strongly that it wasn't necessary to buy store bread if they could make some of their own, simply and effortlessly. So while the stock pots were brewing on the stove, we put together a bowl of basic white dough, which was enough for six loaves of bread. It took almost no time at all to assemble, and while the dough was rising, we made some clarified butter, enough to last about three weeks. But that only took a couple of minutes, so we made some mayonnaise—three separate kinds—and we *still* had time on our hands.

I then showed the class how to make very simple pie and tart crusts that could be frozen. We made four in a few minutes more than it would have taken to make one. What would be a wonderful topping for a fruit pie? Crème Fraîche! So we made some, which we stored in the refrigerator. I reminded them that this wasn't only a dessert item; Crème Fraîche is excellent for enriching cream sauces. By this time the dough needed to be transferred to the loaf pans and given time to rise again.

During the next hour we mixed large quantities of fresh herbs in olive oil. They were placed in jars, to be used in salad dressing, in pasta sauces, stews, or soups. We also made two salad dressings to use alternately throughout the week. In our salad section we have a different salad dressing per salad in order to offer you a wide variety from which to choose.

Then we made vanilla essence, Vanilla Sugar, and while the loaves were baking, we peeled and seeded a bushel of freshly picked autumn tomatoes and placed them inside pint and quart containers to freeze. They would come in very handy and be much appreciated in midwinter when used in sauces or stews, even soups, reminding us in February of the sweet flavorfulness of summer vegetables. We made two separate pesto sauces, and roasted some red peppers to store in oil.

It was getting close to the end of our four-hour session. We took the loaves out of the oven to cool. We strained the stock into quart containers. Then we stepped back and looked at what we had accomplished in less than four hours: four pie crusts, all of which could be frozen; six loaves of bread, which could be frozen; ten quarts of deliciously rich, homemade stock that would last up to three months in the freezer; clarified butter, salad dressings, mayonnaises, herbs in oil, pestos, vanilla essence and sugar, Crème Fraîche, and a substantial amount of fresh tomatoes ready for the freezer. Everyone marveled at how much we had accomplished in so little time. All that was needed was poultry, fish, or meat and some fresh produce from the market and we could have tried almost any recipe in this book. And that is what I mean by Planning Ahead.

I urge you to read each recipe over carefully before starting. When planning the format for this book I wanted to provide as much information as I could for each individual recipe so that you never have to look up additional pages. I have included storing suggestions, recipes for leftovers, freezer and refrigerator life when called for, the basic yield of each recipe, and the approximate time it takes to make each one. I have mentioned marinating times, soaking times, and the point at which you should preheat the oven.

The kitchen is the heart of so many homes. It should be treated with all the respect and honor that is its due. Nothing should be spared when planning a meal, except for your own precious time. I hope this three-part section helps prove that with a small amount of planning ahead; with good equipment, tools, and appliances; and with a well-stocked pantry, freezer, and refrigerator, cooking will become more fun, more exciting, and simpler than you can imagine.

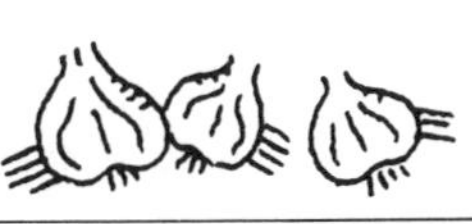

Begin the habit of saving leftover chicken, duck, goose, or turkey parts in a large plastic bag in your freezer. Whenever you find yourself running low on stock, you will have an ample supply of poultry necks, wings, and backs to make yourself a wonderful stock. I suggest you freeze the stock in smaller quantities because many of the recipes in this book call for 2, 3, or 4 cups of stock. It would be convenient if you had just the right amount for those recipes measured out beforehand. Don't forget to label and mark the new stock with the date it was made. Stock usually lasts in the freezer for 3 months.

CHICKEN STOCK

Make this at least a day ahead of time.

5 pounds chicken parts: backs, necks, and wings
2 large onions, peeled and quartered
2 cloves garlic, peeled and crushed
1 carrot, trimmed
8 sprigs Italian parsley
2 bay leaves
5 sprigs fresh thyme or 1 teaspoon dried
2 teaspoons salt
1 teaspoon black peppercorns, bruised

Place the chicken in a 10-quart stockpot. Add water to fill the vessel three-quarters full. Add the rest of the ingredients. Bring to a boil and simmer, covered, for 2 hours. Remove cover and simmer 1½ hours more.

Line a large colander with a cotton kitchen towel. Strain the chicken stock through the lined colander into a large bowl. Discard the solids. Ladle the stock into 1-quart containers. Chill overnight. Next day, remove and discard the fat from the top of the containers. Freeze whatever you will not use within the next 4 days.

Yields: approximately 5 quarts

Preparation time: 3 hours 30 minutes (excluding refrigeration time)

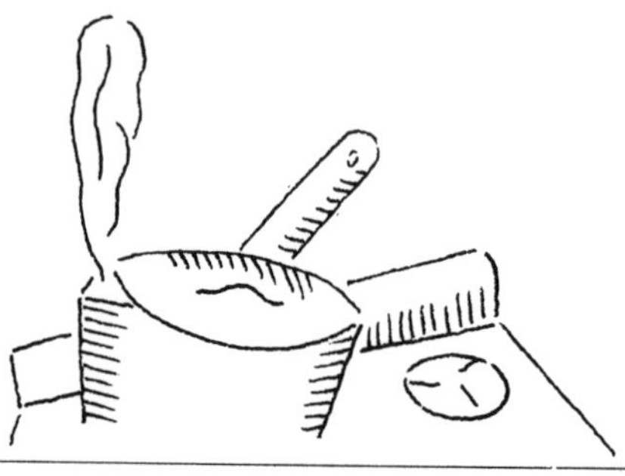

BEEF STOCK

This stock can be used to deglaze, for sauces, to braise vegetables and meats, and as an addition to soups. It must be made at least a day ahead of time.

5 to 6 pounds beef bones, cracked into several pieces
Leftover meat or fat trimmed from steak
2- to 3-pounds fresh chuck steak or shinbone with meat
2 carrots, cut into 1-inch pieces
4 large onions, quartered, unpeeled
10 sprigs parsley
2 parsnips
3 cloves garlic, peeled and crushed
2 bay leaves
2 tablespoons fresh thyme or 2 teaspoons dried
2 teaspoons salt
2 teaspoons crushed black peppercorns

Preheat oven 450°F.

Place all the bones and meat in a large roasting pan. Roast for 1 hour. Remove from oven and transfer all the bones and meat to a 10-quart stockpot. On top of the stove, over high heat, deglaze the roasting pan with a cup of hot water, scraping up all the brown bits. Add to the stockpot. Fill the pot three-quarters full with water. Add all the vegetables and seasonings. Bring to a boil. Simmer, covered, for about 2 hours. Remove the cover and simmer 1 hour more.

Line a large colander with a cotton kitchen towel. Strain the beef stock through the lined colander into a large bowl. Discard the solids. Chill overnight. Next day, remove and discard all the fat from the top. Pour into containers and store in the refrigerator or freezer.

Yields: approximately 5 quarts

Preparation time: 4 hours (excluding refrigeration time)

TO BRUISE PEPPERCORNS

Place peppercorns in a sturdy plastic bag. Lay it on your cutting board and hit it a couple of times with the broadside of your cleaver. This will crack the hull and core and release the flavor and aroma.

TO CRUSH PEPPERCORNS

Follow instructions as above only hit the peppercorns a few more times, breaking them apart for a coarser consistency.

BASIC WHITE BREAD

This recipe makes six loaves. If you have freezer space, make them all, otherwise you can halve the recipe and make three loaves.

3 tablespoons active dry yeast
1 cup plus 3 tablespoons lukewarm (110°F) water
1 tablespoon sugar
4 cups lukewarm (110°F) milk
1 cup (2 sticks) butter, melted and cooled to almost room temperature
¼ cup honey
6 egg yolks
12 to 13 cups unbleached white flour
3 tablespoons salt
1 egg white, lightly beaten

Dissolve the yeast in the water along with the sugar in the bowl of an electric mixer. Let it stand for 5 minutes. Add the milk, butter, and honey. Mix at medium speed until blended. Add the egg yolks. Add half the flour and salt. Mix at low speed for about 5 minutes. Add all but 1 cup of the remaining flour.

Mix at low speed for 5 minutes more. Turn the dough out onto a lightly floured surface. Knead with the remaining 1 cup flour until smooth and elastic. This will take about 8 minutes. Place it in a buttered bowl. Cover and let rise for 1 hour. Divide into 6 pieces. Place into buttered loaf pans or small casseroles, or whatever you like to bake your breads in. Let rise again until doubled in size.

Meanwhile, preheat oven to 350°F.

Gently brush the tops with the egg white. Bake for 40 to 45 minutes, or until the loaves sound hollow when tapped on the top.

Yields: 6 loaves

Preparation time: 2 hours 45 minutes (including rising time)

I do like a little bit of butter to my bread.
—A. A. Milne, *When We Were Very Young*

BASIC CRUST FOR PIES AND TARTS

Use these right from the freezer. They will be crisper when baked. Use them for any recipe in the Desserts section or for any savory tart. These crusts last for up to three months in the freezer.

4 cups unbleached white flour
¾ cup (1½ sticks) butter, cut into small pieces
¾ cup (1½ sticks) margarine, cut into small pieces
½ cup plus 2 tablespoons water

Place the flour in the bowl of a food processor with the metal blade in place. Add the butter and margarine. With five to six on-off motions, process the mixture until crumbly. With the motor running, add the water all at once. Process until the dough starts to stick together. Turn it out onto a lightly floured surface. Quickly gather the pastry into a ball. Flatten it into a disk. Wrap it in plastic wrap and refrigerate for 30 minutes.

Unwrap the dough and cut it into 4 pieces. With a floured rolling pin on a floured surface, roll each piece out to about ⅛-inch thickness. Fit the dough into 9-inch pie plates or tart pans. Wrap each in foil, label, and freeze.

Yields: 4 piecrusts or tarts
Preparation time: 45 minutes

CLARIFIED BUTTER

Clarified butter is needed for a great many of the recipes that require you to sauté meats, fish, or vegetables. I specify when to use plain butter and when to use clarified butter because they each give you a different result. Clarified butter, having no milk residue, doesn't burn.

1 cup (2 sticks) butter

Place the butter into a small saucepan and melt over low heat. Skim the foam off the top. Pour the clear butter into a crock, leaving the milky residue in the bottom of the pan. Store in the refrigerator covered and dated. It will keep for up to 3 weeks in the refrigerator.

Yields: ¾ cup

CRÈME FRAÎCHE

Crème Fraîche is excellent for cooking because it won't curdle when allowed to boil. It adds richness and flavor to many sauces and is also an excellent topping for fruit and desserts.

Always keep heavy cream on hand inside your refrigerator. So many delicious recipes call for it.

2 cups heavy cream
2 tablespoons buttermilk

Heat the cream until very hot, not boiling. Pour it into a container. Stir in the buttermilk. Cover and let it stand at room temperature until it is very thick, for about 24 hours. Store in the refrigerator for up to 3 weeks.

Yields: 2 cups

VANILLA BEANS IN VODKA

Buy Madagascar vanilla beans. They are the biggest and best sold today. If you're making custards, puddings, pie fillings, Crème Chantilly, Crème Anglaise, or Crème Brûlée, take a bean out of the vodka, cut the tip, and squeeze some of the essence into your recipe. It makes a major difference to the taste. Return that bean to the vodka, and it will continue to work. This lasts for years.

12 whole vanilla beans
3 cups vodka

Place the vanilla beans in a tall jar with a tight-fitting lid. Pour the vodka over them. Store at room temperature for about 3 weeks; it takes that long to soften the beans.

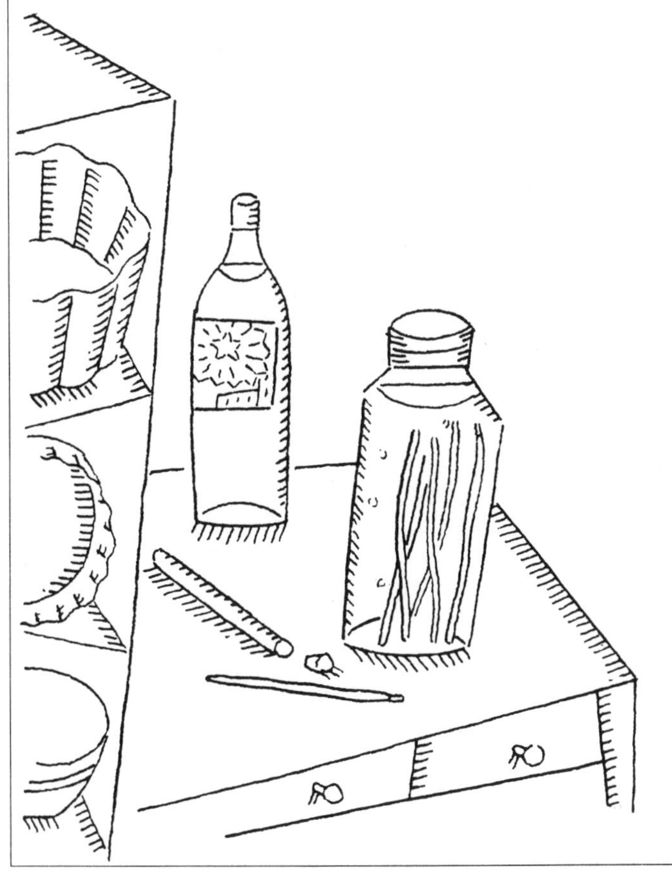

You may have to add a little vodka from time to time to top up the jar so that the vanilla beans are covered at all times.

VANILLA SUGAR

Open a box of confectioners' sugar into a plastic container. Take a fresh vanilla bean, split it lengthwise, scrape some of the seeds into the sugar, and mix well. Place the slit vanilla bean in the plastic container and store for 3 or 4 days. This is wonderful sprinkled over cookies, tarts, fruit pies, or in frostings.

BASIC MAYONNAISE

Mayonnaise is produced simply by adding the oils in droplets to the egg yolks while the blender or food processor is running. The result is best when all ingredients are at room temperature.

3 egg yolks
3/4 cup olive oil
3/4 cup safflower oil
2 tablespoons lemon juice or wine vinegar
1/2 teaspoon salt
1/8 teaspoon cayenne pepper

Place the egg yolks in the bowl of a food processor or blender. With the motor running, add the oil by droplets. After the egg yolks have absorbed all the oil, add the lemon juice or vinegar, the salt, and the cayenne. Process just to blend. Scrape into a container with a tight-fitting lid. Store in the refrigerator for up to 10 days.

Yields: 1 3/4 cups

Preparation time: 10 minutes

TO MAKE HERB MAYONNAISE:

Add 1/2 cup fresh herbs, finely minced, to the finished mayonnaise.

Herb Mayonnaise is wonderful as a dressing for cold mussels. It's also great with cold poached fish or chicken.

TO MAKE MUSTARD MAYONNAISE:

Add 1/4 cup Dijon mustard after you add the lemon juice. Then add salt and pepper as specified above.

Mustard Mayonnaise is a little stronger and is wonderful with hard-boiled eggs or as an accompaniment to smoked chicken, duck, or meat.

SALAD DRESSING WITH CAPERS

A great salad dressing to serve with greens, this utilizes roasted peppers, which lend a rich pungency to the dressing. It keeps for about a week.

1 clove garlic, peeled and minced
½ cup finely chopped roasted red peppers
¼ cup capers, drained
1 tablespoon salt
1 teaspoon ground black pepper
2 tablespoons fresh basil or 2 teaspoons dried
1¾ cups olive oil
¾ cup white wine vinegar

Place all ingredients in a 1-quart container with a tight-fitting lid. Shake vigorously for about 1 minute.

Yields: 3 cups

CREAMY DRESSING

For a fuller cream dressing, try this.

¾ cup sour cream
⅛ teaspoon Tabasco
2 cloves garlic, peeled and mashed into 1 teaspoon salt to form a paste
½ teaspoon ground black pepper
½ cup chopped dill

Combine dressing ingredients in a small bowl and mix well.

Yields: 1 cup

ROASTED PEPPERS IN OIL

This is an excellent addition to salads, or wherever you need roasted peppers in a recipe. It's great cut into strips and served as a garnish for paella. I always have a large jar in my refrigerator because it lasts for two months. Try serving it as part of a wonderful antipasto dish.

ANTIPASTO

Serve the roasted peppers with some sprats or any other type of small smoked fish, cucumber sticks, olives, your favorite cheese, and a fresh vegetable of your choice. Pour a little bit of the oil over the antipasto before serving.

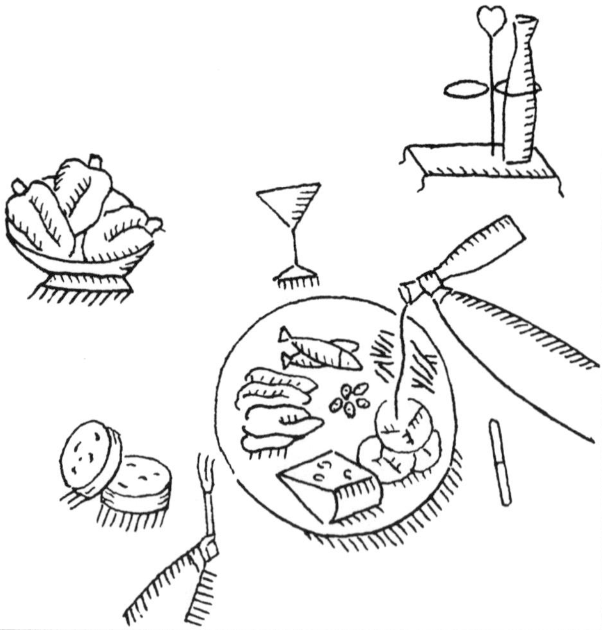

10 red peppers
1 teaspoon coarse salt
1 to 1½ cups olive oil

Preheat the oven to 400°F.

Cut the peppers in half. Remove and discard the seeds. Arrange the peppers, skin side up, in a single layer on a large oiled baking sheet. Sprinkle with the salt. Roast for 30 minutes, or until they feel soft when pricked with a fork. Remove from the oven and let cool. Place the roasted peppers in a 1-quart container with a lid. Pour enough oil over them to cover them. Cover and store in the refrigerator. Bring the oil and peppers to room temperature before serving.

Yields: 10 peppers

Preparation time: 40 minutes (excluding cooling time)

HERBS STORED IN OIL

Rosemary is wonderful for stews and soups. All you need is a couple of tablespoons added to the sauce. Thyme is great for fish. Tarragon can be used for chicken or fish dishes; mint for fish or vegetable dishes; dill for fish, vegetable, poultry, and salads; oregano and basil for pasta sauces or sautéed vegetables. I sometimes add a tablespoon or two of basil or oregano in oil to my scrambled eggs or omelettes.

SUMMER HERBS

Any summer herb can be stored in this manner. Simply substitute four cups of whatever herb you prefer . . . or why not make them all? Stored this way, they maintain their full flavor.

4 cups fresh basil leaves or other herbs
2 cups best-quality olive oil

Using the metal blade in your food processor, process the herbs and oil until the herbs are finely minced. Pour into plastic containers. Cover and store in the refrigerator for up to 3 months.

Yields: approximately 3 cups

PESTO

Make pestos of dill, basil, or parsley (fresh only). Each has a distinctly different flavor, yet all are prepared the same way. Use on hot or cold pasta dishes, or in dips and sauces.

1/4 cup walnuts
1 1/2 tablespoons peeled and minced garlic
2 1/2 cups tightly packed herb leaves
3/4 cup olive oil
1/2 teaspoon salt
1/2 teaspoon ground black pepper

Place the walnuts and garlic in the food processor bowl, with the metal blade already in place. Process for 30 seconds. Add the rest of the ingredients. Puree until smooth. Store in 1-cup containers in the refrigerator for up to 4 months, or in the freezer, where it will keep indefinitely.

Yields: approximately 1 1/4 cups
Preparation time: 10 minutes

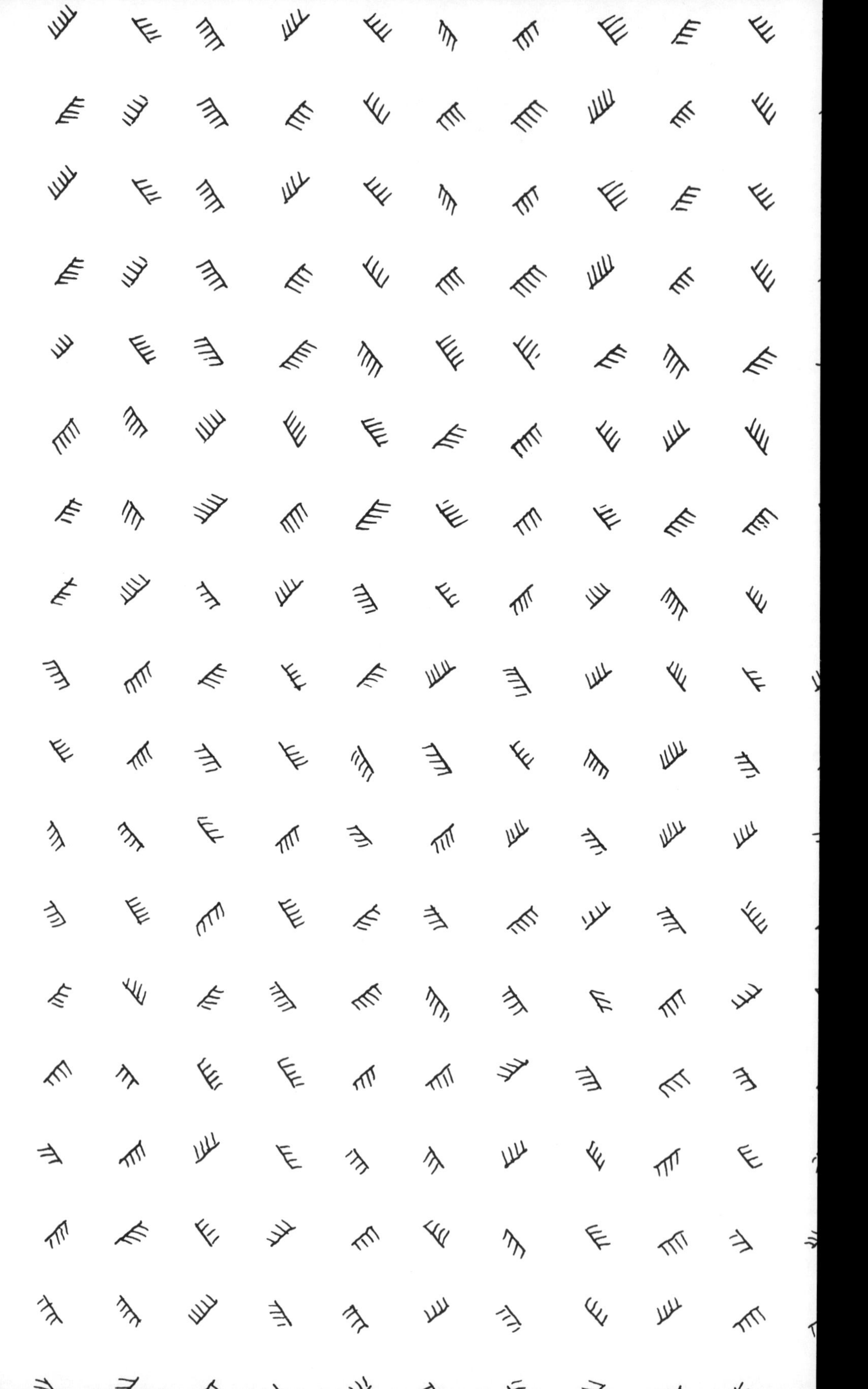

STARTERS

Food is meant to tempt as well as nourish.
—John-Paul Aron

Each spring, just before Loaves and Fishes officially opens for the season, I treat myself to a long bicycle ride around the East Hampton area, knowing that it might be the last time I'll have a chance to do so until the store closes in late autumn.

One of my favorite routes takes me along a curving country road where trees are just beginning to bud and where hidden ponds are filled with ducks and geese. Eighteenth-century clapboard houses are around every bend; white picket fences border well-cared-for gardens, which in a week or more will be abloom with flowers.

Only a month or two has passed since Detlef and I returned from our annual trip abroad, when I get a chance to discover and collect ideas for new recipes. For instance, I found my delicate Salmon Tartare in Lyons, France, my savory Zucchini–Cheese Tart in Alsace, and my fiery Mexican Red Sauce in Guadalajara, Mexico. Thank goodness I have a husband who shares my enthusiasm for good food. There have been countless times when he would sit patiently by while I sat bent over my notebook, trying to capture the essence of some wonderfully unusual dish we had just happened upon. By the time spring rolls around, I've had time to experiment with the new dishes and feel very excited knowing I'll have innovative, exotic recipes to add to our menus.

I turn down a long quiet road with pampas grass growing high on either side, nearly masking the bay from view. Before me is the Atlantic Ocean and a hundred miles or more of fine, white sand. The beach this time of year is nearly deserted, but in a few weeks it will be alive with people.

The store will open in only a few more days. It has been scrubbed, repainted, and restocked. The garden outside has been planted with enough herbs, vegetables, and flowers to last the summer. Bookings for cocktail parties, dinners, weddings, and luncheons are starting to mount up. Everything, it seems, is ready and waiting for the summer season to begin. And so, I hope, am I.

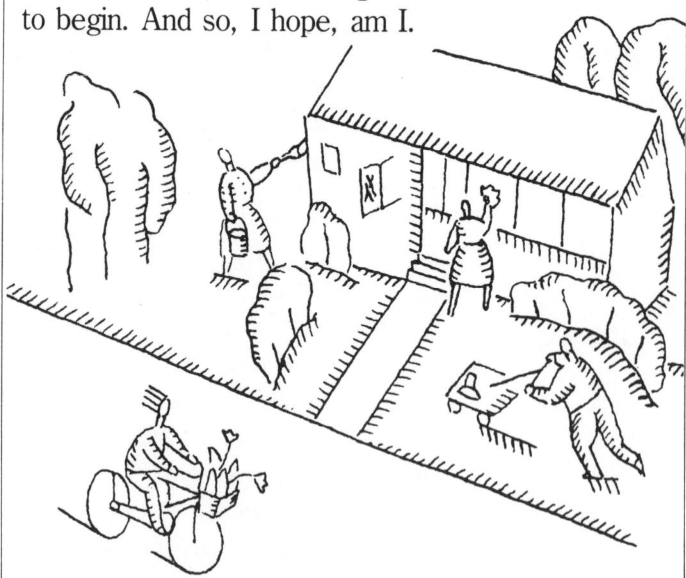

Serve with thick slices of rich black bread and deep bowls of the tangy mustard sauce on the side.

GRAVLAX WITH MUSTARD SAUCE AND FRESH DILL

This has long been a traditional dish in Scandinavian countries. I can't remember a holiday that passed without this delicious marinated fish having a place of honor on our dinner table. It must be made at least three days ahead of the time when you want to serve it.

3-pound piece of salmon fillet, skin left on, all bones removed
1/4 cup coarse salt
1/4 cup sugar
3 tablespoons ground black pepper
1 1/2 bunches dill
3 tablespoons brandy

SAUCE
3/4 cup Dijon mustard
1/4 cup heavy cream
1 tablespoon lemon juice
1/4 teaspoon ground black pepper
1 tablespoon sugar

Place the salmon, skin side down, on a piece of wax paper. Mix the salt, sugar, and pepper in a small bowl. Sprinkle one-quarter of it over the bottom of a glass dish. Rub half of the remaining salt mixture into the fish. Lay 1 bunch dill over the fish. Set aside the remaining dill in the refrigerator to use, chopped, as garnish later on. Fold the fish in half, flesh on flesh, and transfer it to the glass dish. Sprinkle it with brandy and the rest of the salt mixture. Cover the dish with plastic wrap and weight it down with a brick. Store in the refrigerator for 3 days, turning the fish once each day. Shortly before serving take the salmon out of the marinade and discard the dill and marinade. Slice the salmon on the diagonal in paper-thin slices.

Any leftover gravlax chopped fine makes a great addition to a green salad.

To prepare the sauce, mix all the ingredients in a small bowl, being sure to blend them well.

Garnish the gravlax with reserved dill.

Yields: 8 to 10 servings

Preparation time: 25 minutes (excluding marinating time)

BROILED MUSSELS

What could be a better appetizer than fresh mussels sprinkled with bread crumbs and broiled in butter, garlic, and parsley?

3 dozen mussels, scrubbed and debearded
1 cup dry white wine
2 cloves garlic, peeled and minced
2 tablespoons chopped parsley
2 tablespoons butter, softened
¼ teaspoon salt
¼ teaspoon ground black pepper
2 tablespoons bread crumbs

Preheat the broiler.

Place the clean mussels and the wine in a heavy saucepan. Steam until the mussels open, about 5 minutes. Remove from the heat. Drain, reserving 3 tablespoons of the cooking liquid. Discard the top shell of each mussel and place the mussels, flesh side up, on a baking sheet.

Combine the remaining ingredients in a small bowl. Place a dollop of this mixture on top of each mussel. Broil until browned, about 4 or 5 minutes.

Yields: 6 servings
Preparation time: 20 minutes

TO CLEAN MUSSELS

Cover the mussels with cold water. Add a little salt and a tablespoon of flour or cornmeal. I prefer flour, since cornmeal has a tendency to coat the shells. Wiggle your hands in the water to dissolve the flour and salt. Wait 10 minutes or so, giving the mussels time to feed and disgorge any sand or grit. Debeard them just as you drop them into the steamer or saucepan.

BROILED CLAMS WITH GARLIC BUTTER

40 cherrystone clams, on the half shell

GARLIC BUTTER SPREAD

3 cloves garlic, peeled and minced
4 medium shallots, peeled and chopped
3 tablespoons walnuts
¾ cup parsley leaves
¼ cup white wine
1 cup (2 sticks) butter, softened
½ cup fine bread crumbs
Salt to taste
¼ teaspoon ground black pepper
¼ cup grated Parmesan cheese (optional)

Garlic Butter can be made ahead of time and stored for up to 2 weeks in the refrigerator.

Preheat the broiler.

Place the garlic, shallots, walnuts, parsley, wine, butter, bread crumbs, salt, and pepper in the bowl of a food processor fitted with the metal blade. Process until all the ingredients are combined and form a smooth paste.

Spread a little of the garlic butter over each clam. Place the clams on a baking sheet. Sprinkle with cheese.

Broil for 7 to 8 minutes, or until nicely browned. The clams should be hot, but not overcooked.

Yields: about 10 servings

Preparation time: 20 minutes

CURRIED MUSSELS

Allow 1 pound mussels per person.

5 quarts small mussels, scrubbed and debearded
1 cup dry white wine
1 cup peeled and finely chopped onion
1 bay leaf
4 sprigs fresh thyme or ½ teaspoon dried
1 stalk celery, halved

CURRY DRESSING

½ cup olive oil
2 tablespoons red wine vinegar
1 clove garlic, peeled and minced
½ teaspoon salt
1 tablespoon curry powder

Place the mussels in a large saucepan. Add the wine, onion, bay leaf, thyme, and celery. Cook over a high heat, shaking the pan a few times until all the mussels have opened, about 8 to 10 minutes.

To make the dressing, place all the dressing ingredients in a jar with a tight-fitting lid. Shake vigorously.

When mussels are done, drain them in a large colander. Discard the bay leaf, celery, and the thyme sprigs, if you've used fresh thyme. Transfer the mussels to a large bowl, discarding any that did not open. Pour the dressing over the mussels and toss to coat them well. Serve in deep plates.

Yields: 6 servings

Preparation time: 30 minutes

SNAILS AND MUSHROOMS WITH GARLIC BUTTER

40 snails
40 medium mushrooms
Garlic Butter Spread (see recipe for Broiled Clams with Garlic Butter)

Remove the stems from the mushrooms and brush off the tops. Place them, stem side up, on a baking sheet. Place a snail into each mushroom and spread with garlic butter. Broil for 7 or 8 minutes.

Yields: about 10 servings
Preparation time: 15 minutes

SMOKED TROUT SPREAD

Serve this delicious spread with light rounds of crusty French bread to complement the delicacy of the fish, or heap the spread in the center of a pretty bowl and ring it with the tender inner leaves from 2 heads of romaine lettuce.

When I was a young girl, growing up near the Baltic Sea, fish wagons would come along the beach selling small tidbits of smoked fish and fresh shellfish. When I have this spread, it brings me right back to my youth.

2½ pounds smoked trout, boned and skinned
1 tablespoon prepared horseradish, drained
1 small onion, peeled and chopped
Juice of ½ lemon
¼ teaspoon ground white pepper
2 tablespoons heavy cream
3 ounces cream cheese

Place the smoked trout in the bowl of a food processor fitted with the steel blade. Add the horseradish, onion, lemon juice, and pepper. Process until fluffy, about 2 minutes. With the motor still running, add the cream and cream cheese. Process to mix. Chill.

Yields: 2 cups or 12 servings
Preparation time: 10 minutes

SALMON TARTARE

We discovered this unique tartare in Lyons, France. The flavors are so delicately balanced that you are able to savor all of them individually. And the pink salmon looks so beautiful set against a blanket of lush greens.

3 pounds very fresh salmon, filleted, skinned, with all bones removed
1/4 cup lime juice
1 tablespoon brandy
1 1/2 cups finely chopped onion (or scallions, if preferred)
3 cloves garlic, peeled and minced
1 1/2 tablespoons Dijon mustard
1/4 cup finely chopped dill
1/4 cup capers, drained
1 teaspoon ground black pepper
1 teaspoon salt
Dill sprigs (for garnish)

Chop the salmon very fine. Place it in a glass dish or bowl. Add the rest of the ingredients and, using your hands, mix well. Cover and refrigerate for 30 minutes or for up to 24 hours.

Yields: 6 to 8 servings

Preparation time: 20 minutes (excluding marinating time)

FOR COCKTAILS

Spoon the tartare onto thinly sliced blackbread fingers that have been lightly buttered, or spoon the tartare onto rounds of cucumber. Garnish with freshly chopped dill.

FOR A BUFFET LUNCH

Marinate the salmon but use only the lime juice, brandy, garlic, pepper, and salt. When ready, pile the tartare in the center of a serving platter and surround the plate with heaps of onions, mustard, dill, and capers. Then your guests can add and mix according to their individual tastes. Make sure you serve up plenty of buttered black bread on the side.

Whenever you marinate seafood in lemon and lime juice, you are actually "cooking" the fish. It takes 6 to 8 hours for this process to be completed.

SEVICHE

This fresh-from-the-sea salad with its colorful, aromatic herbs and rich spices requires no garnishing, only a clear glass bowl in which to show it off.

1½ pounds scallops, tuna, or any firm-fleshed fish
½ cup lemon juice
½ cup lime juice
1 green pepper, chopped
1 red pepper, chopped
2 stalks celery, chopped
½ bunch parsley, chopped
2 tablespoons chopped cilantro
1 clove garlic, peeled and minced
2 teaspoons minced fresh ginger
2 teaspoons chili powder
¼ teaspoon hot red pepper flakes
¼ teaspoon ground white pepper
½ teaspoon salt

Cut the fish into bite-sized pieces and place in a medium mixing bowl. Add all the other ingredients. Mix well with your hands. Marinate for 6 to 8 hours in the refrigerator. Serve chilled.

Yields: 6 to 8 servings

Preparation time: 15 minutes (excluding marinating time)

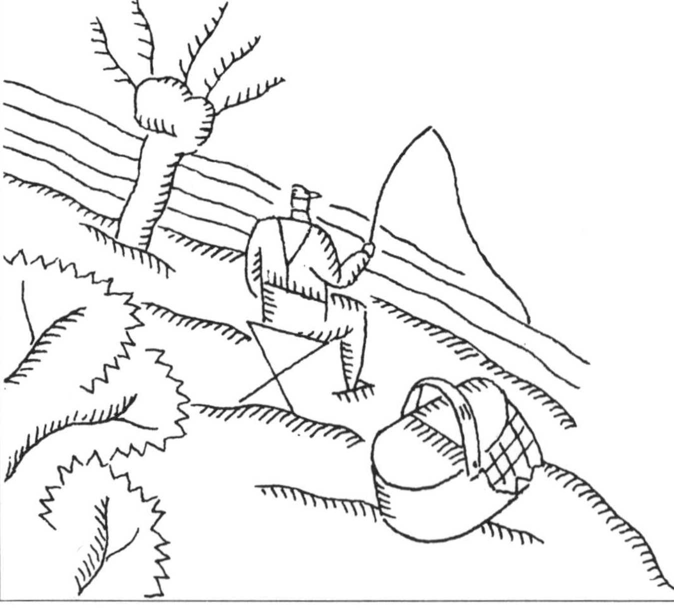

SHRIMP AND ARTICHOKE MARINADE

In larger portions this can be part of a lovely buffet menu, or an excellent luncheon plate, accompanied, of course, by lots of black bread. Make it at least two hours ahead of time.

When shopping for shrimp keep in mind that shrimp should smell of sea water, and the flesh should be firm.

2 pounds shrimp
Two 15-ounce cans artichoke hearts

MARINADE

2 egg yolks
1 cup olive oil
½ cup peanut oil
½ cup white wine vinegar
2 tablespoons coarsely chopped shallots
2 tablespoons Dijon mustard
¼ cup coarsely chopped parsley
¼ cup fresh chives, cut into 1-inch pieces
½ teaspoon salt
½ teaspoon ground black pepper

Peel the shrimp. Place them in a saucepan and cover with water. Bring the water to a boil, remove from the heat, and drain.

Drain the artichoke hearts and cut them in half. Place them along with the shrimp in a glass bowl.

Place the egg yolks, olive oil, peanut oil, and vinegar in the bowl of a food processor fitted with the metal blade. Add the shallots, mustard, parsley, chives, salt, and pepper and process for 30 seconds.

Pour the marinade over the shrimp and artichoke hearts. Mix gently.

Let it marinate for 2 hours or overnight in the refrigerator.

Yields: 6 servings

Preparation time: 25 minutes (excluding marinating time)

Woe to the cook whose sauce has no sting.
—Chaucer

NEW ORLEANS CRAB CLAWS

This "Cajun"-flavored dish was discovered by my daughter, Sybille, also a cook, while she was traveling through the South. She loved the unusual blend of grapefruit juice, curry, and fresh apples.

3 tablespoons butter
1 cup peeled and finely chopped onion
1 clove garlic, peeled and minced
2 ribs celery, finely chopped
2 small carrots, trimmed and finely chopped
1 tart apple, peeled and diced
2½ tablespoons curry powder
½ teaspoon ground cumin
1 bay leaf
¾ teaspoon salt
4 fresh plum tomatoes, diced
3 cups chicken stock
½ cup fresh grapefruit juice
1 tablespoon cornstarch, dissolved in 2 tablespoons chicken stock
2 pounds snow crab claws
2 tablespoons chopped parsley

Melt the butter in a large sauté pan. Add the onion, garlic, celery, and carrots. Sauté over moderate heat for about 3 minutes, stirring occasionally. Add the diced apple and sauté for 2 minutes longer. Add the curry powder, cumin, bay leaf, and salt. Stir well. Add the tomatoes and chicken stock. Simmer over low heat for 15 minutes. Add the grapefruit juice and bring to a boil. While stirring constantly, add the dissolved cornstarch. Then add the crab claws and parsley. Mix gently to coat the claws with the sauce.

Yields: 6 servings
Preparation time: 30 minutes

CRAB-FILLED MUSHROOMS

This is not just another mushroom recipe. The blending of juicy, sweet crab meat and hot curry powder makes this into a delectable appetizer.

If fresh crab meat is unavailable in your area use frozen snow crab meat, which I find works just as well.

6 tablespoons (3/4 stick) butter
2 shallots, peeled and minced
1 clove garlic, peeled and minced
2 teaspoons curry powder
2 tablespoons lemon juice
1 pound snow crab meat, shredded
1/4 teaspoon salt
1/2 teaspoon ground black pepper
1/4 cup minced parsley
32 medium or 18 large mushrooms
3/4 cup (1 1/2 sticks) butter, melted

Preheat the oven to 350°F.

Melt the 6 tablespoons butter in a heavy saucepan. Add the shallots and sauté for 2 minutes. Add the garlic and curry powder. Stir to mix in well. Add the lemon juice, crab meat, salt, pepper, and parsley. Stir until all the ingredients are well blended. Let cool to room temperature.

Remove the stems of the mushrooms and clean them with a soft brush. Dip each mushroom into the melted butter, coating it inside and out. Place the mushrooms, stem side up, on a buttered baking sheet. Pile the crab mixture onto each mushroom. Bake for 12 minutes.

Yields: 8 servings
Preparation time: 25 minutes

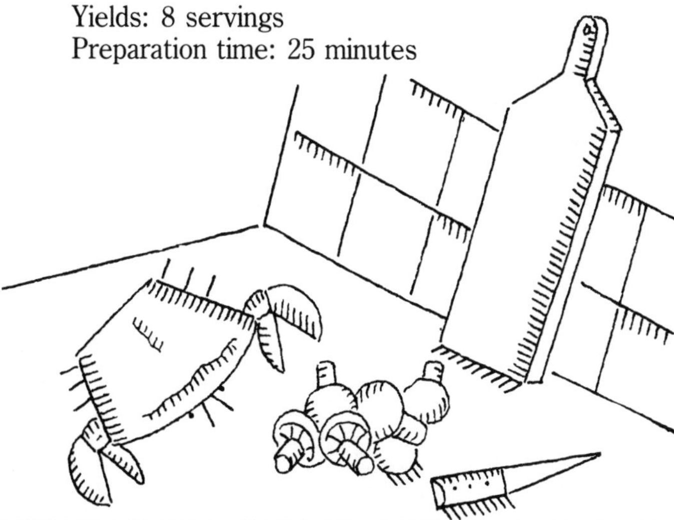

SALT COD MOUSSE

My husband and I had our first taste of this unique dish in Alsace-Lorraine. When I returned home, I worked at trying to re-create the recipe but added hot red pepper flakes. It gave the whole recipe a special boost. Begin preparing this at least a day ahead of time.

1 pound salt cod, boned and skinned
1 large baking potato
2 cloves garlic, peeled
1 cup olive oil
1 tablespoon lemon juice
½ cup heavy cream
½ teaspoon ground black pepper
¾ teaspoon hot red pepper flakes

Wash the cod under running water to remove the excess salt. Allow it to soak in water for at least 24 hours in the refrigerator before using. Change the water twice.

Bake the potato and set aside.

Place the cod in a pan and cover with water. Bring the water to a boil, reduce heat, and let it simmer for 10 minutes. Drain the cod in a colander, pressing out the excess liquid with the back of a large spoon.

Preheat oven to 350°F.

Transfer the cod, along with the garlic, to the food processor bowl, fitted with the metal blade. Scoop out the pulp of the potato into the bowl and with the motor running, slowly add the olive oil, then the lemon juice, and finally the heavy cream. Sprinkle with black pepper and the hot red pepper flakes. Pulse to blend. Scrape the mousse into an ovenproof dish and bake for 20 minutes.

Yields: 10 to 12 servings

Preparation time: 1 hour 15 minutes (excluding soaking time)

It Pays to Advertise

The codfish lays ten thousand eggs
The homely hen lays one.
The codfish never cackles
To tell you what she's done.
And so we scorn the codfish,
While the humble hen we prize,
Which only goes to show you
That it pays to advertise.
—Anonymous

COD SOUFFLÉ FRITTERS

These golden brown fritters look wonderful arranged in a pretty basket lined with a crisp white linen napkin. Serve either hot or at room temperature.

PÂTÉ À CHOUX

1/3 cup water
1/4 teaspoon salt
2 tablespoons butter
1/2 cup unbleached white flour
2 eggs

1 1/2 cups Salt Cod Mousse (see opposite)

4 cups peanut oil

To make the pâté à choux, place the water, butter, and salt in a heavy saucepan and bring to a boil. Add all the flour at once, beating hard, until the dough sticks together to form a ball. Remove from heat and let cool for 5 minutes. Add the eggs and beat with a wire whisk until the dough is a smooth paste. Add the salt cod mousse and blend well.

Heat the peanut oil in a saucepan until it reaches 375°F. Drop the dough mixture by rounded soup-spoonfuls into the heated oil. The fritters should not touch while cooking, so you may need to fry them in three separate batches. Cook until they are golden brown on all sides. This should take approximately 2 to 3 minutes. Using a slotted spoon, transfer them to paper towels to drain.

Yields: 30 fritters or 6 servings
Preparation time: 30 minutes

After you've prepared the dough and added the cod mousse, the mixture may be stored, covered, in the refrigerator for up to 24 hours before crisping them in oil.

AVOCADO DIP

2 ripe avocados, peeled and pitted
Juice of 1 lime
1 fresh plum tomato, minced
2 cloves garlic, peeled and minced
2 medium pickled hot jalapeño peppers, halved, seeded, and minced
¼ teaspoon salt
½ teaspoon ground black pepper
1 tablespoon minced fresh coriander or ½ teaspoon dried

To store leftovers, press a piece of plastic wrap over the container and touching the surface of the dip, making sure all the air has been removed. This way it should last up to 3 days in the refrigerator.

Place avocado flesh in a bowl, add lime juice, then break and mix avocado with your hands. Be sure avocado is thoroughly coated with juice to keep it from discoloring.

Add the remaining ingredients and blend well, keeping the avocado a bit chunky.

Yields: 2 cups

Preparation time: 15 minutes

MEXICAN RED SAUCE

This sauce is good on just about anything—tortilla chips, piled on rice, or served with broiled meats.

If you decide to try this recipe when tomatoes are in season, you can substitute 3 cups diced, ripe, sweet tomatoes for the canned tomatoes in the recipe.

One 28-ounce can tomatoes, drained
⅓ cup fresh cilantro
2 jalapeño peppers, chopped
½ medium onion, peeled and chopped
½ cup fresh parsley
3 cloves garlic, peeled and chopped
½ teaspoon salt
Pinch of sugar

Place all the ingredients in the bowl of a food processor fitted with the metal blade and process until it is a coarse sauce.

Pour sauce into a small pan and heat thoroughly for 2 minutes. Pour into a serving bowl and chill.

Yields: about 2 cups

Preparation time: 10 minutes

GARLIC CLOUDS

Not for garlic lovers only, these heavenly clouds are a must for parties. They whet the appetite and are so simple to make.

1 cup water
6 tablespoons (3/4 stick) butter
1 teaspoon salt
1/8 teaspoon ground black pepper
12 cloves garlic, peeled and minced
1 cup unbleached white flour
4 eggs

EGG WASH

1 egg yolk, mixed with 1 tablespoon heavy cream

Preheat the oven to 425°F.

Bring the water, butter, salt, pepper, and garlic to a boil in a medium saucepan. Remove from the heat. Add the flour all at once. Beat hard for a few seconds. Return the pan to moderate heat and beat the dough until it forms a glossy mass. This should take about 3 minutes. Quickly transfer the dough to the bowl of an electric mixer. With the motor running, add the eggs, one at a time, beating hard after every addition.

Place the dough in a pastry bag and, using the plain large tip, pipe out 1-inch mounds onto a buttered baking sheet. Brush with the egg wash. Bake for 15 minutes. Serve hot or at room temperature.

Yields: 32 clouds

Preparation time: 35 minutes

The garlic clouds could be made as much as 2 weeks ahead of time, wrapped in plastic bags, and frozen. To serve, pop the still-frozen clouds into a 375°F pre-heated oven for 12 minutes, or until heated through. Serve hot.

When cut into small cubes, this savory tart is a fabulous appetizer at cocktail parties. In larger portions it can be part of a buffet lunch. Served hot, cut into hefty wedges, and accompanied by a tossed green salad, this is a wonderful dinner.

If you like, simply substitute sliced tomato for the zucchini to make a tomato–cheese tart.

A bunch of fresh thyme picked in season, chopped up, and stored in the freezer in a sealed plastic bag will retain its flavor so that you can use it throughout the lean winter months.

ZUCCHINI–CHEESE TART

While staying in Colmar, a charming old city in Alsace, my husband and I stopped in at a patisserie. We ordered slices of their cheese tart, one with tomatoes and the other with zucchini. We thought they were delicious. I tried to put the recipe together as soon as I got home.

CRUST

2½ cups unbleached white flour
¾ cup (1½ sticks) butter, chilled and cut into 12 pieces
½ teaspoon salt
2 small egg yolks
5 tablespoons cold water

FILLING

2 pounds (about 6 medium) zucchini
1 cup fresh parsley leaves
3 cloves garlic, peeled
¼ cup fresh basil leaves, coarsely chopped, or 2 tablespoons dried
1 tablespoon coarsely chopped fresh thyme or 1 teaspoon dried
½ teaspoon ground black pepper
½ teaspoon salt
⅔ cup virgin olive oil
5 tablespoons Dijon mustard
¾ pound Appenzeller cheese, grated
⅓ cup finely grated Parmesan cheese

To make the crust, place the flour, butter, and salt in the bowl of a food processor fitted with the metal blade. Pulse 5 times. Add the egg yolks and pulse 2 more times. With the motor running, add the water through the feed tube. Process only until the dough begins to stick together. Transfer the dough to a floured surface and quickly form it into a ball. Set it on a plate and leave it in the refrigerator for 30 minutes to set.

Meanwhile, preheat the oven to 400°F.

Cut the zucchini diagonally into ⅛-inch slices and place them in a large mixing bowl.

Put the parsley, garlic, basil, and thyme in the bowl of a food processor with the blade still in place. Sprinkle with the pepper and salt and process until the herbs are chopped fine. With the motor still running,

Filling the pastry with foil and beans is a common method used to keep the crust from bubbling while baking. In baking terms it is called "baking blind."

add the olive oil through the feed tube. Pour the herb mixture over the zucchini slices and mix well.

Roll out the pastry dough to a ⅛-inch thickness. Fit it into a 18-by-12-by-1-inch pan. Cover the pastry with foil, fitting it gently into the corners. Pour dry beans over the foil, filling the pan. Bake for 15 minutes. Remove the beans and reserve them for another time. Remove the foil and discard. Bake the tart pastry for 5 minutes more, uncovered.

Spread the mustard over the bottom of the crust. Distribute the cheeses over that. Arrange the zucchini in overlapping rows, covering the cheese. Pour whatever herb mixture is left in the bowl over the zucchini.

Reduce the oven temperature to 375°F and bake the tart for 30 minutes more.

Yields: approximately one hundred 1-by-2-inch slices

Preparation time: 1 hour 30 minutes

BUCHERON WITH HERBS

For appetizers, Bucheron can be slivered onto pink radiccio leaves or rounds of warm French bread. We use this cheese at home for snacks, for lunch with thick slabs of grainy bread, and sometimes for dinner when we want something light yet filling.

This recipe is a must! It's simple to prepare and lasts for more than a week in the refrigerator.

2 cups good, fruity olive oil
3 cloves garlic, peeled and halved
¼ cup minced fresh parsley
¼ cup minced fresh chives
3 tablespoons minced fresh basil
1 teaspoon dried thyme
1 teaspoon ground black pepper
1¼ pounds Bucheron goat cheese, cut into ½-inch slices

Heat the olive oil in a saucepan until it starts to smoke. Remove it from the heat and let it stand for 10 minutes. Stir in the garlic, parsley, chives, basil, thyme, and pepper. Let cool to room temperature.

Place the Bucheron in a serving bowl and pour the oil and herb mixture over it. Cover and refrigerate for at least 3 days. Bring to room temperature before serving.

Yields: 6 to 8 servings

Preparation time: 15 minutes (excluding marinating time)

HERBED CHEESE PUFF

A savory pie for any occasion.

If you're considering this as one of your appetizer choices before dinner or at a cocktail party, cut the puff into easy-to-handle pieces, each one no larger than 1 inch by 2 inches.

If this strikes you as a luncheon meal idea, all you have to do is pour the mixture into a buttered 9-inch spring-form pan and bake as directed. Serve it hot, sliced into wedges.

4 tablespoons (1/2 stick) butter
1 cup water
1 teaspoon salt
1/4 teaspoon ground black pepper
1 cup unbleached white flour
4 eggs
1 cup diced smoked ham
6 ounces Swiss cheese, grated
3 tablespoons minced fresh oregano or 1 teaspoon dried

Preheat oven to 400°F.

Combine the butter, water, salt, and pepper in a heavy saucepan and bring to a boil. Add the flour all at once. Stir vigorously until the dough becomes glossy and forms a ball, about 2 or 3 minutes. Put the mixture in the bowl of a food processor fitted with the metal blade, turn on the motor, and add the eggs one at a time. Process until the mixture becomes smooth and shiny.

Spread half the mixture into a buttered 8-by-8-inch baking pan. Sprinkle with the diced ham but only half the grated cheese and half the oregano. Cover with the remaining dough and sprinkle the top with the rest of the cheese and oregano.

Bake for 40 to 45 minutes, or until it is puffy and brown.

Yields: 32 servings

Preparation time: 1 hour 15 minutes

CHICKEN–SPINACH PÂTÉ

This is one of the most versatile pâtés around.

Not only can this be served at cocktail parties scooped onto moist cucumber rounds, but it can also be a delightful first course, part of a large buffet, a light lunch, or served with lots of crusty bread for dinner. Make it at least a day ahead of time.

4 tablespoons (1/2 stick) butter
1 1/2 cups peeled and diced onions
3 cloves garlic, peeled and minced
12 ounces fresh spinach, chopped, or one 10-ounce package frozen chopped spinach, thawed
1 pound chicken breast, boned and skinned, cut into 1-inch pieces
1 1/4 pounds fresh pork, with fat, cut into 1-inch dice

¾ pound smoked bacon, cut into 1-inch pieces
2 eggs
¼ cup brandy
2 teaspoons ground black pepper
2 teaspoons salt
1½ teaspoons dried thyme
½ teaspoon ground nutmeg

Preheat oven to 350°F.

Melt the butter in a heavy pan. Add the onion and sauté over low heat until transparent, about 10 minutes. Add the garlic and spinach and sauté until all the liquid has evaporated. Remove from the heat and let cool.

Place the chicken breast, pork, and bacon in the bowl of a food processor fitted with the metal blade and process until coarsely chopped. Transfer to a mixing bowl. To that add the eggs, brandy, pepper, salt, thyme, and nutmeg. Mix thoroughly with your hands. Add the onion, garlic, and spinach and continue mixing with your hands until well blended.

Press this mixture into a 9-by-5-inch loaf pan or terrine, patting out all the air bubbles. Cover tightly with foil and set the covered pan or terrine inside a slightly larger roasting pan. Add enough boiling water to come halfway up the side of the loaf pan or terrine and bake for 1¾ hours.

Remove from the oven. Place a heavy brick on top of the foil-covered pâté and let cool. Refrigerate for at least 24 hours before serving.

Yields: 1 loaf

Preparation time: 2 hours 15 minutes (excluding refrigeration time)

To keep leftover pâté, make sure it's tightly covered in foil. That way it will last for up to 10 days when stored in the refrigerator.

Serve with thin slices of buttered black bread, mustard on the side, and a small dish of cornichons. If you wish to keep the pâté longer than 5 days, pour melted butter over the top to seal in the flavors, then refrigerate.

If it's impossible for you to purchase duck livers, chicken livers can be used.

If it's the time of year when fresh thyme and rosemary are in season, by all means use them. Use 1 tablespoon freshly minced herbs for every teaspoon of dried herbs.

COUNTRY PÂTÉ

This is an adaptation of a pâté that my mother used to make. It's a hearty pâté in that it includes veal and chicken breasts along with the liver. It is important to prepare this up to a day ahead of time in order to give all the flavors a chance to blend and ripen.

2 tablespoons butter
1 medium onion, peeled and finely chopped
1 clove garlic, peeled and minced
⅓ pound salt pork
½ pound lean fresh pork
1 pound veal
1 pound boned chicken breasts
10 ounces duck livers
2 eggs
2 tablespoons brandy
2 tablespoons dry white wine
¼ cup unbleached white flour
1 teaspoon salt
1 teaspoon ground black pepper
¾ teaspoon each dried thyme and rosemary
½ teaspoon ground nutmeg
2 tablespoons green peppercorns in vinegar, drained

Melt the butter in a small saucepan. Sauté the onion until transparent. Add the garlic and stir. Let cool slightly.

Wash the salt pork under cold running water. Cut into 1-inch pieces. Cut the fresh pork, veal, and chicken breast into 1-inch pieces. Place the pork, veal, and half of the chicken breasts in the bowl of a food processor fitted with the metal blade and process to a fine consistency; scrape into a medium mixing bowl. Place the duck livers, eggs, brandy, wine, flour, salt, pepper, thyme, rosemary, and nutmeg in the same processor bowl, blade still in place, and process for about 30 seconds. Pour this mixture over the meat in the mixing bowl. Add to that the onion–garlic mixture, the remaining pieces of chicken breast, and the green peppercorns. Beat until well blended.

Pack this into a 9-by-5-inch baking pan or any terrine that holds 1½ quarts. Cover with foil. Set inside a large roasting pan. Add enough boiling water to come halfway up the side of baking pan or terrine.

Bake for 1¾ hours, or until all the juices run clear. Remove baking pan or terrine from water bath and place a brick on top of foil to weigh down the pâté. Let cool to room temperature. Refrigerate.

Yields: 1 loaf

Preparation time: 2 hours 15 minutes (excluding refrigeration time)

SPICED EGGPLANT

I always present this mixture piled in a chilled bowl, with squares of pita bread or toasted rounds of French bread. It's even wonderful with tortilla chips. Covered, the eggplant will last for up to 6 days in the refrigerator.

This is an especially good recipe for those who are counting calories yet yearn for something savory with a special zing to it. The entire quart has only two tablespoons of oil.

1 large eggplant
2 tablespoons olive oil
1 cup peeled and finely chopped onion
1 cup finely chopped green pepper
2 cloves garlic, peeled and minced
2 cups finely chopped Italian plum tomatoes
4 tablespoons red wine vinegar
1 tablespoon chopped fresh basil or 1 teaspoon dried
¼ teaspoon cayenne pepper
⅛ teaspoon Tabasco
1½ tablespoons capers, drained
1 teaspoon salt

Preheat the oven to 350°F.

Cut the eggplant in half and place it on an oiled baking sheet, cut side down. Bake for 30 to 40 minutes, or until soft. Let cool.

Heat the oil in a large sauté pan. Add the onions, peppers, and garlic. Sauté over low heat for 5 minutes, being careful not to brown the vegetables. Add the tomatoes, vinegar, basil, cayenne, Tabasco, capers, and salt.

Scoop out the flesh of the eggplant and discard the skin. Mash the pulp to a fine consistency and add it to the onion mixture. Stir well. Simmer over low heat, uncovered, for 15 minutes. Let cool.

Chill in the refrigerator for 3 hours or more before serving.

Yields: 1 quart

Preparation time: about 1 hour (excluding refrigeration time)

SOUPS

Of all the items on the menu, soup is that which exacts the most delicate perfection and the strictest attention.
—Escoffier

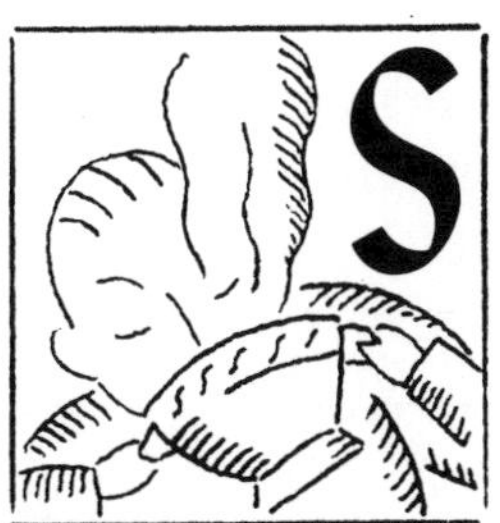

ince it is one of the simplest of foods to prepare, soup often stimulates the ingenuity of a fine cook. With a good homemade stock simmering on the stove, all that's left for you to do is to decide what will be added. It's always wise to use whatever fresh produce is currently available in your markets. That's how my Zucchini–Pepper Soup evolved. A neighbor of ours lugged over a huge basket of very large, freshly picked zucchini from her garden and asked, "Do you think you can make a soup from this?" Since zucchini has such a mild, delicate flavor, I decided that perhaps I should pair it up with the robust green pepper. I experimented until I was sure their individual flavors were left intact without one overpowering the other. It was well worth the time spent. As a chilled soup it is still one of my favorites on those long, hot Long Island summer days.

Sometimes a soup is created because of a certain craving one has for a particular flavor. The Garlic–Chive Soup was my passion. I wanted something subtle, yet distinctive. I experimented until I arrived at just the right balance of color, consistency, and flavor—a light creamy soup with just enough garlic to let you know it's there.

Soup comes in a variety of textures, flavors, colors, strengths, and temperatures, and much of the time these will determine both when and how a soup is to be served. My Chilled Plum Soup, its sweetness mellowed by red wine and presented in a dainty bowl, is an elegant introduction to a dinner of crisp roasted duck. And what could be more gratifying than sitting down to a steaming tureen of Country Vegetable Soup, thick with beans, tender vegetables, savory ham, and a suggestion of garlic and thyme? With a loaf of hot crusty French bread, lots of dairy-fresh butter, and perhaps a dark green salad tossed in a sweet and pungent dressing it becomes a perfect dinner. That, in fact, is one of my earliest recorded memories; having thick, country soup on one of those bitter Scandinavian nights, with my whole family seated around the dining table.

I've selected a variety of my favorite soups from Loaves and Fishes, and some from my own private recipe book. They were chosen for their uniqueness and ease of preparation. I wanted to be sure you wouldn't hesitate before giving any or all of them a try.

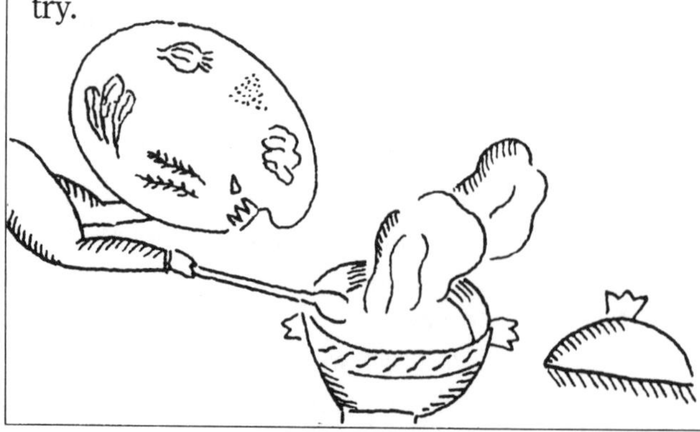

RED CLAM CHOWDER

Plump, tender clams in tomato soup sparked with the sweet yet peppery taste of kohlrabi make an unusual chowder. I chose this vegetable primarily because it is native to my part of the country. In this soup it's superb.

⅓ cup minced lean bacon
3 cups peeled and chopped onion
1 clove garlic, peeled and minced
1½ cups chopped celery
1½ cups peeled and diced kohlrabi
2 cups peeled and diced potatoes
3 cups chicken stock
3 cups peeled and chopped fresh tomatoes or 3 cups canned crushed tomatoes
1 bay leaf
2 tablespoons fresh thyme or 2 teaspoons dried
½ teaspoon ground black pepper
1 pint clam juice
1 pint fresh clams, chopped
½ cup chopped parsley (for garnish)

Sauté the bacon in a large soup kettle for 2 minutes over medium heat. Add the onion and sauté for 3 minutes more. Add the garlic, celery, kohlrabi, potatoes, chicken stock, tomatoes, bay leaf, thyme, and pepper. Bring the soup to a boil and simmer for 15 minutes. Add the clam juice and clams and allow the soup to come to a boil once again. Remove from heat. Garnish with parsley and serve.

Yields: 8 or more servings
Preparation time: 30 minutes

This piquant soup also makes a wonderful sauce for pasta. Try it poured over a bowl of freshly cooked linguine, then sprinkled with grated Parmesan. Add some hot, crusty Italian bread, a leafy green salad, and a bottle of wine and you've made yourself a simple yet wholesome meal. This chowder keeps for 4 days in the refrigerator or for up to 6 weeks in the freezer.

CHEESE CHOWDER

This rich, smooth chowder is best served as a meal in itself. Try warm dark bread, lots of sweet butter, and a freshly cut vegetable salad sprinkled with some tart vinaigrette.

3 strips bacon
2 cups peeled and chopped onions
1 clove garlic, peeled and minced
3 tablespoons unbleached white flour
4 cups chicken stock
1 cup dry white wine
1 bay leaf
3 cups peeled and chopped potatoes
½ teaspoon salt
¾ teaspoon ground white pepper
½ pound Cheddar cheese, grated
1½ cups milk
½ cup heavy cream
Chopped chives (for garnish)

Gruyère cheese can be used instead of Cheddar. This soup reheats very well and can be stored for up to 4 days in the refrigerator.

Brown the bacon in a heavy saucepan over medium heat, drain, and set aside. Using 1 tablespoon of the bacon fat, sauté the onion and garlic for 3 minutes over medium heat. Add the flour and blend in well. Stirring, add the chicken stock. Keep stirring until the mixture is very smooth and there are no lumps of flour.

Add the wine, bay leaf, potatoes, salt, and pepper. Simmer for 15 minutes. Stir in the cheese, then add the milk and heavy cream. Heat through, but do not bring to a full boil.

Crumble the bacon into the soup. Garnish each portion with chopped chives.

Yields: 6 servings

Preparation time: 30 minutes

This chowder can be kept up to 4 days in the refrigerator. When you reheat it, simmer it gently until it reaches the temperature you want.

FISH AND SHRIMP CHOWDER

This is my favorite soup. On chilly evenings, this soothing, creamy chowder, with its chunks of juicy shrimp and abundance of meaty fish is a completely filling meal. I usually have it with some warm whole-grain bread and a crunchy fresh salad tossed in a lemon–herb dressing.

3 tablespoons butter
2 cups peeled and finely chopped onion
2 cups clam juice
2 cups chicken stock
1 bay leaf
¾ teaspoon salt
½ teaspoon ground black pepper
4 cups peeled and diced potatoes (½-inch pieces)
¾ cup milk
1 cup heavy cream
¾ pound tilefish, anglerfish, or any other firm-fleshed fish
1 pound medium shrimp, shelled and cut in half
½ cup minced parsley

Melt the butter in a large soup kettle. Add the onion and sauté until transparent. Add the clam juice, chicken stock, bay leaf, salt, pepper, and potatoes. Bring to a boil, then simmer over low heat for 20 minutes. Add the milk, cream, and fish. Bring to a boil again and add the shrimp. Stir and simmer for 1 minute. Add the parsley and serve.

Yields: 6 servings

Preparation time: 35 minutes

ITALIAN SAUSAGE SOUP

It was in Rome on a nippy February afternoon when Detlef and I stepped into an Italian restaurant to warm up and have something to eat. We were served this hearty soup with its rich, savory sauce, spicy-hot sausages, and flavorful balance of fresh herbs. You'll love this with a salad, lots of hot Italian bread, and a bottle of your favorite wine.

1¼ pounds spicy-hot Italian sausage, cut into ½-inch slices
2 medium onions, peeled and chopped
3 cloves garlic, peeled and minced
3 cups peeled and chopped fresh tomatoes or one 28-ounce can Italian plum tomatoes, chopped
1½ cups dry red wine
5½ cups chicken stock
1 tablespoon chopped fresh basil or 1 teaspoon dried
1 tablespoon chopped fresh oregano or 1 teaspoon dried
1 medium green pepper, seeded and chopped
2 medium zucchini, diced into ½-inch pieces
½ cup orzo (a rice-shaped Greek pasta)
½ teaspoon salt
½ teaspoon ground black pepper
3 tablespoons chopped parsley (for garnish)
½ cup grated Parmesan cheese (optional)

Since the best fully ripened tomatoes can be found in local markets only during the peak summer months and early fall, I suggest you buy them canned if you have no way of preserving tomatoes. The best are Italian plum tomatoes—they seem to have a much better, richer flavor.

Sauté the sausage in a 5-quart saucepan over medium heat until lightly browned. Remove the sausage to a plate, leaving 2 tablespoons of the fat in the saucepan. Discard the rest of the fat. Add the onions and garlic and sauté for 2 or 3 minutes. Add the sausage, tomatoes, wine, and stock. Bring to a boil. Add the basil and oregano. Simmer, uncovered, over low heat for 15 minutes. Skim off the excess fat. Add the green pepper, zucchini, orzo, salt, and pepper and simmer, covered, for 10 minutes. Garnish with parsley. Sprinkle with Parmesan cheese.

Yields: 10 servings

Preparation time: 45 minutes

We made the quantity of this soup greater than the others because, when frozen, it can be stored for up to 6 weeks in the freezer. Not many soups thaw well, but this one does. If you want to keep it without freezing, it will last for 4 days in the refrigerator.

CELERY

Celery, raw,
Develops the jaw,
But celery stewed,
Is more quietly chewed.
—Ogden Nash

COUNTRY VEGETABLE SOUP

This is a hearty, traditional soup that is easily adapted to whatever produce is available throughout the year. Don't be put off by the length of preparation time needed. The beans soak without needing to be watched, and the soup simmers for almost all of two and a quarter hours.

1 pound white beans, soaked in water overnight
1½ pounds smoked ham, cut into bite-sized pieces
4 cups peeled and chopped onion
4 cloves garlic, peeled and minced
3 cups peeled and chopped fresh tomatoes or one 28-ounce can Italian plum tomatoes, with juice
12 cups chicken stock
6 cups water
1½ bay leaves, crumbled
2 tablespoons chopped fresh thyme or 2 teaspoons dried
1 cup chopped parsley
4 stalks celery, chopped
4 carrots, peeled and sliced
3 medium zucchini, cut into bite-sized pieces
1 tablespoon salt
1 teaspoon ground black pepper
Chopped parsley (for garnish)

Drain the soaked beans and place them in a 10-quart pot. Add the ham, onion, garlic, and tomatoes and heat over medium flame for 2 minutes. Add the chicken stock, water, bay leaves, thyme, and parsley. Bring to a boil. Simmer for about 1½ hours. Add the celery and carrots and simmer for another 15 minutes. Add the zucchini, salt, and pepper and simmer for 10 minutes more. Garnish with parsley.

Yields: 4 to 6 quarts

Preparation time: 2 hours 15 minutes (excluding soaking time)

GARLIC–CHIVE SOUP

This soup comes from a pure love of garlic. A delicate bouquet emanates from this light, creamy soup, making it a perfect prelude to any savory lamb or beef dinner.

2 tablespoons peeled and minced garlic
2 teaspoons coarse salt
5 cups chicken stock
6 tablespoons (¾ stick) butter
⅓ cup unbleached white flour
1 cup heavy cream
⅛ teaspoon ground white pepper
⅛ teaspoon turmeric
¼ cup chopped chives (for garnish)

Mash the garlic and salt together to make a paste. Place it in a 3-quart saucepan and add the chicken stock. Bring this to a boil, then simmer for 20 minutes.

Melt the butter in a separate heavy saucepan. Sprinkle in the flour and cook over low heat for 2 minutes, stirring constantly. Remove from the heat. Add 3 cups of the garlic–chicken broth to this mixture and stir until it starts to thicken. Pour in the rest of the broth and blend. Add the cream, pepper, and turmeric. Return to the heat and bring the soup to a boil, stirring all the while. Let it simmer for 3 minutes, then remove from the heat. Add the chives and serve.

Yields: 6 servings
Preparation time: 35 minutes

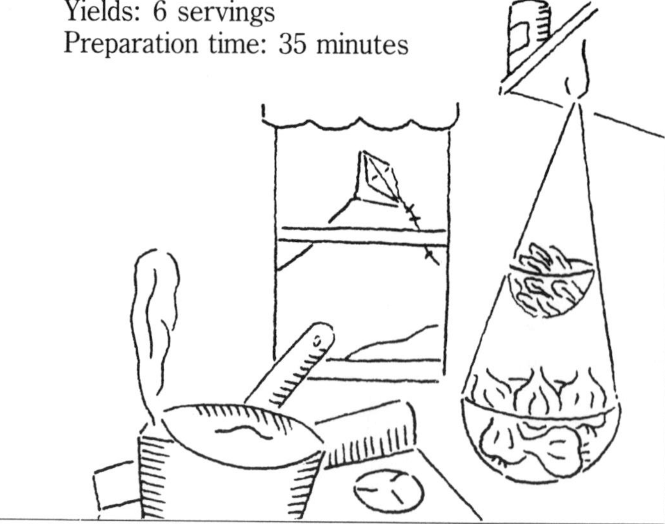

SPINACH SOUP

Hot or chilled, as an introduction to a festive dinner or on its own as a luncheon meal, this light soup with its hint of nutmeg is one of the most popular soups at Loaves and Fishes.

2 tablespoons clarified butter
3 cups peeled and coarsely chopped onion
3 cups chicken stock
1½ pounds fresh spinach or two 10-ounce packages frozen spinach, thawed
3 tablespoons butter
2 tablespoons unbleached white flour
3 cups milk
1½ teaspoons salt
1 teaspoon freshly ground black pepper
½ teaspoon freshly grated nutmeg

Melt the clarified butter in a heavy saucepan. Add the onion and sauté over low heat until transparent; do not brown. Add the chicken stock and bring to a boil. Simmer for about 10 minutes. Add all the spinach, saving 6 perfect leaves for garnish. Bring the soup to a boil again, then remove from the heat. Let cool.

Meanwhile, melt butter in a heavy saucepan. Stir in the flour and cook for 2 minutes. Continue stirring as you slowly add the milk. Bring it to a boil and remove from the heat.

Pour the spinach mixture into the bowl of a food processor fitted with the metal blade and puree until smooth. Combine the spinach and milk mixtures in a saucepan. Add the salt, pepper, and nutmeg. Reheat until hot, but not boiling.

Yields: 6 servings
Preparation time: 30 minutes

TO SERVE CHILLED

Let the soup cool for 30 minutes, then chill it in the refrigerator for at least 4 hours or overnight. Serve in chilled bowls and garnish with a spinach leaf topped with a dollop of sour cream.

This soup will keep for up to 4 days in the refrigerator. Simmer it gently. Garnish with a drop of sour cream crossed with a sprig of fennel.

PEA AND FENNEL SOUP

I first tasted fennel in Baune, France, served in long, thin strips hidden inside a thick bouillabaisse. I was captivated by this new, exotic taste and wanted to create a soup using fennel as its predominant flavor. I tried combinations of many vegetables and finally arrived at this perfect blend. Served hot or cold, this is one of the most elegant of soups, and is a beautiful introduction to almost any meal.

2 tablespoons safflower oil
2 cups peeled and coarsely chopped onion
1 large fennel bulb, coarsely chopped
4½ cups chicken stock
1 cup dry white wine
¾ teaspoon ground white pepper
1¼ teaspoons salt
4½ pounds fresh shelled peas or two 10-ounce packages frozen peas, thawed
1 cup heavy cream
Fennel sprigs (for garnish)

Heat the oil in a large saucepan. Add the onion and fennel and sauté over a low heat for 5 minutes. Add the chicken stock, wine, pepper, and salt. Bring to a boil, then simmer for 20 minutes. Remove from the heat. Add the peas, cover, and allow the soup to cool for 30 minutes.

Puree in the bowl of a food processor or in a blender; this may have to be done in several batches.

Return the soup to the saucepan. While reheating over low flame, add the cream and stir. Serve garnished with fennel sprigs.

Yields: 8 servings

Preparation time: 1 hour 15 minutes

ZUCCHINI–PEPPER SOUP

A delicate green color and a smooth, refreshing vegetable taste make this a perfect first course. It can be served hot or chilled and goes very well with almost any main course.

4 small zucchini, cut into ½-inch pieces
2 green peppers, seeded and coarsely chopped
1½ cups peeled and coarsely chopped onion
4 cups chicken stock
1½ cups sour cream
4 sprigs chopped parsley, leaves only
1 teaspoon salt
½ teaspoon ground black pepper

GARNISH

1 small zucchini, thinly sliced
½ cup sour cream
8 sprigs dill

Place the zucchini, peppers, onion, and chicken stock in a saucepan and bring to a boil. Reduce the heat and allow it to simmer for 15 minutes. Remove from the heat and let cool for 15 minutes.

Pour half the soup mixture and half the sour cream into the bowl of food processor fitted with the metal blade. Add the parsley, salt, and pepper. Whirl until smooth. Add the rest of the ingredients and process until smooth.

Serve in bowls with a slice of zucchini topped with a dollop of sour cream and decorated with a sprig of fresh dill.

Yields: 8 servings

Preparation time: 50 minutes

HOT

When reheating the soup, never allow it to boil. Soups made with sour cream will curdle as soon as they reach the boiling point, so be careful.

CHILLED

If you plan to serve the soup chilled, refrigerate it for at least 4 hours after it has been pureed.

A zester is a very popular and useful gadget that produces strips of citrus fruit peels.

SUMMER TOMATO SOUP

The combination of tangy oranges, sweet juicy tomatoes, and only the slightest suggestion of allspice makes this a uniquely piquant first course. It will need to be chilled for at least four hours beforehand.

2 tablespoons safflower oil
2 cups peeled and chopped onion
1 clove garlic, peeled and minced
3 cups chicken stock
3 cups peeled and chopped fresh tomatoes or 3 cups canned crushed tomatoes
1 teaspoon salt
1/4 teaspoon ground black pepper
1/4 teaspoon ground allspice
1 1/2 cups orange juice
Rind of 1 orange, grated
1/4 cup heavy cream
Strips of orange zest (for garnish)

Heat the safflower oil in a large soup pot. Add the onion and sauté over low heat until it becomes transparent. Add the garlic, chicken stock, tomatoes, salt, pepper, and allspice and simmer for 12 minutes. Let cool slightly.

Puree half the soup in the bowl of a food processor fitted with the metal blade and pour into a serving blowl. Repeat with the other half.

Add the orange juice, rind, and cream to the bowl of soup. Stir well and chill for at least 4 hours. Garnish with orange zest strips.

Yields: 6 servings

Preparation time: 40 minutes (excluding refrigeration time)

WHITE GAZPACHO

Thick with crunchy fresh vegetables, spiced with a touch of garlic and onions, and sweetened with slices of chilled grapes, this popular soup makes a perfect meal or first course during the summer months.

3 cucumbers, peeled, seeded, and chopped
3 cloves garlic, peeled and minced
2¼ cups chicken stock
2½ cups yogurt
3 tablespoons white wine vinegar
2 teaspoons salt
2 teaspoons ground white pepper
2 red peppers, seeded and finely chopped
1½ green peppers, seeded and finely chopped
1 medium red onion, peeled and minced
½ cup white or red seedless grapes, halved
½ cup heavy cream

Place the cucumber, garlic, and chicken stock in the bowl of a food processor fitted with the metal blade. Process for about 2 minutes.

Combine the rest of the ingredients in a separate bowl. Add the cucumber mixture. Mix well, chill, and serve.

Yields: 3 quarts
Preparation time: 20 minutes

CHILLED PLUM SOUP

In Scandinavian countries and provinces of northern Germany, fruit soups are traditionally served prior to any poultry dinner. This soup needs no stock and is a refreshing combination of fresh plums and red wine in a chilled creamy soup. It can also be served as an exotic dessert.

USING FRESH PLUMS

Fresh Italian plums have a very short season—from the middle of August to the end of September. If, during that time, you would like to use fresh plums in this recipe, this is what to do:
Halve and pit 3 cups plums. Place them in a saucepan with 2 cups water and ½ cup sugar. Simmer for 10 minutes, then drain, reserving the liquid for later use. Proceed with the recipe.

Two 28-ounce cans whole purple plums in heavy syrup
1½ cups water
½ teaspoon ground cinnamon
1 bay leaf
½ teaspoon ground white pepper
⅛ teaspoon salt
¾ cup red Burgundy wine
1½ tablespoons cornstarch
¾ cup heavy cream
Grated rind and juice of 1 lemon
1½ cups sour cream
2 tablespoons brandy

Drain the plums, reserving the syrup. Remove the pits and finely chop the plums. Place them in a large saucepan. Add the syrup, water, cinnamon, bay leaf, pepper, and salt. Simmer for 5 minutes.

Combine the wine, cornstarch, and heavy cream. Slowly pour this mixture into the soup, stirring constantly. Bring to a full boil. Remove from the heat.

In a large serving bowl, mix the lemon rind, lemon juice, sour cream, and brandy. Using a wire whisk, slowly beat 2 cups of the soup into the sour cream mixture. Once that's been thoroughly mixed, pour in the rest of the soup. Stir and chill for at least four hours.

Yields: 6 to 8 servings

Preparation time: 30 minutes (excluding refrigeration time)

CHILLED RASPBERRY SOUP

In Scandinavia, for weddings and other special occasions, families often serve a chilled fruit–wine soup, followed by lots of homemade bread and freshly baked ham, and accompanied by some authentic rhubarb wine. This soup is so easy to make and is so pretty, light, and always a welcome surprise when served before a dinner of roast duck or chicken.

Fresh raspberries have such a short season that we never expect anyone to cook them into a recipe. Use frozen raspberries. It's much better to serve fresh raspberries with Crème Fraîche or with a trickle of raspberry sauce, or to use them to blanket a crisp tart shell.

Three 10-ounce packages frozen raspberries in light syrup, thawed
2½ cups water
½ teaspoon ground cinnamon
½ teaspoon ground white pepper
⅛ teaspoon salt
1 cup Beaujolais wine
1½ tablespoons cornstarch
¾ cup heavy cream
Juice and grated rind of 1 lemon
2 cups sour cream
2 tablespoons Framboise

Puree the raspberries. Strain them into a medium saucepan, discarding the seeds. Add the water, cinnamon, pepper, and salt and simmer for 2 minutes.

In a separate bowl, mix together the wine, cornstarch, and heavy cream. Pour this into the soup, stirring constantly. Bring the soup to a full boil and remove from the heat.

Place the lemon rind, lemon juice, sour cream, and Framboise in a large serving bowl and mix. Using a wire whisk, gradually beat 2 cups of the soup into the sour cream mixture. Then add the rest. Stir and chill for at least four hours.

Yields: 6 to 8 servings

Preparation time: 30 minutes (excluding refrigeration time)

SALADS

Let the salad maker be a spendthrift with oil, a miser with vinegar, a diplomat with salt, and a madman with mixing.
—Spanish proverb

Salads give free creative rein to an imaginative cook. They can range anywhere from a one-vegetable side dish dressed in a simple vinaigrette, to a seductive first course designed to open the palate, to a more complicated mixture intended to serve as a full meal. Salads can be made from almost anything—every conceivable vegetable, almost any cut of meat, fish, poultry, pasta, grains, beans, and, on occasion, a flower or two. For example, the lavender flower from the slender chive plant not only decorates a salad bowl but has its own pleasant, shalloty taste.

If someone were to ask me what my favorite salad is, I would have a hard time answering. The Mexican Chicken Salad is a huge hit at Loaves and Fishes, as well as in my own kitchen at home. But then I think of the Lobster–Potato Salad and remember how luscious that tastes—fresh lobster chunks sharing a light dressing with slices of earthy new potatoes. I remember, too, dining on the Radish Sprouts, Goat Cheese, and Pear Salad and thinking of how this recipe mixes such wonderful, diverse tastes: the salty goat cheese, the sweet crunchy pear, and the peppery radish sprouts. Let's just say, then, that the best salads seem to develop from a democratic blending of colors, textures, flavors, and tastes.

I have supplied each salad recipe with its own distinct dressing. There's nothing better than a fruity, virgin olive oil with a tart vinegar, yet it doesn't suit every salad. Each one demands its own sparkling complement. There are no difficult or complicated recipes in this chapter. I wanted to make sure you tried all of these hand-picked ideas in the hope that you may, from them, glean a few of your own.

MELON, SHRIMP, AND AVOCADO SALAD

Sybille was visiting in California and sampled this salad at an outdoor buffet. The textures are perfectly balanced, and the tastes are so complementary. This is an excellent first course for grilled fish or Moroccan Lamb Stew.

1 pound shrimp, shelled and cooked
2 small cantaloupes or 1 large honeydew melon
2 ripe avocados
Juice of 1 lemon
⅓ cup peeled and finely chopped onion

CURRY DRESSING
½ cup olive oil
2 tablespoons red wine vinegar
1 clove garlic, peeled and minced
1 tablespoon curry powder
1 egg yolk
2 tablespoons heavy cream

Fresh mint (for garnish)

I suggest you assemble all the ingredients first, then mix them together only once, with your hands. This salad breaks up easily and should be handled gently.

Place the shrimp in a large salad bowl. Peel and seed the melon, then cut into bite-sized pieces. Add to the shrimp. Pit and peel the avocado; cut into bite-sized pieces and add to the salad. Sprinkle the avocado with lemon juice so it won't discolor. Add the onion.

To make the dressing, combine ingredients in a lidded container. Shake well and pour over the salad. Toss gently with your hands. Garnish with mint.

Yields: 6 to 8 servings.
Preparation time: 20 minutes

To get the most flavor from saffron soak it in 1/4 cup of warm water for 5 minutes. This will soften the strands and release the flavor. Add it to whatever recipe you're preparing.

PAELLA SALAD

I wanted to use all these good ingredients in a substantial salad that would taste just as good the day after it was prepared.

4 chicken breasts, skinned and boned
1/4 cup olive oil
2 cups peeled and finely chopped onion
3 cloves garlic, peeled and minced
1 1/2 cups converted rice
4 cups chicken stock
1 teaspoon curry powder
1 teaspoon salt
1/2 teaspoon Tabasco
1/2 teaspoon saffron threads
2 1/2 cups marinated artichoke hearts, drained, reserving 1/4 cup marinade
2 green peppers, chopped
6 scallions, chopped
2 stalks celery, chopped
1 cup green olives, pitted and chopped
1/2 cup pimiento, chopped
1 1/2 pounds shrimp, shelled and cooked

DRESSING

2 cups mayonnaise
1 tablespoon curry powder
1/2 teaspoon turmeric
1 teaspoon ground black pepper
2 teaspoons salt

Cut the chicken breasts into bite-sized chunks and set aside.

Sauté the onion and garlic in the olive oil over medium heat for about 3 minutes. Add the rice, chicken stock, curry powder, salt, Tabasco, and saffron. Stir once and cover. Bring the rice to a boil and simmer for 10 minutes over low heat. Add the chicken chunks and simmer for 7 minutes more. Remove from the heat and pour into a large salad bowl. Add the artichoke hearts and pour the reserved marinade over the rice and chicken. Add the peppers, scallions, celery, green olives, pimiento, and shrimp.

To make the dressing, mix all the ingredients together separately and pour over the salad, mixing it well with your hands, making sure it is thoroughly blended.

Yields: 6 to 8 servings
Preparation time: 40 minutes

SHRIMP AND ORZO SALAD

Fresh pink shrimp with Greek pasta tossed in a creamy mustard dressing make a satisfying meal when served with a green, leafy salad. In smaller portions, this salad also makes an ideal first course. It's best served the same day it's prepared.

12 ounces orzo (a rice-shaped Greek pasta)
1½ pounds raw shrimp
1 small red pepper
1 tablespoon olive oil
¼ teaspoon salt
¼ teaspoon ground black pepper
¾ cup mayonnaise
1½ tablespoons Dijon mustard
1 tablespoon dry white wine
5 scallions, green parts only, sliced
½ cup chopped dill
¾ teaspoon salt
½ teaspoon ground black pepper
6 sprigs dill (for garnish)

Preheat the oven to 400°F.

Boil the orzo in 1½ quarts water until done, about 12 minutes (it should be al dente). Drain, then run cold water over the orzo to cool it down quickly. Place the pasta in a large mixing bowl.

Poach the shrimp. Let cool slightly and shell. Add to the orzo. Cut the red pepper in half, remove the seeds, sprinkle with olive oil, salt, and pepper. Place it on a baking sheet and roast for 20 minutes. Remove and let cool.

Dice the peppers into ½-inch pieces and add to the orzo along with the rest of the ingredients. Mix the salad gently but thoroughly with your hands. Garnish with dill.

Yields: 6 servings
Preparation time: 45 minutes

TO POACH SHRIMP

Bring 1 quart water, 1 tablespoon lemon juice, and ½ teaspoon salt to a boil. Add the shrimp. Bring to a boil once again. As soon as the shrimp turn pink, they are done. This usually takes between 2 and 3 minutes. Drain. Run under cold water and the shrimp are ready to be shelled. It is not necessary to remove the black vein except for the sake of aesthetics.

SHRIMP AND CRAB MEAT SALAD

A mild salad, naturally sweetened by the succulent shellfish.

You can substitute frozen cooked crabmeat or canned crabmeat when fresh is not available.

1¾ pounds medium shrimp, shelled and cooked
1¼ cups snow crab meat, cooked
1 cucumber, peeled, seeded, and diced
1 tablespoon peeled and minced onion

DRESSING

1 cup mayonnaise
1 tablespoon mustard
3 tablespoons lemon juice
½ teaspoon salt
½ teaspoon ground black pepper
¾ cup finely chopped dill

Green leafy lettuce (for garnish)

Place the shrimp, crab meat, cucumber, and onion in a large salad bowl.

To make the dressing, mix the ingredients together in a separate bowl. Pour the dressing over the salad and mix gently with your hands until all the seafood is coated. Serve the salad in the center of a platter surrounded by a green leafy lettuce.

Yields: 6 servings
Preparation time: 20 minutes

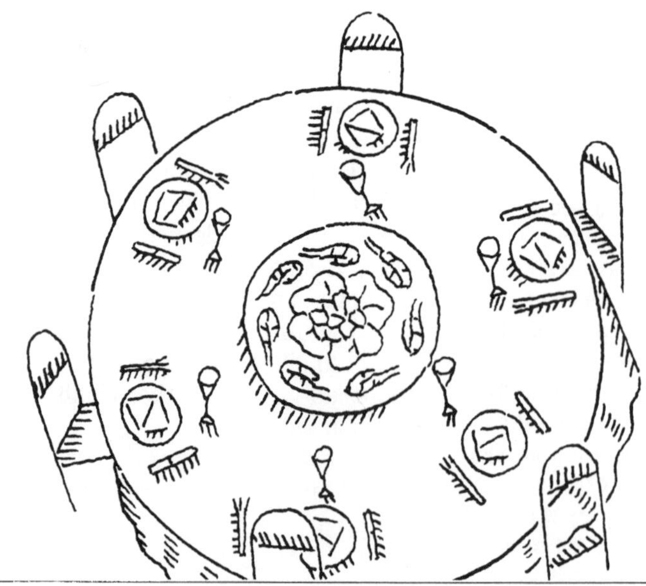

CURRIED SEAFOOD SALAD

I wanted to include this Loaves and Fishes favorite because of its versatility. The freshness of the seafood mixed with a mellow curry flavoring and a hint of chutney makes this salad an ideal first course, or an appetizing lunch served inside a sweet, juicy melon. I also recommend it for dinner, served with a leafy spinach salad and warm corn muffins.

½ pound small shrimp, shelled and cooked
½ pound snow crab meat, cooked
½ pound tilefish, filleted, poached, and broken into bite-sized pieces
4 scallions, chopped
1 cup chopped celery
¾ cup water chestnuts, sliced

DRESSING

1 cup mayonnaise
¼ cup mango chutney
1 tablespoon lemon juice
1 tablespoon curry powder
½ teaspoon salt

1 head romaine lettuce (to line platter)

Place the shrimp, crab meat, tilefish, scallions, celery, and water chestnuts in a large mixing bowl.

To make the dressing, combine the ingredients in a separate bowl and mix. Pour the dressing over the seafood and vegetables and toss gently with your hands.

Line a platter with lettuce leaves and arrange salad on top.

Yields: 6 servings
Preparation time: 30 minutes

TO POACH FISH

Pour 1 cup water and ½ cup dry white wine into a shallow skillet. Add ½ teaspoon salt, ½ stalk celery, and 1 bay leaf. Bring the liquid to a boil and simmer for 2 minutes. Add the fish and poach at a slow simmer for 4 or 5 minutes, or until the fish flakes apart. Lift the fish fillet out of the liquid and let cool. Save the poaching liquid for use in sauces or soups. It keeps for up to 3 days in the refrigerator or 2 months in the freezer.

LOBSTER SALAD

Lobster, like fresh raspberries, should never have its unique taste overpowered. This salad was created to present the sweet, white meat of the lobster without too much trimming. This can be served as either a main course or a first course.

2½ pounds cooked lobster meat
2 cups finely chopped romaine lettuce
¼ cup capers in vinegar, drained

DRESSING

¼ cup vinegar from capers
1 cup mayonnaise
½ cup chopped parsley
½ teaspoon salt
½ teaspoon ground black pepper

Italian parsley sprigs (for garnish)

Cut the lobster meat into bite-sized morsels and place in a large salad bowl. To that add the chopped lettuce and capers.

To make the dressing, blend the ingredients together in a separate bowl. Pour the dressing over the lobster mixture and mix gently with your hands. Make sure all the meat is coated with the sauce. Garnish with parsley.

Yields: 6 servings
Preparation time: 15 minutes

TO COOK LOBSTERS

Pour enough water into a 10-quart pan to fill it half full. Add 2 tablespoons of salt and bring it to a boil. Plunge four 1½ pound lobsters into the water, head first. When the water returns to a running boil, cover the pan and start timing. The lobsters should be ready in 12 minutes.

LOBSTER–POTATO SALAD

What could be a better combination than the simplest of foods served with the most sublime? The earthy potato and the succulent lobster, dotted with tangy capers, make a marvelous lunch.

2 pounds small white potatoes
3 cups lobster meat, cooked
2/3 cup chopped dill
4 scallions, green parts only, chopped
3 tablespoons capers in vinegar, drained
2 tablespoons vinegar from capers
1 1/2 tablespoons lemon juice
3/4 teaspoon salt
3/4 teaspoon ground black pepper
3/4 cup mayonnaise
Dill sprigs (for garnish)

Boil the potatoes for 15 minutes, then drain. .Let them stand until they are cool enough to handle, then cut them into bite-sized pieces. Place them in a large salad bowl. Cut the lobster into bite-sized pieces and add that to the potatoes. Sprinkle with dill, scallions, capers, caper vinegar, lemon juice, salt, and pepper. Finally add the mayonnaise and mix the salad gently with your hands, being careful not to break the potatoes. Garnish with dill sprigs.

Yields: 6 servings
Preparation time: 45 minutes

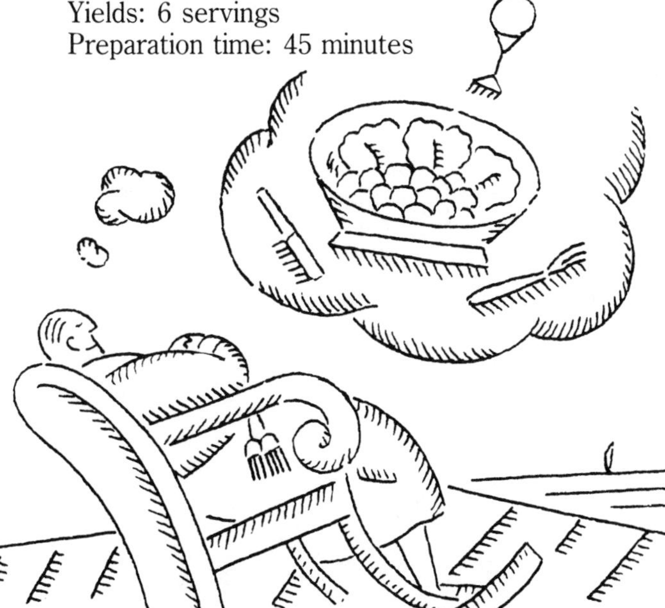

One cannot think well, love well if one has not dined well.
—Virginia Woolf

If you're planning this dish as part of a large buffet, arrange the salad in the center of a large platter and place bowls of salted peanuts, grated coconut, sliced bananas, and chopped green peppers around the plate as possible additions to be sprinkled over the salad.

CURRIED CHICKEN SALAD

We make over fifty pounds of this salad every morning and by afternoon it's completely sold out.

3 pounds chicken breasts, boned and skinned
1 medium onion, peeled and halved
1 bay leaf
6 sprigs parsley
1 parsnip, peeled and halved
½ teaspoon salt
¼ teaspoon ground black pepper
1 clove
1 cup water chestnuts, sliced
½ cups scallions, cut on the diagonal
Rind of 2 limes, grated

DRESSING

1 cup mayonnaise
2 tablespoons soy sauce
⅓ cup curry powder
1 cup mango chutney, finely chopped

Combine the chicken breasts and onion in a large saucepan, cover with cold water, and bring to a boil. Add the bay leaf, parsley, parsnip, salt, pepper, and clove. Simmer for about 10 or 12 minutes, or until the chicken is done.

Using a slotted spoon, transfer the chicken to a strainer and let cool until comfortable enough to handle. Discard the rest.

Cut the cooked chicken breasts into bite-sized pieces. (I like them in chunks about 1 inch square.) Place them in a large salad bowl. Add the water chestnuts, scallions, and lime rind.

To make the dressing, mix all the ingredients in a separate bowl and pour over the chicken. Mix gently but thoroughly with your hands.

Yields: 6 to 8 servings
Preparation time: 40 minutes

CHICKEN BROTH

Boil the leftover chicken broth until it's reduced to half its original amount. It can be frozen and used for soups or stews.

ORIENTAL CHICKEN SALAD

Tender chicken, crisp snow peas, and crunchy water chestnuts, mixed into a highly seasoned Oriental dressing, make this a tasty meal.

2½ pounds chicken breasts, boned and skinned
1 medium onion, peeled and halved
½ stalk celery
1 bay leaf
½ teaspoon salt
¼ teaspoon ground black pepper
4 cups water
⅓ pound snow peas, trimmed and cut on the diagonal
1 bunch scallions, cut on the diagonal
1 cup water chestnuts, sliced

DRESSING

½ cup mayonnaise
½ cup sesame tahini
3 tablespoons lemon juice
2½ tablespoons dry sherry
3 tablespoons dry white wine
4 teaspoons Dijon mustard
1½ tablespoons soy sauce
1½ tablespoons sugar
2 tablespoons peeled and minced ginger
¼ teaspoon hot red pepper flakes
½ teaspoon ground black pepper

Place the chicken, onion, celery, bay leaf, salt, and pepper in the water and bring to a boil over high heat. Reduce the heat and poach the chicken for about 12 minutes. Check for doneness, being careful not to overcook. When the chicken is ready, transfer it to a platter. Strain the broth and save it for another use.

When the chicken is cool enough to handle, slice it into bite-sized chunks and place in a medium salad bowl. To that add the snow peas, scallions, and water chestnuts.

To make the dressing, combine the ingredients either in your food processor or in a separate bowl. Blend until you have a smooth sauce and pour it over the chicken. Mix very well with your hands.

Yields: 8 servings
Preparation time: 30 minutes

I usually serve this with a side dish of Green Bean Salad tossed in a creamy horseradish dressing, some warmed Buttermilk–Corn Bread, and a chilled bottle of my favorite white wine.

MEXICAN CHICKEN SALAD

I created this dish because of my passion for Mexican food. It's a special treat for those of you who share my enthusiasm. Freshly cut cilantro gives this spicy salad an intoxicating bouquet.

3 pounds chicken breasts, boned and skinned
4 ounces canned peeled green chilies, drained and chopped
1 large pickled jalapeño pepper, seeded and minced
1/3 cup peeled and finely chopped onion
4 fresh Italian plum tomatoes, finely chopped
1/2 cup finely chopped cilantro

DRESSING
1/3 cup olive oil
2 tablespoons white wine vinegar
2 large cloves garlic, peeled and minced
3/4 teaspoon salt
1/2 teaspoon ground black pepper

Pour water into a medium saucepan until it is three-quarters full. Add the chicken breasts and simmer until done, about 10 to 12 minutes. Remove the chicken and cut into bite-sized chunks. Place in a large salad bowl. To that add the green chilies, jalapeño pepper, onion, tomatoes, and cilantro.

To make the dressing, combine the ingredients in a lidded container and shake vigorously. Pour over chicken salad and mix well, using your hands.

Yields: 6 servings
Preparation time: 30 minutes

GREEN BEAN SALAD

2 pounds fresh green beans

DRESSING
1 cup sour cream
1/2 cup freshly grated horseradish
1/4 cup peeled and minced white onion
3/4 teaspoon salt
3/4 teaspoon ground black pepper
1/3 cup chopped parsley

Blanch the green beans until crisp, then shock them under cold water. While the beans are cooling, mix the dressing ingredients together. Pour this over the green beans in a salad bowl and serve at room temperature or chilled.

Yields: 6 servings

Preparation time: 15 minutes

SMOKED CHICKEN SALAD

Smoked chicken lends its intriguing flavor to all the other ingredients.

Smoked chicken breasts are available in specialty food stores.

3 boned smoked chicken breasts (about 2½ pounds)
1 medium onion, peeled and minced
1 red pepper, sliced into ½-inch pieces
¾ cup fresh shelled peas
½ cup finely chopped parsley

It would be wise to make this salad up to 8 hours before you need it because then you would be allowing all the flavors more time to blend.

DRESSING

⅔ cup mayonnaise
2 teaspoons white wine vinegar
1 teaspoon salt
1 teaspoon ground black pepper

Remove the skin and fat from the smoked chicken breasts. Cut the chicken into bite-sized chunks and place in a salad bowl. Add the onion, red pepper, peas, and parsley.

To make the dressing, mix the ingredients in a separate bowl, then pour over the chicken. Blend well with your hands.

Yields: 6 servings

Preparation time: 20 minutes

FOR COCKTAILS

If you chop up the vegetables and chicken very small, this salad can be spooned onto cucumber rounds or spread over buttered black bread and served as appetizers. The salad keeps for up to 4 days in the refrigerator.

DUCK SALAD

Wild rice adds texture to this sweet, pungent salad.

2 ducks
1 medium onion, peeled and quartered
1⅓ cups wild rice
1 teaspoon salt
4 scallions, chopped
Zest of 2 oranges

DRESSING

¼ cup red wine vinegar
6 tablespoons olive oil
2 teaspoons salt
2 teaspoons ground black pepper
2 cloves garlic, peeled and minced
½ cup mango chutney, chopped

Watercress sprigs (for garnish)

Place the ducks and onion in a stock pot, cover with cold water, and bring to a boil. Simmer, covered, for 2 hours. Let the ducks cool overnight in their broth. This will help to keep the meat moist.

Place the rice in a saucepan with 3 cups water and the salt and bring to a boil. Simmer for about 25 minutes, until the rice is al dente; drain.

Pull the duck meat from the bones and cut into bite-sized chunks. Place the meat in a bowl and add the cooked rice, the scallions, and the orange zest.

To make the dressing, mix the ingredients separately and pour over the duck salad. Toss by hand to make sure it is mixed well.

Yields: 6 to 8 servings

Preparation time: 2 hours 30 minutes (excluding cooling time)

COLD SESAME NOODLES

This is not for the faint-hearted.

1 pound spaghettini
2 tablespoons vegetable oil

DRESSING

1/4 cup peeled garlic cloves
1/2 cup peanut oil
1/2 cup sesame tahini
1/2 cup strong tea
1/2 cup soy sauce
1/4 cup dry sherry
1/4 cup sherry vinegar
1/4 cup sugar
2 teaspoons ground black pepper
1/8 teaspoon cayenne pepper

1 green pepper, chopped
1 red pepper, chopped
1 small zucchini, cut lengthwise and sliced
1 small yellow squash, cut lengthwise and sliced
6 scallions, chopped
1/4 pounds snow peas, blanched and sliced on the diagonal
1 cup water chestnuts, sliced
1/4 cup peeled and minced ginger

Boil the spaghettini in salted water until it's al dente. Drain and transfer the noodles to a medium serving bowl. Sprinkle with the vegetable oil and mix so that the noodles won't stick. Set aside.

To make the dressing, pulse the garlic in the bowl of a food processor until finely chopped. Add the peanut oil, sesame tahini, and tea. Pulse to blend. Add the remaining ingredients and pulse to blend. Pour this mixture over the noodles. Add the chopped vegetables and mix well with your hands.

Cover and store in the refrigerator until ready to serve or serve at room temperature.

Yields: 6 to 8 servings
Preparation time: 30 minutes

This fiery salad, in small portions, makes an excellent first course to, say, a duck dinner. As a side salad it goes extremely well with any grilled meats or poultry courses. Garnish with chopped scallions. If you find this a bit too hot for your palate, cut down on the cayenne pepper.

Sesame tahini, also called sesame paste, is made from 100 percent ground hulled sesame seeds.

This lasts for about three days when stored in the refrigerator. It's best served at room temperature.

SESAME–BROCCOLI SALAD

A simple salad, with a rousing, fiery dressing. If you're serving lamb or beef, or Swordfish Steaks in Lime–Soy Marinade, have this salad before or after the main course. It has a marinating time of two hours.

2 heads broccoli
¼ cup sesame oil
2 teaspoons hot red pepper flakes

DRESSING

2 cloves garlic, peeled and minced
1 teaspoon salt
2 tablespoons red wine vinegar
⅓ cup olive oil

You are not required to cook the broccoli because during the marinating process the dressing "cooks," or tenderizes, the vegetable for you.

Cut off the broccoli tops into 2½-inch-long florets and place them in a mixing bowl. Peel the stems, discarding the lower woody part, and cut them into bite-sized pieces. Place with the florets.

Heat the sesame oil over a medium flame to the point before it starts to smoke. Remove from the heat, add the hot red pepper flakes, and allow them to steep for 10 minutes. Then pour the oil over the broccoli.

To make the dressing, combine the ingredients in a container with a tight-fitting lid. Shake vigorously and pour over the salad. Toss well, using your hands. Marinate for 2 hours in the refrigerator.

Yields: 6 servings

Preparation time: 20 minutes (excluding marinating time)

FUSILLI AND FETA WITH FRESH SORREL

Sorrel distributes its lemony flavor throughout this robust salad. You can serve this as a full meal. It can also be packed for picnicking on the beach. The sun has a way of blending all its special flavors.

3/4 pound fusilli noodles
3/4 pound feta cheese, cut into 1/2-inch cubes
1/4 cup peeled and minced red onion
1/2 cup diced sun-dried tomatoes, drained
1 cup Niçoise black olives, pitted
3 cups fresh sorrel leaves

DRESSING

1 clove garlic, peeled and minced
1/2 teaspoon salt
3/4 teaspoon pepper
3 tablespoons red wine vinegar
1/2 cup olive oil

Boil the fusilli until just done, about 10 minutes. Drain and transfer to a mixing bowl. Add the feta cheese, onion, tomatoes, olives, and sorrel.

To make the dressing, combine all the ingredients in a container with a lid and shake well. Pour the dressing over the salad and mix lightly with your hands. Serve at room temperature.

Yields: 6 to 8 servings
Preparation time: 30 minutes

Among the varied stories of how macaroni got its name, this is the one I like best. It's about an Italian woman who shaped pasta dough into small squares, cooked it in her favorite sauce, and served it up to her husband for his approval. According to this story, he nearly swooned with ecstasy, crying out, "ma caronies, ma caronies." Translated, this means "my little dears, my little dears."

FRESH PEAS WITH DILL

Sweet and delicate, yet cool and crunchy. Serve this with veal, chicken, or fish. During sugar snap pea season try using them instead of snow peas.

3 cups fresh peas, shelled from 3 pounds pea pods
1 pound snow peas, trimmed
1 small onion, peeled and finely chopped

DRESSING

¾ cup sour cream
⅛ teaspoon Tabasco
2 cloves garlic, peeled and mashed into 1 teaspoon salt to form a paste
½ teaspoon ground black pepper
½ cup chopped dill

Blanch and shock both types of peas separately. Cut the snow peas in half, on the diagonal. Place both types of peas in a bowl and add the onion.

To make the dressing, combine the ingredients in a small bowl and mix well. Pour the dressing over the pea salad and toss with your hands to make sure it's coated evenly.

Yields: 6 to 8 servings
Preparation time: 20 minutes

BLANCHING AND SHOCKING PEAS AND SNOW PEAS

Place the shelled peas into rapidly boiling water for only 5 seconds, or until they turn bright green. Drain and quickly plunge them into very cold water for about a minute.

The snow peas might take a little less time, depending on their freshness and maturity.

WARM RADICCIO SALAD

With its distinctive flavor and the hint of vinegar, this salad opens the palate and starts dinner off wonderfully.

2 small heads radiccio lettuce
2 tablespoons red wine vinegar
6 tablespoons olive oil
¾ teaspoon salt
¾ teaspoon ground black pepper
½ cup paper-thin slices peeled red onion

Cut the radiccio heads into quarters. Discard the cores. Separate the leaves and set aside.

Combine the vinegar, oil, salt, and pepper in a large sauté pan and heat until the mixture starts to

Radiccio is imported from Italy or Belgium. Its crisp, pretty leaves range in color from pastel pink to a rich, ruby red. When the leaves are separated, they turn into miniature, edible bowls. For appetizers, place a slice of goat cheese in each of these fragile "bowls" and sprinkle with fresh chopped chives.

boil. Add the radiccio and onion. Sauté over high heat, stirring constantly, for 1 minute. At the point when the lettuce starts to wilt, remove it from the heat. Divide onto six salad plates and serve warm.

Yields: 6 servings
Preparation time: 15 minutes

CUCUMBER SALAD WITH FRESH DILL

I remember having this at least twice a week when I was growing up because it was a family favorite. It was also a practical salad, since cucumber and dill grew in great abundance around our farm. It is crisp with a sweet and pungent taste, and is a wonderful complement to whole broiled fish and boiled new potatoes.

European, also called "seedless," cucumbers have no wax coating. We leave the skin on for both color and texture. Any leftovers from this salad will keep for up to 24 hours in the refrigerator.

2 European cucumbers
1 teaspoon salt
2 cloves garlic, peeled and minced
½ cup peeled and finely chopped red onion
¼ cup chopped dill
1 teaspoon sugar
1 teaspoon ground white pepper
2 tablespoons white wine vinegar
1½ cups sour cream

Slice the cucumbers very thin. Sprinkle with salt and place them in a colander for 15 minutes. Then press out as much liquid as you can with the back of a large spoon. Transfer the cucumber slices to a salad bowl. Add the rest of the ingredients and mix gently but thoroughly with your hands.

Yields: 6 to 8 servings
Preparation time: 30 minutes

GAZPACHO SALAD

This salad is so easy to assemble. It contains all the ingredients of red gazpacho—minus the soup—and makes a wonderful main course.

If you want to try a variation, substitute for the eggs, mozzarella, and olives some cooked, cubed chicken breasts, crumbled blue cheese, and crisp bacon bits. Try experimenting with different herbs besides the basil, too—this is a very adaptable salad.

1 head romaine lettuce
1 large red onion, peeled and diced
2 European seedless cucumbers, cut lengthwise, cored, and diced into ½-inch cubes
4 tomatoes, cut into ½-inch cubes
2 green peppers, seeded and cut into ½-inch pieces
1 pound mozzarella cheese, cut into ½-inch cubes
6 eggs, hard-boiled, shelled, and quartered
½ cup oil-cured black olives
1 cup fresh basil leaves, chopped

DRESSING

¾ cup olive oil
¼ cup red wine vinegar
1 clove garlic, peeled and crushed
¾ teaspoon salt
⅛ teaspoon Tabasco
½ teaspoon sugar

Line a shallow bowl or platter with large leaves of romaine. Shred the rest of the lettuce and sprinkle over the romaine. Pile the onion in the center, ring the cucumbers around the onion, the tomatoes should rim the cucumbers, next the peppers, then the mozzarella, until the platter is filled to the outer edge. The egg quarters should be placed decoratively near the center. Sprinkle the olives and basil on top of the salad.

To make the dressing, combine all the ingredients in a jar with a top and shake vigorously. Then trickle it over the entire salad.

Yields: 6 servings
Preparation time: 20 minutes

THREE-PEPPER SALAD

One of the newer salads from Loaves and Fishes, this makes a good first course to any hearty meal and is excellent as part of a buffet. The colors are glorious. This salad is best served at room temperature.

2 red peppers
2 green peppers
2 yellow peppers
⅓ cup olive oil
1 teaspoon salt

DRESSING

½ teaspoon peeled and minced garlic
½ teaspoon salt
2 tablespoons red wine vinegar
6 tablespoons olive oil
⅛ teaspoon Tabasco
2 teaspoons Dijon mustard
½ teaspoon sugar

1½ tablespoons chopped chives (for garnish)

Preheat oven to 425°F.

Cut the peppers lengthwise into quarters. Discard the seeds. Using a little of the oil, grease a large baking sheet. Place the peppers in a single layer across the pan, skin side down. Pour the rest of the olive oil over the peppers and sprinkle with salt. Roast for 20 minutes. Let cool to room temperature.

To make the dressing, mash the garlic and salt into a paste and add this to the remaining ingredients. Shake vigorously in a lidded jar.

Overlap the peppers on a platter and spoon the dressing over them. Sprinkle with chives and serve.

Yields: 6 servings
Preparation time: 35 minutes

Queen Victoria's chef, Francatelli, used garlic with extreme discretion. First he would assemble all the ingredients. Then he would carefully fold in the dressing and, just before serving, he would pop a clove of garlic into his mouth, chew it well, lift the bowl up, and gently breathe over the salad.

RADISH SPROUTS, GOAT CHEESE, AND PEAR SALAD

This salad combines the crunchy sweetness of pears, the salty creaminess of goat cheese, and the peppery overtone of radish sprouts. It's a meal in itself.

1 head romaine lettuce, rinsed and separated
8 ounces radish sprouts, rinsed and torn into bite-sized pieces
¾ pound Bucheron cheese, cut into 1-inch dice
4 ripe pears, cut into 1-inch dice

I usually prefer using Comice pears in this salad, but if you find them unavailable use Anjou or Bosc pears.

DRESSING

¼ cup red wine vinegar
¾ cup olive oil
1 teaspoon salt
½ teaspoon ground black pepper
½ teaspoon sugar
1 tablespoon fresh rosemary or 1 teaspoon dried

Arrange a bed of romaine leaves on 6 separate plates. Divide the radish sprouts, diced Bucheron, and diced pears into 6 portions and place on top of the lettuce leaves.

To make the dressing, combine all the ingredients by shaking them in a jar with a tight-fitting lid. Pour dressing over each portion.

Yields: 6 servings

Preparation time: 15 minutes

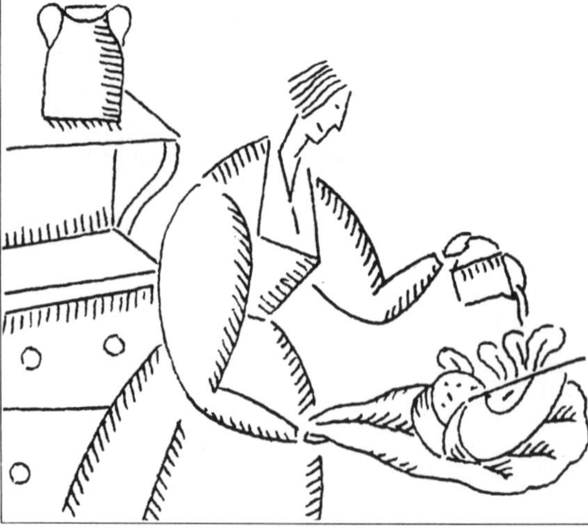

BEET, CELERY, AND APPLE SALAD

The combination of textures and tastes makes this salad very special. It's a good balance to any hearty meal. Serve on the side as a colorful addition to a buffet or as a refreshing first course.

Don't peel the beets before cooking them. They lose both their color and flavor. In fact, only remove their tops, leaving a good inch protruding from either end before placing them in the pot to boil. Once cooked, their skins come off very easily. A drop of vinegar or cream of tartar added to the pot helps them keep their rosy color.

2 pounds beets, tops removed leaving 1-inch on either end
½ cup peeled and thinly sliced red onion
1½ cups chopped celery
1½ cups cored and chopped tart apples

DRESSING

1 cup sour cream
2 tablespoons heavy cream
2 tablespoons lemon juice
¼ cup grated fresh horseradish or prepared horseradish, drained
1 teaspoon salt
¾ teaspoon ground black pepper
½ cup finely chopped parsley

Cover the beets with water and bring to a boil. Simmer for 25 to 30 minutes, depending on the size of the beets. Drain and let cool until they are easy to handle. Peel the beets and cut into ¼-inch sticks. Place in a mixing bowl and add the onion, celery, and apples.

To make the dressing, combine all the ingredients in a separate bowl and pour over the vegetables. Mix gently with your hands. Serve chilled.

Yields: 6 servings

Preparation time: 45 minutes (excluding refrigeration time)

Lemon balm, also called sweet balm or Melissa, is an herb with lemon-scented leaves. This item can be purchased at specialty food and produce stores.

POTATO SALAD

This is my mother's recipe, which I've adjusted by adding some cream. It helps to "gentle" the vinaigrette and brings out the earthy taste of the potato.

3 pounds new potatoes
½ cup chicken stock
½ cup heavy cream
2 cloves garlic, peeled and mashed into 1 teaspoon salt to make a paste
5 scallions, green parts only, chopped

DRESSING

5 tablespoons olive oil
¼ cup white wine vinegar
¼ cup Dijon mustard
1 teaspoon salt
1½ teaspoons ground black pepper

Lemon balm sprigs or 1 teaspoon lemon zest (for garnish)

Boil the potatoes until just done. Drain and let stand until they are cool enough to handle. Pour the chicken stock and cream over the potatoes and mix with your hands. Stir in the garlic paste and scallions. Marinate at room temperature for 30 minutes.

To make the dressing, combine all the ingredients in a container with a tight-fitting lid. Shake vigorously. Pour over the potato salad and toss carefully, using your hands.

Garnish with lemon balm sprigs or lemon zest and serve.

Yields: 6 to 8 servings

Preparation time: 1 hour 15 minutes (including marinating time)

Wild rice may seem expensive, but remember it *triples* in quantity when it's cooked, so a little goes a long way. Another note to remember—never overcook the rice; it shouldn't split open, or it will lose its unusual texture and taste. Always serve it al dente.

WILD RICE SALAD

This is a favorite at Loaves and Fishes, since it goes with almost any food. The hazelnuts give this salad its crunch. A wonderful present for a friend would be this recipe and a box of wild rice.

10 ounces wild rice
½ teaspoon salt
⅓ cup red wine vinegar
¼ cup olive oil
3 scallions, chopped
½ cup hazelnuts, toasted and halved
1 orange
1 cup seedless red grapes, halved
1 teaspoon salt
1 teaspoon ground black pepper

Place the rice in 2 quarts water with the ½ teaspoon salt and bring to a boil. Simmer for 25 minutes. The rice will be slightly underdone, or al dente. Drain and transfer to a salad bowl. Add the wine vinegar, olive oil, scallions, and toasted hazelnuts. Zest the orange and add that to the salad. Peel off the rind and cut the orange into small pieces. Stir into the salad. Add the grapes, salt, and pepper and mix the salad thoroughly with your hands. Let it stand for 30 minutes at room temperature to develop the flavor.

Yields: 8 servings
Preparation time: 1 hour

LENTIL–SAUSAGE SALAD

This salad can be made ahead of time. It keeps up to 3 days in the refrigerator. Bring it to room temperature before serving.

You can substitute any sausage for the one we've suggested, as long as it has lots of flavor.

One wet, chilly night in summer, Detlef and I chose to eat at a warm, cozy bistro that was just outside of Paris. We were served this salad as a first course. When I got back to Sagaponack, I made the salad adding cumin, to give it a touch more interest. I have since been serving this salad year-round as either a first course or a full meal. Try it with Cucumber Salad with Fresh Dill as a side dish, and some Bran–Whole Wheat Bread.

1 pound lentils
12 hot Italian sausages
1 tablespoon olive oil
2 medium red onions, peeled and finely chopped
3 stalks celery, diced
2 cucumbers, peeled, seeded, and diced
2 sweet red peppers, seeded and diced
2 green peppers, seeded and diced
4 cloves garlic, peeled and minced
2½ teaspoons salt
2 teaspoons ground black pepper
2 teaspoons ground cumin

DRESSING

¾ cup lemon juice
¾ cup olive oil
1½ tablespoons fresh oregano or 1½ teaspoons dried

Cook the lentils in 5 quarts water for about 12 minutes, or until they're just done. Don't overcook them. Drain and place the lentils in a salad bowl.

Sauté the sausages in olive oil until done. Let cool slightly, then slice. Mix with the lentils. Add the other salad ingredients and toss with your hands.

To make the dressing, combine all the ingredients in a lidded container and shake well. Pour the dressing over the lentil salad and toss again with your hands, making certain the dressing is well blended.

Yields: 8 to 10 servings
Preparation time: 35 minutes

LAMB, MINT, AND SPINACH SALAD

I love the appearance of leafy green spinach leaves mingled with tender pink slices of roast lamb. This salad is at its peak when served at room temperature right after it's been prepared.

1¼ pounds roast lamb, cut into thin strips
1 cup fresh mint leaves, coarsely chopped
2 cups fresh spinach leaves, coarsely chopped
½ cup red peppers roasted in oil, drained and cut into strips
1 cup paper-thin slices peeled red onion
½ teaspoon salt
½ teaspoon ground black pepper

DRESSING

1 clove garlic, peeled
1 teaspoon coarse salt
3 tablespoons red wine vinegar
½ cup olive oil
½ teaspoon sugar
½ teaspoon ground black pepper

Combine the lamb with the mint, spinach, red peppers, onion, salt, and pepper.

To make the dressing, mash the garlic and coarse salt into a paste and place this, together with the rest of the dressing ingredients, in a container with a tight-fitting lid. Shake thoroughly, then pour over the lamb salad. Toss the salad with your hands.

Yields: 6 servings

Preparation time: 20 minutes

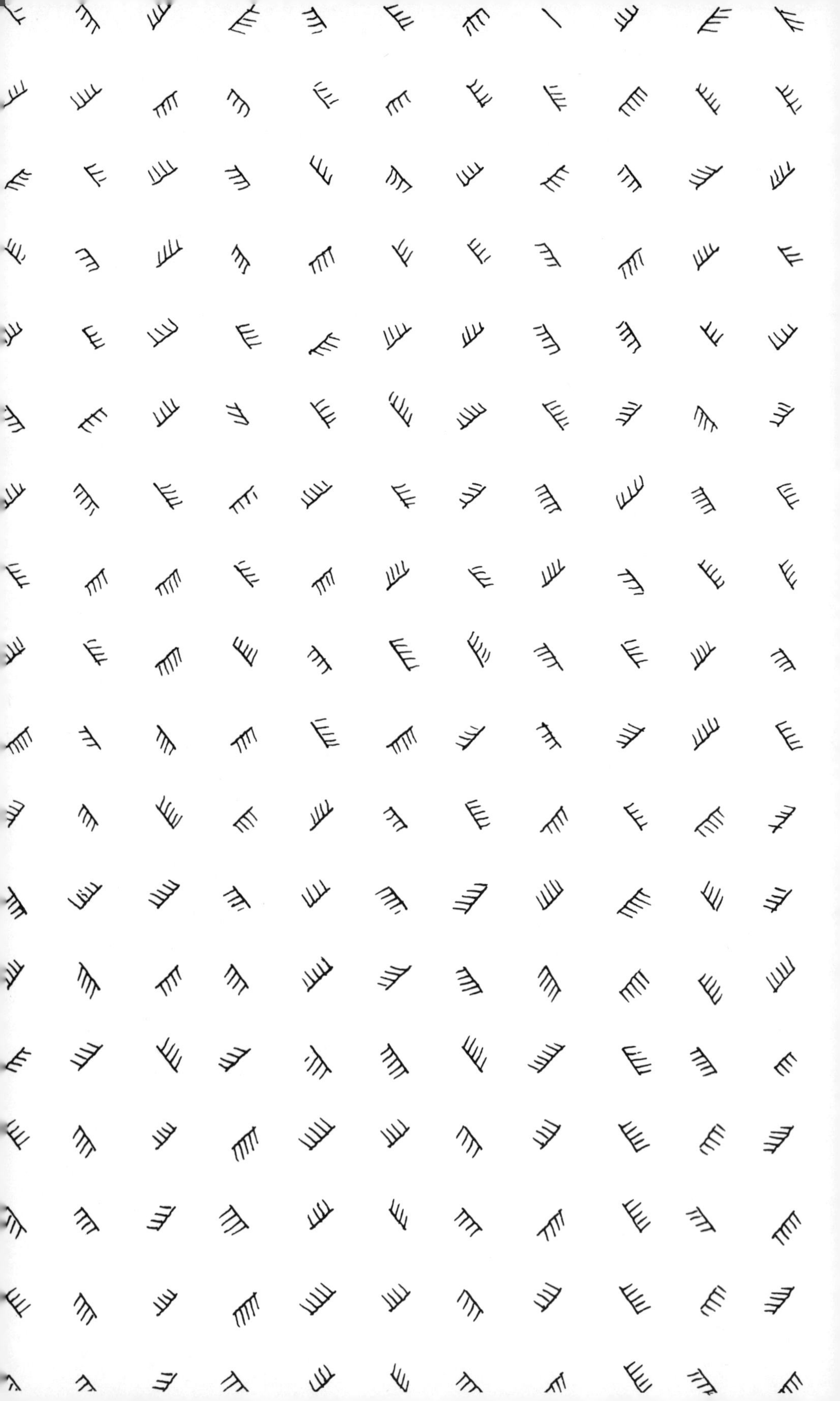

EGGS

An egg which has succeeded in being fresh has done all that can be reasonably expected of it.
—Henry James

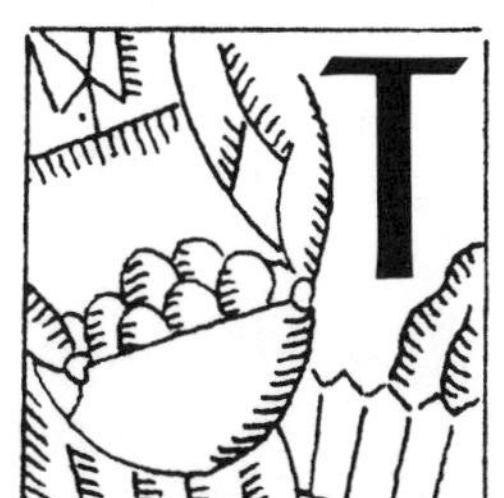

he very first chore I can remember as a child was that of gathering the morning eggs. Our hens were free-roaming, which means my job wasn't as easy as it sounds. Up well before dawn, my apron held out in front of me, I wandered over acres of farmland, with a retinue of clucking hens following at a distance. When I'd come upon a cluster of hidden eggs, the hens would cluck. The more difficult the eggs were to find, the more the hens would carry on. I never figured out whether they were cheering me on or laughing at all the trouble I went through each day. Anyway, when my apron was full, they would slowly escort me across the fields right up to our kitchen door. My mother would take the eggs and gently set them in a large basket. And, by the end of the day, they were all gone. It used to amaze me.

I never have to send my son or daughter out scouting for eggs. A wonderful farmer delivers a large supply of fresh eggs to Loaves and Fishes every morning. And by the time the sun is setting, I see we've used up the day's supply and marvel at how many sauces, dressings, salads, breads, cakes, pastries, pies, cookies, soufflés, mousses, and custards we have produced and how the simple, humble egg was essential in making all of these dishes. I love eggs—scrambled, baked, fried, or poached—in the morning, or late at night after a long evening out, and so I have carefully selected a variety of egg recipes that are delicious and simple to prepare. I hope you try them.

An Egg

A box without hinges,
key, or lid,
Yet golden treasure
inside is hid.
—J.R.R. Tolkien,
The Hobbit

APFELPFANNKUCHEN (APPLE PANCAKES)

We always arose before dawn on the farm, had our breakfast, then headed out to deal with our individual chores. By midmorning we were ravenous, and that's when we would have Apfelpfannkuchen—our second breakfast, served with homemade plum jam or fresh peach preserves. I added the touch of Calvados to bring out the apple taste, and now I serve it at home for breakfast, lunch, or brunch.

2 tablespoons Calvados
4 Granny Smith apples, peeled and thinly sliced
6 eggs, at room temperature, separated
1 cup unbleached white flour
1½ cups milk
½ teaspoon vanilla extract
6 tablespoons (¾ stick) clarified butter
2 teaspoons ground cinnamon
¼ cup sugar

Preheat the oven to 200°F.

Sprinkle the Calvados over the apple slices and set aside.

With an electric mixer, beat the egg whites until they hold soft peaks. Transfer to another bowl. Pour the egg yolks into the mixer bowl and add the flour. Mix at medium speed until creamy. Add the milk and the vanilla. Mix to blend well. Fold in the egg whites.

Heat some of the clarified butter in a 9-inch skillet. Pour in 1 cup of the batter and cover with about one-sixth of the apple slices. Allow the pancake time to set and brown nicely. Slide it out of the pan, onto a large lid. Then return it to the skillet, apple side down. Sauté, shaking the pan now and then, until the pancake is browned on the other side and the apples seem tender yet firm.

Slide the pancake onto a serving platter, folding it omelette style. Keep it warm in the oven. Repeat the process until you have 6 apple pancakes.

Sprinkle them with a combination of the cinnamon and sugar and serve.

Yields: 6 servings

Preparation time: 30 minutes

TO TURN THE PANCAKE

Select a handled pot lid which has a relatively flat surface. When the pancake is ready to be turned over, slide it onto the lid, cooked side down. Then, in one simple movement, turn the lid over, returning the pancake to the pan, cooked side up.

ARTICHOKE–CHEESE TART

An unusual blend of artichoke and savory cheese.

CRUST

1½ cups unbleached white flour
10 tablespoons (1¼ sticks) butter, cut into 10 pieces
1 egg yolk
¼ cup cold water

FILLING

3 tablespoons olive oil
2 cloves garlic, peeled and minced
3 cups canned artichoke hearts, drained and quartered
4 eggs
½ cup ricotta cheese
⅓ cup grated Parmesan cheese
½ teaspoon salt
½ teaspoon ground black pepper
½ pound mozzarella cheese, cut into 1-inch pieces

Place the flour and butter in the bowl of a food processor fitted with the metal blade and pulse 6 or 7 times until mixture has the consistency of small peas. With the motor running, add the egg yolk and water. Process until the dough starts to stick together. Scrape it onto a floured surface. Using your hands, quickly work the dough into a smooth ball. Cover with plastic wrap and refrigerate for 30 minutes. Turn onto a lightly floured surface and roll into a circle about ⅛-inch thick. Fit the pastry into a 9-inch pie plate. Cut off the overhanging dough and flute the edges.

Preheat the oven to 375°F.

Heat the olive oil in a sauté pan. Add the garlic and artichoke hearts and sauté over low heat until fragrant. This should take about 5 minutes. Set aside to cool.

Meanwhile, combine the eggs, ricotta, Parmesan, salt, and pepper in a bowl and beat until blended.

Spread the artichoke mixture evenly over the bottom of the pie shell. Pour the egg mixture over that and top with the mozzarella, pushing it in slightly. Bake for 40 minutes, or until golden and set.

Yields: 6 servings

Preparation time: 1 hour 30 minutes (including refrigeration time)

FRESHNESS TEST

If an egg sinks to the bottom of a pan of cold water, it's fresh. If it's only moderately fresh, one end may bob toward the top. If an egg rises to the top and floats, pluck it out of the water and throw it away.

GOAT CHEESE TART

This tart can be made a day ahead of time and reheated in a 350°F oven for 12 minutes.

Ever since Sybille created this tart, it's been one of the most popular ones at Loaves and Fishes. Serve it with the Sesame–Broccoli Salad for lunch or present it as a first course.

CRUST

1½ cups unbleached white flour
6 tablespoons (¾ stick) butter
6 tablespoons (¾ stick) margarine
2½ to 3 tablespoons cold water

FILLING

1 tablespoon butter
¾ cup peeled and chopped shallots
9 ounces Bucheron goat cheese
1 cup heavy cream
3 eggs
¼ cup chopped dill
Pinch of ground white pepper

Whenever you shop for cheese, always ask for a taste before buying any. You can't tell its freshness by merely looking at it. Goat cheese should have a pleasant, pungent taste. You needn't use Bucheron for this recipe. Experiment. Maybe you'll discover some wonderfully exotic cheese that would turn this tart into your very own creation.

Preheat the oven to 350°F.

To make the crust, place the flour, butter, and margarine in the bowl of a food processor fitted with the metal blade. Pulse until the mixture is the size of small peas. With the motor running, add the water all at once. Turn it off as soon as the dough begins to stick together. Do not overprocess. Turn the dough out onto a floured surface and work quickly into a ball. Chill in the refrigerator for 30 minutes.

To make the filling, melt the butter. Add the shallots and sauté until transparent, about 5 minutes. Set aside. Place the goat cheese in the bowl of the food processor with the metal blade in place and process until smooth, about 15 seconds. Add the cream and eggs and mix until well blended. Add the dill and pepper and blend.

Line a 9-inch tart pan with the dough. Spread the shallots evenly over the bottom of the unbaked tart shell. Pour in the cheese mixture to fill the crust. Bake for 30 to 35 minutes, or until golden brown and set. Cut into wedges and serve either hot or at room temperature with a green leafy salad.

Yields: 6 to 8 servings

Preparation time: 1 hour 30 minutes (including refrigeration time)

SMOKED STURGEON TART

A guaranteed winner whether served for lunch or as a first course. This tart has a light, creamy texture enriched with just enough smoked fish and cheese to make it a substantial meal.

CRUST

2 cups unbleached white flour
¾ cup (1½ sticks) butter, well chilled
⅓ cup ice water

FILLING

You can substitute smoked salmon for the sturgeon and end up with an equally exquisite dish.

½ pound smoked sturgeon, finely chopped
1 cup grated Swiss cheese
2 tablespoons peeled and minced shallots
4 eggs
1 cup heavy cream
1 cup milk
½ teaspoon ground nutmeg
½ teaspoon salt
Dash of cayenne pepper

Preheat the oven to 350°F.

Combine the flour and butter in the bowl of a food processor and process with the metal blade until you have crumbs the size of peas. Add the ice water and process until it forms a ball. Roll out the dough and use it to line a 10-inch quiche pan.

Scatter the sturgeon over the bottom of the quiche shell. Sprinkle with the cheese and shallots.

Place the eggs, cream, milk, nutmeg, salt, and cayenne in the food processor bowl. With the metal blade in place, whirl until smooth. Pour over the sturgeon mixture and bake for 40 minutes. Serve warm or at room temperature. Cut into 8 wedges. This would go well with the Fresh Peas with Dill salad.

Yields: 8 servings
Preparation time: 1 hour

I think we should get rid of the mystique of soufflés right now. They really are simple. When you beat the egg whites, they only need to stand in soft peaks. When the air bubbles are heated, they expand, and that's what causes the soufflé to rise. When you fold the beaten egg whites into the base, use a rubber spatula and don't stir. You don't want to deflate the egg whites too much. Five large egg whites can carry 1 cup of solids—1 cup of steamed, chopped spinach or minced mushrooms, for example. The cheese that is added to a soufflé melts to become part of the base.

Simmering the garlic beforehand, then pureeing it with milk brings out a special sweetness.

You can also make 6 individual soufflés by spooning this mixture into six 1-cup buttered ramekins and baking them for 15 minutes.

GARLIC–CHEESE SOUFFLÉ

Don't be intimidated by the word *soufflé*. This is really one of the easiest of dishes to prepare.

1 head garlic, cloves separated and peeled
1 tablespoon fresh thyme or 1 teaspoon dried
1 bay leaf
1/3 cup olive oil
2/3 cup water
1 cup milk
1 1/2 cups heavy cream
5 tablespoons butter
1/3 cup unbleached white flour
5 eggs, separated
1/4 teaspoon ground black pepper
1/4 teaspoon salt
1 cup grated Swiss cheese
1/4 cup freshly grated Parmesan cheese

Place the garlic, thyme, bay leaf, olive oil, and water in a small, heavy saucepan. Simmer, covered, over low heat for 30 minutes.

Meanwhile, preheat the oven to 425°F.

When the garlic is cooked, drain and discard the bay leaf. Transfer the garlic mixture to the bowl of a food processor, with the metal blade in place. Add the milk, and puree for about 15 seconds, or until the mixture is smooth. Add the cream and process for 2 seconds more. Set aside.

Melt the butter in a heavy saucepan. Add the flour and stir for about 2 minutes over low heat. Add the garlic puree all at once and bring to a boil, stirring constantly. Remove from the heat. Using a wire whisk, beat in the egg yolks one at a time until they are well incorporated. Add pepper and salt. Fold in the Swiss and Parmesan cheeses.

In a mixing bowl, beat the egg whites until they hold soft peaks. Fold them into the soufflé, trying not to deflate them too much.

Pour the mixture into a buttered shallow 2 1/2-quart casserole. Bake for 20 minutes.

Yields: 6 servings

Preparation time: 1 hour 30 minutes

Eggplant and cilantro would make a delicious filling for an omelette.

EGGPLANT–CILANTRO PIE

Mixed with crisp, sweet red peppers and rich melted cheese and surrounded by a buttery pastry shell, this pie becomes a hearty, full meal. The eggplant should be slightly undercooked so that it retains its shape and distinct flavor.

CRUST

2 cups unbleached white flour
½ teaspoon salt
¾ cup (1½ sticks) butter, chilled and cut into 12 pieces
2 tablespoons lemon juice
3 tablespoons cold water

FILLING

3 tablespoons olive oil
1½ cups peeled and minced onion
1 red pepper, diced
Eggplant, skin left on, cut into 1-inch chunks (about 4 cups)
5 eggs
1 cup heavy cream
1 cup milk
1 teaspoon salt
¾ teaspoon ground black pepper
½ cup chopped cilantro
½ pound Gruyère cheese, grated

Place the flour, salt, and butter in the bowl of a food processor and pulse 5 times using the metal blade. Add the lemon juice and water and process for 3 seconds. Using your hands, scrape the dough onto a floured surface and work it until it forms a smooth ball. Cover with plastic wrap and refrigerate for 30 minutes.

Preheat the oven to 375°F.

Heat the olive oil in a large sauté pan, add the onion and red pepper, and sauté over low heat for about 5 minutes. Add the eggplant and sauté for 5 minutes more. Remove from the heat and let cool slightly.

Roll the dough out on a lightly floured surface until it is a circle approximately ⅛-inch thick and 14 inches in diameter. Fit the circle into an 11-by-1½-inch quiche pan.

Break the eggs into the bowl of a food processor

fitted with the metal blade. Add the cream, milk, salt, and pepper and process until the mixture is well blended.

Spoon the eggplant mixture over the crust. Sprinkle with the cilantro. Follow with the Gruyère. Then slowly pour in the egg mixture, making sure it is evenly distributed.

Bake for 45 minutes, or until nicely browned. Allow to set for 10 minutes. Cut into 6 wedges and serve.

Yields: 6 servings

Preparation time: 1 hour 15 minutes (including refrigeration time)

OMELETTES

Break 3 eggs into a bowl. Add salt, pepper, and some chopped chives or other herbs you fancy. Add 1 tablespoon water and beat with a fork. Heat a small omelette pan. Brush it with enough melted butter to cover the inner surface. Pour the eggs into the pan, add whatever filling you wish, and heat until the top of the omelette is soft and the underside is set. This shouldn't take more than 30 to 40 seconds. Don't worry about rolling a perfect omelette. It's infinitely more important to have it cooked just so.

There is no such thing as a pretty good omelette.
—French Proverb

This pie can be made 1 day ahead of time and reheated in a 350°F oven for 15 minutes.

MUSHROOM AND LEEK PIE

The leek and mushroom grew around us in great abundance. So, although this recipe was conceived on the farm, I've updated it in my own kitchen because these two products seem to be available all year round.

CRUST

1⅓ cups unbleached white flour
¼ teaspoon salt
⅛ teaspoon ground black pepper
4 tablespoons (½ stick) butter, cut into small pieces
4 tablespoons (½ stick) margarine
1 egg yolk
¼ cup cold water

FILLING

2 tablespoons butter
2 leeks, white parts only, chopped
2 cups sliced mushrooms
4 eggs
1 cup sour cream
¼ cup heavy cream
⅛ teaspoon cayenne pepper
½ teaspoon salt
½ pound mozzarella cheese, cubed

Place the flour, salt, pepper, butter, and margarine in the bowl of a food processor and, using the metal blade, pulse 5 to 6 times. Add the egg yolk. Turn on the motor and while it is running, add the water. Process until the dough sticks together; this will take only about 10 seconds. Transfer the dough to a floured surface. Form into a disk. Cover with plastic wrap and refrigerate for 30 minutes.

Preheat the oven to 425°F.

Melt the butter in a large skillet. Add the leeks and mushrooms and sauté over medium heat for 5 minutes. Remove from the heat and let cool to room temperature.

Beat the eggs, sour cream, heavy cream, cayenne, and salt with a fork until the mixture seems well blended. Set aside.

Roll the dough into a large circle about ⅛-inch thick. Fit it into a 10-inch quiche pan. Prick with a fork to reduce shrinkage. Bake the shell for 8 min-

TIPS ON STORING

It's been said that eggs lose more quality in 1 day at room temperature than in 1 week in the refrigerator. They should be stored large end up, to keep the yolks centered. Never wash eggs before refrigerating them, since their porous shells have been treated with a harmless mineral to slow the loss of carbon dioxide. Leave the eggs inside the carton, since it keeps them from losing moisture.

utes. Remove from the oven. Reduce the oven temperature to 375°F.

Spread the mushroom–leek mixture over the bottom of the shell. Then sprinkle with the mozzarella. Pour the egg–cream mixture carefully over that and bake for 40 minutes. Let it rest for 5 minutes before serving.

Yields: 6 to 8 servings

Preparation time: 1 hour 30 minutes (including refrigeration time)

EGGS, POTATOES, AND CHEESE

A deliciously filling casserole made from our most basic of foods. This recipe combines layers of tender cooked potatoes and slices of mozzarella, sprinkled with sharp Parmesan and held together with a moist, creamy egg mixture.

6 medium potatoes, boiled, peeled, and sliced in 1/4-inch pieces
1 1/2 teaspoons salt
1 teaspoon ground black pepper
3 cloves garlic, peeled and minced
1/2 cup chopped parsley
1 pound mozzarella cheese, sliced thin
3/4 cup grated Parmesan cheese
3/4 cup (1 1/2 sticks) butter, melted
6 eggs
1 cup half-and-half

Preheat the oven to 350°F.

Butter a shallow 12-by-9-inch casserole. Layer the bottom with half the potatoes. Sprinkle with half the salt, pepper, garlic, and parsley. Cover with half the mozzarella. Sprinkle with half the Parmesan. Repeat for one more layer, using all the ingredients in the same order. Trickle the melted butter over the casserole and bake for 20 minutes. Remove from the oven.

Beat the eggs and half-and-half with a fork. Pour over the potato–cheese mixture. Return the casserole to the oven, and bake for 30 minutes more. Serve hot with a crisp vegetable salad.

Yields: 4 to 6 servings

Preparation time: 1 hour

ZWIEBEL KUCHEN

This tart when cut into bite-sized pieces makes a wonderful appetizer to serve with drinks.

During Oktoberfest, farmers near Stuttgart, Germany, start down from the top of the mountains, stopping at every farm on the way to taste their homemade wines. Zwiebel Kuchen is served to them at each farm so that they may cleanse their palates before continuing on their way. By the time they reach the bottom, I'm pretty sure it doesn't matter to them what the Zwiebel Kuchen tastes like, but here's a recipe that's straight from my mother's kitchen.

CRUST

1¼ cups plus 2 tablespoons unbleached white flour
1 teaspoon sugar
1 teaspoon salt
1 tablespoon active dry yeast
½ cup lukewarm (110°F) milk
2 tablespoons butter, softened

FILLING

5 cups peeled and thinly sliced onion
2 tablespoons butter
3 eggs, beaten
¼ teaspoon cayenne pepper
¾ teaspoon salt
½ teaspoon crushed caraway seed
½ cup sour cream
¾ cup half-and-half
1½ cups grated Swiss cheese

IMPORTANT NOTE

Remember that tarts with custardy fillings using eggs and cream will curdle if baked at a temperature higher than 375°F.

Preheat the oven to 350°F.

To make the crust, place ¾ cup of the flour, the sugar, salt, and yeast in the bowl of an electric mixer. Add the warm milk and butter. Beat hard for about 2 minutes, making sure the dough is smooth. Add another ½ cup of flour and stir to blend. Place in a warm place and let it rise until doubled in size.

To make the filling, sauté the onion in the butter over low heat until transparent, about 10 minutes. It should not brown. Remove from the heat and let cool for 5 minutes.

Beat together the eggs, cayenne, salt, caraway seed, sour cream, and half-and-half and set aside.

Butter a 9-inch tart pan with a removable bottom. Pat the dough into a 10-inch circle and fit it into the pan. Arrange the onion over the bottom of the tart. Carefully pour the egg mixture over the onion and sprinkle with the cheese.

Place the tart on a rack in the center of the oven. Bake for about 40 minutes, or until nicely browned and puffed.

Serve hot or at room temperature cut into wedges.

Yields: 8 servings

Preparation time: 1 hour 30 minutes

This tart can be made a day ahead of time and reheated in a 350°F oven for 12 minutes.

FRESH BASIL FRITTATA

Traditionally, frittatas are started on the stove in a frying pan, then transferred to the broiler. We've come up with this way to cook frittata that places the whole meal in the oven, so that no one needs to watch over it. We have so much basil growing in our garden behind Loaves and Fishes that this seemed the most natural "pie without a crust" to make.

This particular recipe can be halved to serve six. Bake in a buttered casserole or baking pan half the size of the one recommended in this recipe. This is also wonderful to serve with cocktails. Cut the frittata into small bite-sized pieces and serve at room temperature.

¾ cup unbleached white flour
1½ teaspoons baking powder
15 eggs
1 cup (2 sticks) butter, melted
3 cups ricotta cheese
1½ pounds Gruyère cheese, grated
¾ teaspoon salt
1 teaspoon ground black pepper
1¼ cups chopped basil

Preheat the oven to 350°F.

Place the flour, baking powder, eggs, and butter in the bowl of an electric mixer and blend well. Add the ricotta, Gruyère, salt, pepper, and basil. Mix enough to blend.

Pour onto a buttered 12-by-17-inch baking sheet with 1-inch raised edge. Bake 40 minutes, or until the frittata is set and browned. Serve at room temperature.

Yields: 10 to 12 servings

Preparation time: 1 hour

SALMON FRITTATA WITH FONTINA AND FRESH DILL

This dish served at brunch with Super Bran Muffins, honey butter, and a slice of cantaloupe with lemon is an absolute hit every time!

12 eggs
¾ teaspoon ground black pepper
2 cups sour cream
½ cup unbleached white flour
1 teaspoon baking powder
6 tablespoons (¾ sticks) butter, melted and cooled
5 ounces smoked salmon, minced
5 scallions, minced
⅓ cup minced dill
¾ pound Italian fontina cheese, diced into ½-inch pieces

Preheat the oven to 375°F.

Break the eggs into a large mixing bowl. Sprinkle with the pepper and beat with a wire whisk until frothy. Add the sour cream, flour, and baking powder. Whisk again until the mixture is well blended. Add the melted butter, salmon, scallions, dill, and fontina. Mix well.

Pour the mixture into a buttered shallow 3-quart casserole and bake for 35 minutes, or until a knife inserted in the center comes out clean. Let the frittata set for 10 minutes before serving.

Yields: 6 to 8 servings

Preparation time: 50 minutes

EGGS WITH MUSTARD AND CHIVES

Wedges of hard cooked eggs, blanketed in a sharp mustard sauce and garnished with chopped chives, this is excellent for buffets—tasty and easy to prepare.

12 eggs, hard boiled

SAUCE

4 tablespoons (½ stick) butter
½ cup peeled and minced shallots
¼ cup minced chives
½ cup port wine
1½ cups heavy cream
3 tablespoons mustard
¼ teaspoon ground black pepper
½ teaspoon salt

2 tablespoons chopped chives (for garnish; substitute scallions if chives are unavailable)

Preheat the oven to 250°F.

Shell the eggs, cut them into quarters, and place them on a serving platter. Keep the eggs warm in the oven while you are making the sauce.

To make the sauce, melt the butter in a large sauté pan. Add the shallots and chives. Sauté for 3 minutes over medium heat, tossing and stirring constantly. Add the wine. Over high heat, reduce the wine to half. Add the cream, mustard, pepper, and salt. Reduce longer until the sauce starts to thicken, about 5 minutes. Pour the sauce over the eggs and garnish with the chives.

Serve with new potatoes and cucumber salad.

Yields: 6 servings

Preparation time: 20 minutes

HARD-BOILED EGGS

Take the eggs from the refrigerator, place them in a pot, and cover with cold water. Bring to a rolling boil and simmer for exactly 6 minutes. Then run the eggs under cold water to stop the cooking process. Shell and serve.

SOFT-BOILED EGGS

Follow the same instructions as for hard-boiled eggs, except simmer for only 3 minutes. Run the eggs under cold water and they're ready.

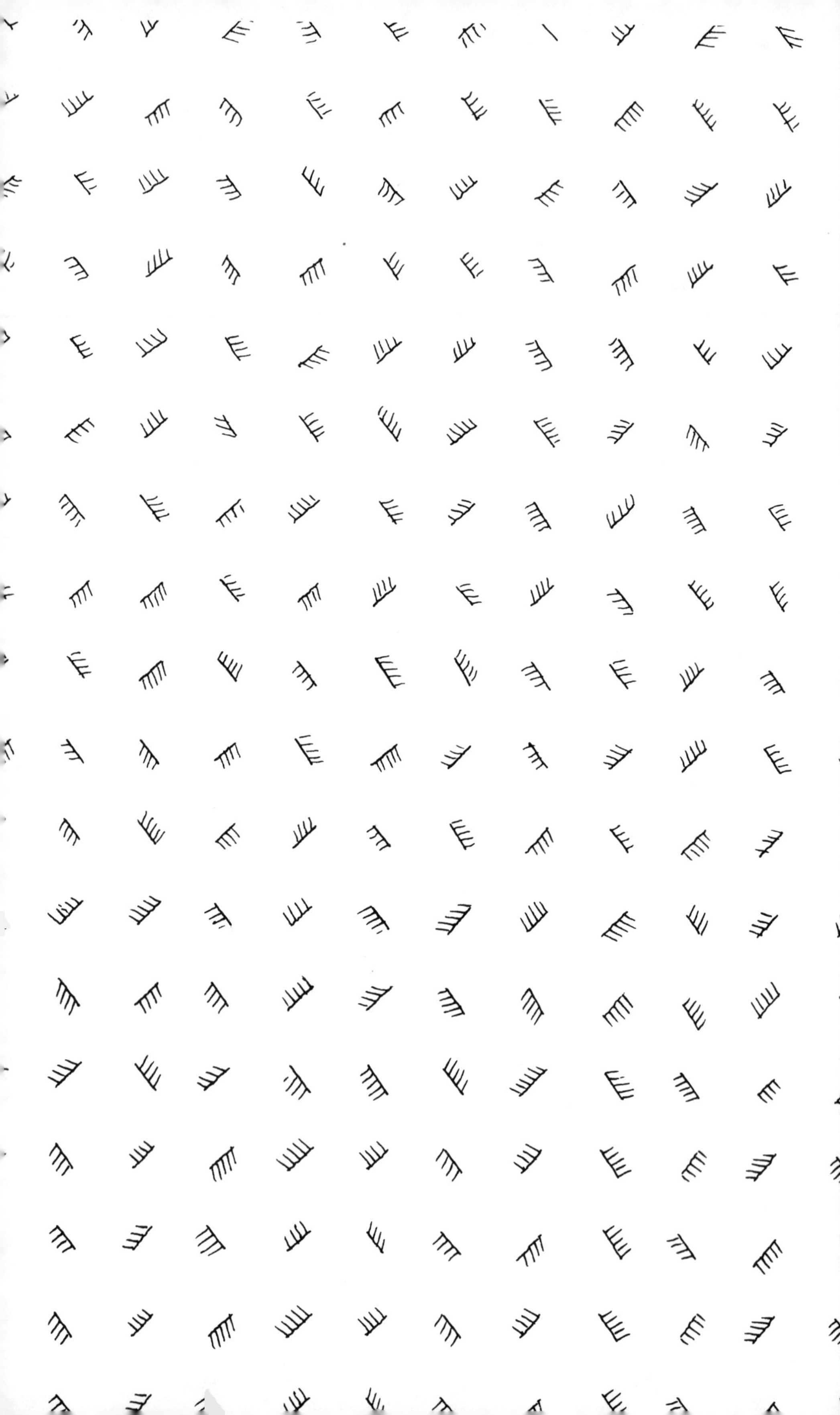

FISH

Let not the Sauce
Be better than the Fish.
—Old French proverb

During a cooking course I was teaching, I invited a local fisherman to come to one of our sessions so that he could demonstrate to my students how best to select fish. He advised pressing a finger into the side of the flesh; if it was resilient and sprung back into position, it was fresh. If the indentation of your finger remained, it wasn't. "The gills should be bright red, the eyes should be clear. If a fish smells fishy, don't buy it, it's old. Fish should smell of the sea, that's all." He skillfully showed all of us how quickly he could clean a fish, and he made each student in turn have a go at it. It was much simpler than all of them had thought. He held up a bag of the fishbones and heads and said, "Here's for the stock." For the following week I set about trying to dismiss the various taboos about fish;

that it's bland, too difficult to prepare, that the sauces are too complicated, and that it turns dry and leathery in the blink of an eye.

Many of the recipes in this section will forever dispel these questions and problems. All I can say is that fish is truly the simplest and most satisfying of foods you can purchase and prepare. Grilled Fresh Tuna Steaks with Lemon Sauce is wonderful on its own for a dinner, but if there are any leftovers they can go into making a fresh salad for the next day's lunch. Almost any fish can be pan-sautéed (that's how I prefer it), yet I've added some spectacularly tasty, easy, and unusual sauces to go with the fish, many of the recipes taking only twenty minutes to prepare.

SHELLFISH IN CREAM SAUCE

A traditional, easy-to-make cream sauce. If you like, you can use weakfish or bass instead of shellfish. Place the fish inside a buttered casserole, bake for 10 minutes at 400°F, and cover with the sauce.

18 mussels, scrubbed
½ cup dry white wine
2 live lobsters (1½ pounds each)
1 pound bay scallops
1½ pounds medium raw shrimp, shelled

CREAM SAUCE

½ cup (1 stick) butter
¼ cup unbleached white flour
3 cloves garlic, peeled and minced
1 cup clam juice
1½ cups heavy cream
1½ cups dry white wine
¾ teaspoon ground white pepper
⅛ teaspoon cayenne pepper
1 cup minced fennel
1 bay leaf

Chopped dill (for garnish)

Preheat the oven to 400°F.

Steam the mussels in the ½ cup wine, until they open. Drain and set aside, reserving the juice for another time.

Bring a large pot of water, one-quarter full, to a rolling boil. Plunge the lobsters in head first. Cover and simmer for 12 minutes. Cut the lobsters into 2-inch pieces and set aside.

Place the scallops and shrimp in a large ovenproof casserole and set aside.

To make the sauce, melt the butter in a heavy saucepan. Add the flour and garlic and sauté over low heat for 2 minutes, stirring constantly. Remove from the heat. Add the clam juice, cream, and wine. Return to the heat, stirring until the sauce is bubbling and starts to thicken. Remove from the heat.

Add the pepper, cayenne, fennel, and bay leaf. Stir well and pour the sauce over the scallops and shrimp. Bake for 20 minutes. Add the mussels and lobster and bake for 5 minutes more. Garnish with dill and serve.

Yields: 6 servings
Preparation time: 1 hour

If there are any leftovers the next day, place them in individual baking shells, sprinkle with grated Parmesan or buttered bread crumbs and bake in a 375°F oven until browned. It's quick and makes a beautiful light lunch.

An easy and tasty dinner buffet. Guests can help themselves to the seafood they like. Serve with buttered rice mixed with fresh herbs. The sauce can be prepared 2 days ahead of time and stored in the refrigerator until needed.

BAKED SEAFOOD SAGAPONACK

A beautifully rich, wholesome, and authentic local dish, which takes less than an hour to prepare. Be sure to serve lots of warm, crusty Italian bread to soak up the delicious creamy tomato sauce.

SAUCE

2 tablespoons butter
2 tablespoons olive oil
1½ cups peeled and chopped onion
1 cup diced leek (white parts only)
½ cup chopped fennel
5 cloves garlic, peeled and minced
3 pounds ripe tomatoes, chopped, or drained canned tomatoes
1½ cups dry white wine
1½ cups chicken stock
2 tablespoons chopped fresh basil or 1 teaspoon dried
1 tablespoon chopped fresh thyme or ½ teaspoon dried
1 tablespoon chopped fresh oregano or 1 teaspoon dried
½ teaspoon hot red pepper flakes
Salt and pepper to taste
½ cup heavy cream

3 pounds fillet of anglerfish, tilefish, or any firm-fleshed fish
1 pound raw shrimp, shelled
2 whole live lobsters, cut into serving-sized pieces
2 dozen mussels, scrubbed and steamed open (for garnish)
½ cup capers, drained (for garnish)
Chopped parsley (for garnish)

If you can't bear to cut up the lobsters while they are still alive, have your fishmonger do it for you.

To make the sauce, heat the butter and oil in a large, heavy nonaluminum sauté pan. Add the onion, leek, and fennel. Sauté over low heat for about 5 minutes, stirring occasionally. Add the garlic, tomatoes, wine, and chicken stock and bring the mixture to a boil. Lower the heat and let it simmer. Add the basil, thyme, oregano, hot red pepper flakes, and salt and pepper. Cover the pan and simmer for 20 minutes. Remove the cover and simmer for 5 minutes more. Add the cream. Increase the heat to high for 5 minutes to reduce the sauce. Remove from the heat and let cool slightly.

Meanwhile, preheat the oven to 375°F. To assemble, bake, and serve, pour half the sauce into a large shallow baking dish. Add all the fish, except for the mussels. Pour the remaining sauce over the fish. Bring to a simmer on top of the stove. Cover with a piece of buttered parchment paper, buttered side down, and bake for 10 to 12 minutes. Remove from the oven. Discard the paper and garnish with the mussels, capers, and parsley.

Yields: 8 servings

Preparation time: 1 hour

MUSSEL STOCK

Using ½ cup dry white wine and 3 cloves garlic, steam 4 pounds mussels until they open. Strain the stock through a kitchen towel. Pour it into a container, mark with the date, and store it in the freezer for up to 3 months. Mussel stock can be used in fish soups, fish stews, bouillabaisse, and in any lobster sauce or fish sauce recipe. It is delicious.

SEAFOOD PAELLA

A bed of rice tinted saffron yellow, red lobster shells filled with succulent pink meat, black shells steamed open revealing the plump mussels inside—flavored with garlic, onions, and hot sausages, this recipe is well worth the effort.

1 pound hot sausage links
2 pounds raw shrimp, shelled
2 live lobsters (about 1¼ pounds each)
1½ dozen littleneck clams
2 dozen mussels
½ cup dry white wine
4 tablespoons (½ stick) butter
1 large onion, peeled and chopped
4 cloves garlic, peeled and minced
2 cups raw rice
½ teaspoon salt
½ teaspoon ground black pepper
¾ teaspoon saffron threads
6 cups strong chicken stock
2 red peppers, seeded and chopped
1 green pepper, seeded and chopped
Chopped parsley (for garnish)

Preheat the oven to 375°F.

Brown the sausage links in a skillet over medium heat and set aside until cool enough to handle. Cut each link diagonally into 3 pieces.

Fill a medium saucepan three-quarters full of water and bring to a boil. Add the shrimp and simmer until they turn pink, about 2 minutes. Drain and set aside.

Pour water into a large pot until it reaches 1 inch and bring to a boil. Add the lobsters, cover, and steam for 10 minutes. Set aside until they are cool enough to handle. Cut them into serving-sized pieces, leaving the shells on.

Bring the same water to a boil again and add the clams. Cover and steam until they open, about 4 minutes. Drain and set aside.

Place the mussels and wine in a saucepan, cover, and bring to a boil. Steam until they open, about 3 minutes. Drain and set aside.

Heat the butter in a heavy skillet. Add the onion and garlic. Sauté over medium heat for 5 minutes.

Save the stock as you cook each individual shellfish and to that add the shells of the shrimp, an onion, 4 cloves garlic, a bay leaf, and a stalk of celery, and let it boil for an hour, covered. Remove the lid and let

it simmer for another 30 minutes. Let cool. Strain. Then seal in a container marked with the date. So while the paella is being assembled, you will be making a delicious stock for future use. It will keep frozen for up to 3 months and can be used in all recipes calling for clam or fish stock.

Add the rice, salt, pepper, saffron, and 5 cups of the chicken stock. Stir once. Cover and simmer until the rice is al dente, about 12 minutes. Remove from the heat.

Fold in the red and green peppers, the sausage pieces, and the shrimp. Transfer the paella to a buttered casserole. Scatter the lobster pieces, clams, and mussels over the rice and pour on the remaining cup of chicken stock. Cover with foil and bake for 30 minutes, or until heated through. Sprinkle with chopped parsley and serve.

Yields: 8 servings

Preparation time: 1 hour 30 minutes

CLAMS AND SAUSAGE IN PARSLEY SAUCE

We first sampled this in the south of France. It serves as an excellent buffet offering or as a party dish. You can also try pouring it over cooked linguine.

6 dozen littleneck clams
1/4 cup olive oil
3 cups peeled and finely chopped onion
4 large cloves garlic, peeled and minced
2 red peppers, seeded and diced
1/4 cup unbleached white flour
1 1/4 cups clam juice
1 cup dry white wine
2 cups minced parsley
1/2 teaspoon hot red pepper flakes
3 cups sliced chorizo sausages

Scrub the clams and set aside. Heat the oil in a large sauté pan. Sauté the onion, garlic, and red peppers for 5 minutes over low heat. Sprinkle the flour over the vegetables. Stir to mix well. Add the clam juice, wine, parsley, and hot red pepper flakes. Stirring constantly, bring the mixture to a boil. Simmer for 5 minutes. Add the sausage and the clams. Cover and bring to a boil. Simmer just until the clams open. This will take no more than 5 minutes.

Yields: 6 servings

Preparation time: 30 minutes

ANGLERFISH IN LOBSTER SAUCE

A very easy, infinitely satisfying meal with a delicate, creamy sauce flavored with sherry and a drop of brandy. Although I have designated two hours as the preparation time, in reality an hour and a half are for simmering.

1 live lobster (2 pounds)
4 cups mussel stock (see recipe for Baked Seafood Sagaponack)
2 cups water
1 medium onion, unpeeled and quartered
3 stalks celery, cut in thirds
1 bay leaf, broken in half
4 tablespoons (1/2 stick) butter
3 tablespoons unbleached white flour
1 cup heavy cream
1 tablespoon tomato paste
2 tablespoons dry sherry
1 tablespoon brandy
3/4 teaspoon ground black pepper
3 pounds anglerfish, cut into serving-sized pieces
Chopped parsley (for garnish)

Steam the lobster in a large pot of boiling water for 15 minutes. Remove, cut in half, and take out all the meat, reserving the shells. Chop the meat finely and set it aside.

Place the lobster shells in a large stockpot. Add the mussel stock, water, onion, celery, and bay leaf. Bring to a boil and simmer over low heat, covered, for 1 hour. Uncover and simmer over medium heat for 30 minutes. Strain the stock through a colander lined with a cotton kitchen towel. Discard the solids. Save the stock.

Melt the butter in a large, heavy saucepan. Add the flour, stir, and simmer over low heat for 2 minutes. Add the lobster stock. Stirring constantly, bring the sauce to a boil. Add the cream, tomato paste, sherry, brandy, and pepper. Stir well. Add the fish pieces and bring to a boil. Simmer until the fish is done, about 6 to 8 minutes, depending on the thickness of the pieces. Add the chopped lobster meat and heat through.

BUYING FRESH LOBSTERS

Make sure the lobster is very active and that its shell is black, even bluish in color. For those who enjoy the unique flavor of the "coral" roe, female lobsters can be distinguished by 2 soft feelers located where the body meets the tail.

Serve the fish on a platter with the sauce poured over it. Garnish with chopped parsley.

Yields: 6 servings

Preparation time: 2 hours

SPICY SHRIMP AND ANGLERFISH

A gingery pepper sauce sweetened with brown sugar and Madeira wine, this is delicious served over rice.

1/3 cup olive oil
12 scallions, chopped
1/4 cup peeled and minced ginger
6 cloves garlic, peeled and minced
1/4 cup peeled and minced fresh horseradish
2 cups peeled and finely chopped tomatoes
1/4 cup Madeira wine
1/4 cup soy sauce
1/4 cup light brown sugar
1 1/2 teaspoons hot red pepper flakes
2 pounds raw shrimp, shelled
2 pounds anglerfish, cut into bite-sized pieces
Chopped parsley (for garnish)

Place the olive oil, scallions, ginger, garlic, and horseradish in a large skillet and sauté for 5 minutes over medium heat. Add the tomatoes, wine, soy sauce, sugar, and hot red pepper flakes. Sauté for 10 minutes more. Add the shrimp and fish and simmer until just done, about 8 to 10 minutes.

Transfer to a serving platter and sprinkle with parsley.

Yields: 6 to 8 servings

Preparation time: 30 minutes

FISH STEW WITH SAFFRON

Friends of ours in Sienna, Italy, took us one evening to an underground restaurant. We had this dish served to us with pasta instead of potatoes. I've adjusted the recipe according to what fish and vegetables were available at the time, and have often used orzo. This has been my family's favorite meal for years.

3 tablespoons olive oil
2 cups peeled and finely chopped onion
3 large cloves garlic, peeled and minced
1 green pepper, finely chopped
5 cups finely chopped tomatoes
1 cup diced fennel
3 cups clam juice
2 cups dry white wine
1 bay leaf
2 tablespoons fresh basil or 2 teaspoons dried
1 tablespoon fresh thyme or 1 teaspoon dried
1 strip (4-by-1-inch) orange peel
¼ teaspoon saffron threads
½ teaspoon hot red pepper flakes, or to taste
½ teaspoon ground black pepper
2½ cups peeled and chopped potatoes (or 1 cup of either pasta shells or orzo, if preferred)
20 clams, scrubbed
1 pound squid, cleaned and cut into ¼-inch rings
1 pound bass, cut into bite-sized pieces
1 pound raw shrimp, shelled
⅓ cup chopped parsley (for garnish)

Heat the olive oil in a large sauté pan. Sauté the onion, garlic, and green pepper over low heat for 5 minutes, stirring occasionally. Add the tomatoes, fennel, clam juice, wine, bay leaf, basil, thyme, orange peel, saffron, hot red pepper flakes, black pepper, and the potatoes or pasta. Bring the stew to a boil, then simmer, covered, over low heat for 15 minutes.

Add the clams, cover the pan, and simmer until the clams open. Add the squid, bass, and shrimp. Cover and simmer just until all the fish are done, about 2 minutes. Serve in deep soup bowls, garnished with parsley.

Yields: 6 servings
Preparation time: 30 minutes

The gentle art of gastronomy is a friendly one. It hurdles the language barrier, makes friends among civilized people, and warms the heart.
—Sam Chamberlain, author and gourmet

FLOUNDER FILLETS WITH BLACK BEANS

This spicy dish can be assembled in the morning and cooked that evening—twenty-five minutes for the preliminaries and eighteen minutes to bake. Serve with lemon rice and a green leafy vegetable, drizzled with herb butter.

¼ cup fermented black beans, rinsed well and finely chopped
3 cloves garlic, peeled and minced
3 tablespoons peeled and minced ginger
½ teaspoon sugar
2 scallions, green parts only, thinly sliced
2 pounds flounder fillets

SAUCE

¼ cup safflower oil
½ teaspoon sesame oil
2 tablespoons soy sauce
1 teaspoon oyster sauce
1/16 teaspoon cayenne pepper
½ teaspoon ground black pepper

1 scallion, green part only, cut into long, thin diagonal strips (for garnish)

Preheat the oven to 400°F.

Mix together the beans, garlic, ginger, sugar, and scallions. Lay the fillets, dark side up, on a surface. Spread the mixture evenly over each piece, keeping it ½ inch from the edges. Roll up the fillets and place them in a generously buttered glass or earthenware baking dish.

To make the sauce, mix together the safflower oil, sesame oil, soy sauce, oyster sauce, cayenne, and black pepper. Pour the sauce around the fillet rolls. Bake for 16 to 18 minutes.

Transfer the rolls to a warm serving platter and pour the sauce around the fish. Garnish with the scallion strips and serve.

Yields: 6 servings

Preparation time: 45 minutes

Fermented black beans and oyster sauce are easily found in the gourmet section of almost any supermarket or at any Oriental food store.

FAST-FRY FILLETS

Dust the fillets lightly with a combination of flour, salt, and pepper and panfry them in some clarified butter with a handful of herbs thrown in. A minute or two on each side until they're lightly browned and that's it! You may also dust the fillets with some grated Parmesan cheese and panfry them that way.

Serve this with cucumber salad and some Danish Roasted New Potatoes for a typical Scandinavian meal.

FISH FRICKADELLERS WITH CAPER SAUCE

This Danish fish recipe was often served in our home when I was growing up. The consistency is rather like a quenelle, but more flavorful. I wanted to include this recipe because it can transform a simple fish like flounder into a very exciting meal.

MINCED FISH

½ cup (1 stick) butter, at room temperature
¼ cup unbleached white flour
⅓ cup peeled and minced shallots
⅓ cup chopped parsley
2½ pounds fillet of flounder, cut into 1-inch pieces
2 teaspoons salt
1 teaspoon ground black pepper
3 eggs
½ cup heavy cream

FOR SAUTÉING

4 tablespoons clarified butter
½ cup flour

SAUCE

2 tablespoons butter
2 tablespoons flour
1½ cups chicken stock
⅓ cup heavy cream
2 egg yolks
1 tablespoon Dijon mustard
⅓ cup capers, drained and crushed
¾ teaspoon salt
½ teaspoon ground black pepper

Parsley sprigs (for garnish)

To make the minced fish, cream the butter and flour in the bowl of a food processor, using the metal blade. Add the shallots, parsley, flounder, salt, and pepper. Puree the mixture until smooth. Add the eggs and cream and process for 15 seconds. Scrape the fish mixture into a bowl. Cover and chill for 3 hours or up to 12 hours.

Preheat oven to 200°F.

To sauté the frickadellers, heat the butter in a

large sauté pan. Place the flour on a piece of wax paper. Shape the fish mixture into twelve 3-inch disk-shaped patties. Dip each into the flour to cover both sides. Sauté the frickadellers for about 3 minutes on each side, over medium heat. Transfer to a large, deep serving platter and keep warm in preheated oven while you're making the sauce.

To make the sauce, melt the butter in a heavy saucepan. Add the flour and simmer the roux for about 1 minute over medium heat. Stirring constantly, add the chicken stock and cream all at once. Stir with a wire whisk while letting the sauce come to a full boil. Remove from the heat. Add the egg yolks and whisk them in quickly. Add the mustard, capers, salt, and pepper. Stir well.

Spoon some of the sauce around the frickadellers. Garnish with the parsley sprigs and serve. Pour the rest of the sauce into a small bowl and serve on the side.

Yields: 6 servings

Preparation time: 45 minutes (excluding refrigeration time)

FLOUNDER FILLETS WITH SHRIMP MOUSSE AND LETTUCE SAUCE

Pink shrimp mousse, flavored with sherry and a hint of cayenne, surrounded by delicate fillets of flounder. Complemented with a fresh, cool lettuce sauce spiked with a dash of Tabasco and flavored with fresh mint leaves, served cold, this is an excellent party dish.

8 small flounder fillets
Juice of 1 lemon
½ teaspoon ground black pepper
1 teaspoon salt

MOUSSE
1¾ pounds raw shrimp, shelled
3 egg whites
1½ teaspoons salt
⅛ teaspoon cayenne pepper
2 teaspoons tomato paste
1 tablespoon finely chopped parsley
2 tablespoons dry sherry
1¾ cups heavy cream

SAUCE
2 cups shredded and tightly packed romaine lettuce
¼ cup peeled and finely chopped onion
½ cup yogurt
½ teaspoon Tabasco
½ teaspoon ground black pepper
½ teaspoon salt
2 cups sour cream
¼ cup whole mint leaves

Preheat the oven to 350°F.

Sprinkle the flounder with the lemon juice, pepper, and salt. Line a buttered 9-by-5-inch glass loaf pan with the fish, white side against the glass, letting part of the flounder hang over the edge.

To make the mousse, place the shrimp, egg whites, salt, cayenne, tomato paste, parsley, and sherry in the bowl of a food processor with the metal blade in place and puree until the mixture is very fine, about 15 seconds. With the motor running, slowly add the cream, pouring through the feed tube. Process until thoroughly blended. Spoon mousse mixture into the fish-lined loaf pan. Fold the flounder ends over the top. Cover loaf pan with a piece of buttered parchment paper, buttered side down, and set it inside a larger roasting pan. Pour enough boiling water into roasting pan to reach halfway up the loaf pan. Bake for 50 minutes. Let cool, then chill overnight.

To make the sauce, puree the lettuce, onion, yogurt, Tabasco, pepper, and salt in the food processor, using the metal blade, until fine, about 3 seconds. Add the mint and sour cream. Process just to blend. Serve the sauce with the chilled flounder and mousse.

Yields: 8 servings

Preparation time: 1 hour 30 minutes (excluding refrigeration time)

COD STEAKS WITH FENNEL BUTTER

If cod doesn't appeal to you, substitute striped bass, tilefish, sea trout, or any other lean fish.

We ate a great deal of cod when I was young, growing up near the Baltic Sea. And here again, cod is available to me throughout the year.

Fennel, with its distinctive taste, can be found in produce markets year-round, too.

6 cod steaks, each 3/4 inch thick
1 teaspoon salt
3/4 teaspoon ground black pepper
1/2 fennel bulb, coarsely chopped
1/2 cup (1 stick) butter
1/3 cup dry white wine

Preheat the broiler.

Sprinkle the cod steaks with the salt and pepper and place them on a buttered baking sheet with a 1-inch raised rim.

Place the fennel and butter in the bowl of a food processor. Process with the metal blade until smooth. Spread the fennel butter evenly over the six steaks. Pour the wine around them.

Broil for 12 minutes. The fish should be cooked through, moist and flaky without turning it.

Serve with the pan juices.

Yields: 6 servings

Preparation time: 25 minutes

GRILLED FRESH TUNA STEAKS WITH LEMON SAUCE

This is a big time-saver. During the hour that the tuna is marinating, you will be able to steam the vegetables, concoct a simple salad, set the table, and have a drink. The fish takes only a few minutes to cook, and the marinade gives this dish a tangy herbal flavoring.

Swordfish, mako shark, or any firm-fleshed fish would be equally good in this recipe.

MARINADE

1/3 cup mustard
1/3 cup lemon juice
2 cloves garlic, peeled and minced
3 tablespoons fresh rosemary, minced, or 3 teaspoons dried
1 1/3 cups olive oil
2 teaspoons salt
1 teaspoon ground black pepper

3 pounds fresh tuna, cut into 3/4-inch steaks

SAUCE

4 tablespoons (1/2 stick) butter
3 tablespoons unbleached white flour
1 1/2 cups chicken stock
1/3 cup heavy cream
1/2 teaspoon salt
1/2 teaspoon ground black pepper

Rosemary sprigs and 1 lemon, sliced (for garnish)

To make the marinade, combine all the ingredients in the bowl of a food processor with the metal blade in place and puree for 30 seconds, or until smooth and creamy. Pour the marinade into a glass or stainless-steel casserole. Place the tuna steaks in the marinade, pushing down on them to make sure they are completely covered with sauce. Marinate at room temperature for 1 hour.

Preheat a grill or broiler until very hot. Preheat the oven to 200°F.

Take the tuna from the casserole dish, reserving the marinade for the sauce. Grill the steaks over hot coals until done. It should take about 4 minutes on each side. It's best to check for doneness, since the

To check for doneness, make a small slit in the fish with a knife. The meat shouldn't look transparent and the consistency should be flaky.

time varies depending on how hot the coals are. If you're using your broiler, the time is about the same.

Arrange the grilled fish on a warm platter and place inside the preheated warm oven while you prepare the sauce.

To make the sauce, melt the butter in a heavy saucepan. Add the flour. Simmer, stirring, until all the lumps are gone. Add the chicken stock, stirring constantly until the sauce begins to bubble. Add the cream, salt, and pepper. Bring to a bubbling boil again. Remove from the heat. Add the marinade and stir.

Cover the fish lightly with the sauce. Serve the rest on the side. Garnish the platter with rosemary sprigs and lemon slices.

Yields: 6 servings

Preparation time: 1 hour 20 minutes (including marinating time)

If there are any leftovers, this would make an ideal salad the next day. For Salad Niçoise, add blanched green beans to the tuna chunks and dress with a vinaigrette.

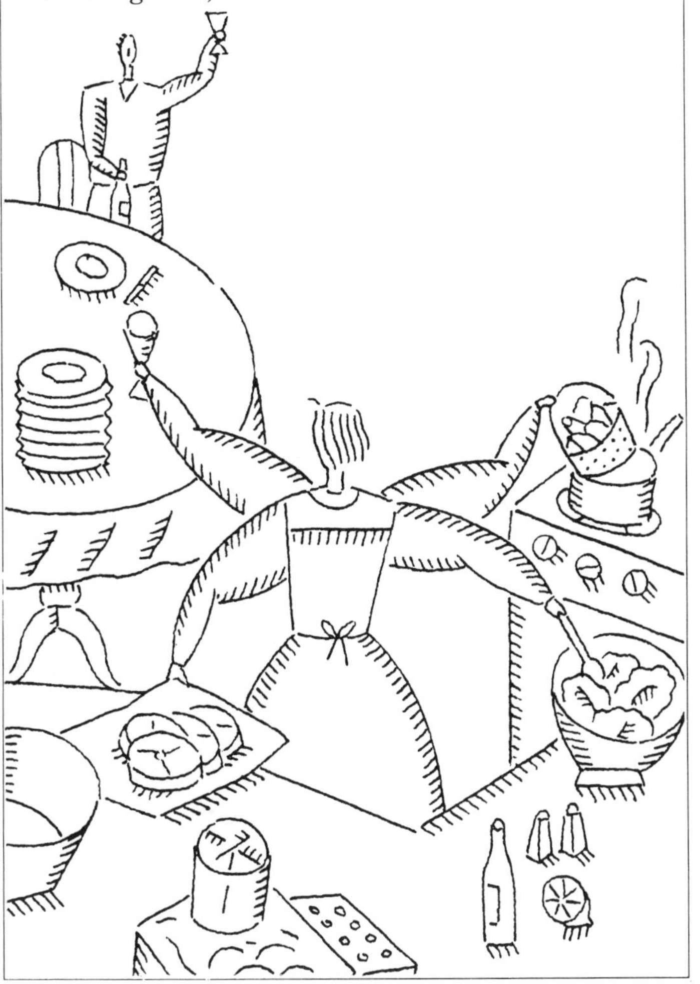

SWORDFISH STEAKS IN LIME–SOY MARINADE

In Mexico we had many fish dishes served with lime. It really lends a special taste that complements the fish.

4 pounds swordfish, cut into 8 steaks

MARINADE
1/3 cup soy sauce
2 teaspoons grated lime peel
1/4 cup lime juice
2 cloves garlic, peeled and minced
1 tablespoon Dijon mustard
1/4 cup peanut oil
1/4 cup finely chopped scallion
1/2 teaspoon ground black pepper

1 scallion and 1 strip of lime peel, cut into julienne strips (for garnish)

Arrange the swordfish pieces in a glass or stainless-steel flat dish with sides high enough to hold the marinade.

To make the marinade, combine the soy sauce, grated lime peel, lime juice, garlic, mustard, oil, chopped scallion, and pepper in a small bowl. Mix well. Pour over the swordfish. Cover the dish and place in the refrigerator for 2 to 4 hours, depending on when you need it.

Preheat the broiler until hot.

Place the fish on a broiler pan; broil for 4 to 5 minutes on each side, or until the flesh is flaky.

Transfer to a large serving platter; pour the juices from the broiling pan over the fish. Garnish with the julienne strips of scallion and lime peel.

Yields: 8 main course servings or 16 first-course servings

Preparation time: 15 minutes (excluding marinating time)

FOR STARTERS

Cut the swordfish into bite-sized pieces and broil for about 3 to 4 minutes.

TO SERVE 16 GUESTS

Double all the ingredients and follow the same instructions.

TO SERVE 24 GUESTS

Triple the ingredients, except for the soy sauce—the amount should be 3/4 cup. Broil in 2 batches, keeping the first batch warm on a serving platter in a preheated 250°F oven.

SWORDFISH FILLETS WITH BASIL AND CAPERS

Another simple meal to prepare. The fresh tomatoes and basil could go with a variety of other fish, too.

Salt and pepper to taste
4 pounds swordfish, sea bass, or tilefish fillets, cut into serving-sized pieces

SAUCE
2 tablespoons olive oil
2 cups peeled and finely chopped onions
2 cloves garlic, peeled and minced
4 large fresh tomatoes, peeled and cut into wedges
½ cup chopped fresh basil or 3 teaspoons dried
2 teaspoons salt
¾ teaspoon ground black pepper
¼ teaspoon cayenne pepper
¼ cup capers, drained

Fresh basil leaves and ¼ cup capers, drained (for garnish)

Preheat the oven to 400°F.

Lightly salt and pepper the pieces of fish on both sides and place them in a buttered ovenproof casserole.

To make the sauce, heat the oil in a large sauté pan. Add the onion and garlic. Sauté for about 5 minutes over a medium heat; don't let them brown. Add the tomatoes, basil, salt, pepper, cayenne, and capers. Bring to a boil. Simmer for 10 minutes, stirring occasionally. Pour the sauce around the fish. Bake for 15 to 18 minutes, or until the fish is just done.

Garnish with fresh basil leaves and capers.

Yields: 8 servings

Preparation time: 45 minutes

If you happen to have leftovers, cut them into hefty chunks and add them to a salad of greens and vegetables. Swordfish is marvelous cold.

MARINATED BAKED SALMON FILLETS

This is really two dishes in one. Remember, this needs two days to marinate. If you assemble it on Friday, it makes a perfect dinner for Sunday night.

MARINADE

1/3 cup coarse salt
1/4 cup ground black pepper
1/3 cup sugar
2 bunches dill, finely chopped
1/4 cup brandy
One 5-pound salmon, filleted (yields 2 fillets)
6 tablespoons (3/4 stick) butter
1 1/2 cups dry white wine

SAUCE FOR HOT SALMON

3 tablespoons butter
2 tablespoons unbleached white flour
Pan juices
Salt and pepper to taste

SAUCE FOR COLD SALMON

1 cup finely chopped romaine lettuce
3/4 cup sour cream
2 tablespoons dry white wine
1/8 teaspoon Tabasco
2 cloves garlic, peeled and minced
2 tablespoons heavy cream

After the holidays I decided to try something different with the gravlax we had left over from a dinner party. I baked the fillets and poured the pan juices over them, and they were wonderful for dinner that evening. Two fillets were left over, and I served them cold the next day for our own lunch, providing a cold sauce for the fillets. Since then this has been a very popular item at Loaves and Fishes parties.

To make the marinade, mix the salt, pepper, and sugar together in a bowl. Sprinkle one-fourth of the mixture and one-fourth of the chopped dill over the bottom of a glass dish just large enough to hold the fillets. Place one salmon fillet in the dish and sprinkle it with another one-fourth of the salt mixture, one-fourth of the dill, and one-half of the brandy. Rub another one-fourth of the salt and dill mixtures on the second fillet and lay that over the first fillet, seasoned sides facing. Sprinkle with the rest of the salt, dill, and brandy. Cover with plastic wrap and weight it down with a brick. Refrigerate for 2 days, turning the fish once each day.

Preheat the oven to 400°F.

Take the salmon from the dish, discarding the

marinade, and pat dry with paper towels. Cut the fillets into 6 or 8 serving-sized pieces. Place them in a buttered baking dish. Dot each piece with some butter. Pour the wine around the fish and bake for 15 minutes, or until just done. Save the juices. Arrange the fish on a hot serving platter and keep it warm inside the turned-off oven.

To make the sauce for hot salmon, melt the butter in a small, heavy saucepan over medium heat. Add the flour and stir well until all the lumps disappear, about 1 minute. Add the fish pan juices all at once. Stirring constantly, bring the sauce to a boil. Add salt and pepper to taste. Pour the sauce over the salmon and serve.

To serve the fillets cold, place the salmon on a platter after it has been baked, cover, and chill for a few hours or until the next day. To prepare the cold sauce, simply combine all the ingredients and mix well. Spoon the sauce over the salmon and serve.

Yields: 6 to 8 servings

Preparation time: 20 to 30 minutes (excluding marinating time)

SALMON ROLL FILLED WITH SOLE MOUSSE

This is a spectacular dish to serve for a formal dinner or as an elegant first course. However, you should prepare it the day before, since it needs that much time for the mousse to set properly. The pink salmon ringing the fluffy sole mousse is masked with a delicate green sauce, slightly pungent, slightly peppery.

POACHING LIQUID

3 cups dry white wine
2 cloves garlic, peeled and mashed
1 tablespoon black peppercorns
1 onion, peeled and quartered
1 stalk celery
1 lemon, halved

SOLE MOUSSE

1½ pounds fillet of sole or flounder
3 egg whites
1½ cups heavy cream
¾ teaspoon salt
1 teaspoon ground white pepper
¼ cup dry sherry
Juice of 1 lemon
⅛ teaspoon cayenne pepper
¼ cup chopped chives (optional)

1 salmon fillet, approximately 2½ to 3 pounds (from a 9-pound fish, after the skin and bones have been removed)

GREEN SAUCE

2 cups tightly packed watercress leaves
2 cups coarsely chopped parsley, tightly packed
½ cup sliced scallions, green parts only
2 cups mayonnaise
2 tablespoons lemon juice
½ teaspoon salt
¾ teaspoon ground black pepper

To make the poaching liquid, place the ingredients into a large fish poacher. Add enough water to fill the pan three-quarters full. Bring to a boil and simmer for 20 minutes.

To make the sole mousse while the poaching liquid is simmering, place all the mousse ingredients, except for the chives, in the bowl of a food processor with the metal blade in place. Process until smooth, about 3 minutes. Fold in the chopped chives and set aside.

Cut a 24-by-18-inch piece of cheesecloth. Place the salmon fillet on it. Cut a deep pocket, lengthwise, into the fillet, taking care not to cut all the way through. Spoon the mousse into the pocket. Wrap the cheesecloth around the salmon roll and secure with toothpicks. Measure the thickness of the roll before you lower it into the poaching liquid. Poach for 10 minutes per inch of thickness (measured at the thickest part).

Carefully lift the roll out of the poacher. Wrap with foil and place in a French baguette pan overnight in the refrigerator so that the roll will firm up and keep its shape while cooling.

To make the green sauce, place the watercress, parsley, and scallions in the bowl of a food processor, and using the metal blade, puree until smooth. Add the mayonnaise, lemon juice, salt, and pepper. Puree just to blend.

To serve the salmon, unwrap the roll carefully and cut into ½-inch slices. Garnish each serving with two tablespoons of sauce.

Yields: 10 to 12 servings

Preparation time: 1 hour 30 minutes (excluding refrigeration time)

Mankind is divisible into two great classes: hosts and guests.
—Max Beerbohm

WHOLE COLD POACHED SALMON WITH CUCUMBER–DILL SAUCE

This section wouldn't be complete without our version of cold poached salmon. The cucumber–dill sauce is very light and fresh tasting.

POACHING LIQUID

Dry white wine
1 teaspoon salt
6 black peppercorns, crushed
6 sprigs thyme
3 sprigs parsley

One 6-pound salmon, cleaned, head and tail left on

GARNISH

3 lemons, sliced
1 bunch dill
1 cucumber, sliced

SAUCE

1½ cups peeled, seeded, and chopped cucumbers
2 cups fresh dill, cut into 1-inch pieces
1 clove garlic, peeled and minced
1 cup sour cream
1½ cups mayonnaise
½ teaspoon ground black pepper
⅛ teaspoon cayenne pepper
½ teaspoon salt

To poach the salmon, pour enough white wine into your fish poacher to fill it one-fourth full. Add water to make it half full. Add the salt, peppercorns, thyme, and parsley. Bring the liquid to a boil. Simmer for 15 minutes over low heat.

Measure the thickness of the fish before you lower it into the poaching liquid. Bring to a boil and simmer for 10 minutes per inch (measured at the thickest part). Transfer the fish to a large platter. Carefully peel off the skin. Cover and chill. Garnish with the lemon, dill, and cucumbers shortly before serving.

To make the sauce, place all the ingredients in

In the hands of an able cook, fish can become an inexhaustible source of perpetual delight.
—Brillat-Savarin

the bowl of a food processor with the steel blade in place and puree until smooth. Chill at least 4 hours. Serve with the fish.

Yields: 6 servings

Preparation time: 1 hour (excluding refrigeration time)

SALMON MOUSSE

This is a perfect brunch offering.

3/4 pound poached salmon
1 egg white
1/2 cup plus 1 tablespoon heavy cream
3/4 teaspoon salt
1/2 teaspoon ground white pepper
2 tablespoons grated fresh horseradish (optional)

Preheat the oven to 350°F.

Using the steel blade, puree the salmon and egg white in the bowl of a food processor for 2 seconds. With the motor running, add the cream, salt, pepper, and horseradish. Puree until the cream is absorbed into the mousse, about 30 seconds.

Spoon the mixture into an oiled 5-by-9-inch loaf pan. Set the loaf pan into a larger baking pan. Pour hot water into the outer pan until it reaches halfway up the side of the loaf pan. Cover with a piece of buttered parchment paper, buttered side down, and bake for 20 minutes.

Yields: 6 servings

Preparation time: 30 minutes

AN UNFORGETTABLE OMELETTE

Here's an elegant way of using any leftover poached salmon you may have. Prepare the Salmon Mousse as instructed, cut into 6 slices and use as fillings for 6 omelettes. Just before you serve, sprinkle each omelette with some beads of golden caviar.

WHOLE BAKED FISH WITH FRESH THYME

Fish is simply magnificent—moist, and closest to its original taste, when cooked this way. The bones absorb the heat and help cook the fish through, while the natural juices of the fish are retained.

One 5-pound or two 2½-pound whole red snappers or other fish, cleaned, head and tail left intact
1 teaspoon salt
¾ teaspoon ground black pepper
4 cloves garlic, peeled and minced
1 teaspoon ground cumin
2 tablespoons olive oil
1 cup dry white wine
15 sprigs thyme
2 egg yolks
¾ cup Crème Fraîche

Preheat the oven to 400°F.

Butter a shallow glass baking dish and place the fish inside. Mix together the salt, pepper, garlic, cumin, oil, and wine in a small bowl and pour around the fish. Place about 5 sprigs of the thyme inside the fish cavity and spread another 5 sprigs over its top. Bake for 40 minutes if you are using one large fish and 30 minutes for two small ones.

Using two spatulas, carefully transfer the fish to a large serving platter. Keep it warm inside the turned-off oven.

Strain the juices from the baking dish into a 9-inch skillet. Over high heat, reduce the amount by half.

Beat the egg yolks into the Crème Fraîche. While whisking, pour the egg mixture into the pan juices. Remove from the heat as soon as the sauce starts to thicken, or just before it comes to a boil.

Garnish with the rest of the thyme and serve it with the sauce on the side.

Yields: 6 servings

Preparation time: 1 hour

BAKED SEA TROUT WITH BASIL–TOMATO SAUCE

A fresh herbed tomato sauce, mildly tart, makes this dish very flavorful and easy to prepare.

In some markets sea trout is sold as weakfish. If neither one is available, try substituting bluefish. It's equally tasty with this savory sauce.

3 pounds fillet of sea trout, cut into 6 serving-sized pieces
½ cup olive oil
1¼ cups chopped basil
2 teaspoons salt
1 teaspoon ground black pepper

SAUCE

2 cups chopped basil
1 cup chopped oregano
3 large cloves garlic, peeled and chopped
½ teaspoon salt
¼ teaspoon ground black pepper
⅛ teaspoon cayenne pepper
2 tablespoons olive oil
2 tablespoons red wine vinegar
2 cups finely chopped fresh plum tomatoes

Preheat the oven to 400°F.

To bake the fillets, sprinkle half the olive oil over the bottom of an ovenproof casserole large enough to hold the fish pieces without crowding them. Spread the basil evenly over the oil. Sprinkle the fish pieces with the salt and pepper. Place them on top of the bed of basil. Bake for 12 minutes, or until the fish is no longer opaque and flakes easily.

To make the sauce, place the basil, oregano, garlic, salt, pepper, cayenne, olive oil, and vinegar in the bowl of a food processor. Puree with the metal blade for 10 seconds. Transfer the mixture to a small saucepan. Add the tomatoes and heat just until the sauce is hot. Don't let it boil, or it will lose its fresh color and taste.

Serve the fish on a large platter, with a little of the sauce spooned over each piece.

Yields: 6 servings

Preparation time: 25 minutes

WHOLE COLD POACHED FISH WITH CAPER SAUCE

Here's another way to prepare a variety of poached fish other than salmon. The sauce is very rich and creamy, with the tartness of wine vinegar and capers. I have also used it often on sautéed chicken breasts.

Court bouillon should be made and used the same day, or 1 day later at the most.

COURT BOUILLON (OR POACHING LIQUID)

3 cups dry white wine
1 clove garlic, peeled and crushed
1 lemon, cut in wedges
1 carrot, sliced
1 stalk celery, sliced
4 sprigs parsley
8 black peppercorns, bruised

One 5- to 6-pound bass, tilefish, or snapper, cleaned, head removed, tail left on

SAUCE

2 cloves garlic, peeled and crushed
3 tablespoons capers, drained
4 egg yolks, hard-boiled
1 teaspoon salt
½ teaspoon ground black pepper
2 scallions, green parts only, chopped
¾ cup olive oil
¼ cup white wine vinegar
1 cup heavy cream
1 cup coarsely chopped parsley

GARNISH

2 lemons cut into quarters
1 bunch of watercress

To make the court bouillon, pour the wine into a fish poacher and add enough water to fill it one-half full. Add the garlic, lemon, carrot, celery, parsley, and peppercorns. Bring to a boil. Simmer for 15 minutes. Measure the thickest part of the fish to determine the cooking time; allow 10 minutes per inch. Lower the fish into the simmering liquid and poach for the required time.

Transfer the fish to a large platter. Let it stand for a few minutes, then carefully remove the visible skin. Cover with a kitchen towel moistened with water and chill for about 3 hours.

To make the sauce, place the garlic, capers, egg yolks, salt, pepper, scallions, and parsley in the bowl of a food processor and with the metal blade in place, process for 30 seconds. With the motor still running, add the oil in droplets. Add the vinegar and pulse a few times.

In a separate bowl, whip the heavy cream until soft peaks hold. Fold the sauce into the cream and chill for about 20 minutes.

To serve, garnish the fish with the lemon and watercress. Serve the sauce on the side.

Yields: 6 servings

Preparation time: 1 hour (excluding refrigeration time)

GRILLED LOBSTERS WITH HERB BUTTER

6 live lobsters, split in half
3/4 cup (1 1/2 sticks) butter
2 cloves garlic, peeled
1 1/2 teaspoons coarse salt
1/2 cup finely chopped oregano
1/2 cup fresh rosemary

Preheat a grill until very hot.

Place the lobsters, flesh side up, on preheated grill. Melt the butter. Crush the garlic with the salt. Add to the butter along with the oregano and rosemary. Brush the lobster flesh with the herb butter. Grill for 10 minutes. Brush again with the melted butter mixture and turn the lobsters flesh side down. Grill for 3 to 5 minutes more, or until the meat is just done.

Serve the lobsters flesh side up on a large platter with the remaining butter spooned over them.

Yields: 6 servings

Preparation time: 15 minutes

LOBSTER SHELL STOCK

There is so little waste in a lobster. The meat, the roe, and the green tomalley are edible. Even the shell shouldn't be discarded. Place leftover lobsters shells in a large pot, add 4 cups water, 1 quartered onion, 3 stalks celery cut in thirds, and a bay leaf. Bring to a boil and simmer over low heat, covered, for 1 hour. Uncover and simmer over medium heat for 30 minutes more. Strain the stock through a colander lined with a kitchen towel. Discard the solids. Pour the stock into a container, cover it, and mark it with the date. The stock will last up to 3 months in the freezer and is absolutely marvelous for fish stews, soups, or sauces.

CHILLED MARINATED FLOUNDER FILLETS

An advantage to this recipe is that you can make it the day before (the preparation time is only 25 minutes) and have it ready for dinner the following evening. The raisins are added because the Scandinavians like a little sweetness in their dish.

This is a Scandinavian version of a recipe found in Africa and South America. The ingredients change somewhat in the translations, but it still makes a great first course or a wonderful addition to a buffet.

¼ cup lemon juice
2½ pounds flounder fillets
¾ cup unbleached white flour
1 teaspoon salt
½ teaspoon ground black pepper

MARINADE
1 cup olive oil
1 cup vegetable oil
2 cups peeled and thinly sliced white onion
4 cloves garlic, peeled and halved
1¼ cups white wine vinegar
3 tablespoons raisins
2 tablespoons fresh thyme or 1 teaspoon dried
1¼ cups water
1 teaspoon sugar

Sprinkle the lemon juice over the flounder and let it sit for 5 minutes. Mix the flour, salt, and pepper and spread the mixture on a piece of wax paper. Coat both sides of each fillet with the flour mixture and set aside.

Heat the olive and vegetable oils in a large, deep skillet. Sauté the fillets over medium heat for 1 minute on each side and place on paper towels to drain. Transfer them to a large, deep platter. Repeat this procedure until all the fish fillets are sautéed.

To make the marinade, discard all but ½ cup of the oil from the skillet. Add the onion and sauté until transparent. Add the garlic, vinegar, raisins, thyme, water, and sugar. Simmer for 1 minute. Let cool for 15 minutes, then pour the marinade over the fish. Cover the platter with plastic wrap and chill for 12 to 24 hours before serving.

Yields: 6 servings

Preparation time: 25 minutes (excluding refrigeration time)

PAN-SAUTÉED SOFT-SHELL CRABS WITH BROWN BUTTER SAUCE

¾ cup unbleached white flour
¼ teaspoon cayenne pepper
½ teaspoon ground black pepper
¾ teaspoon salt
1 dozen soft-shell crabs, cleaned
½ cup clarified butter
2 tablespoons lemon juice
2 tablespoons finely chopped tarragon

Mix the flour, cayenne, pepper, and salt together and place on wax paper. Coat the crabs on both sides with the flour mixture. Set aside.

Heat half the butter in a large skillet. Sauté the crabs for 4 minutes on each side over medium heat until nicely browned. Transfer to a warm platter. Add the rest of the butter to the skillet. Heat until amber colored. Remove from the heat. Add the lemon juice and pour the sauce over the crabs. Sprinkle with tarragon and serve.

Yields: 6 servings
Preparation time: 15 minutes

Lo, luscious now as an infant's lisp,
The strawberry, tart and juicy,
And soft-shelled crabs as sweet and crisp
As a nocturne by Debussy.
—Ogden Nash

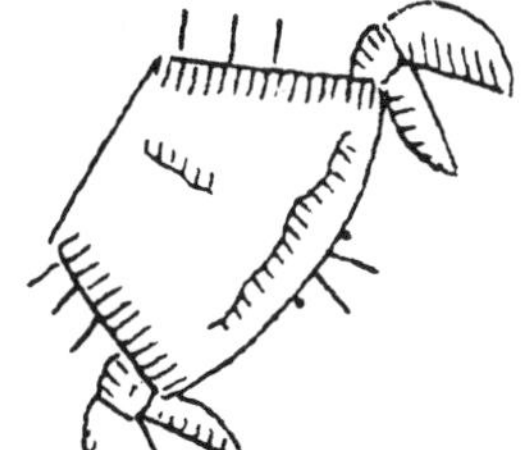

SAUTÉED SCALLOPS AND LEEKS IN CRÈME FRAÎCHE SAUCE

This is a very new idea of ours and is already very much in demand. The tender bay scallops in a white, creamy wine sauce are sweetened with sautéed leeks and flavored with shallots. The preparation time is so fast that the rest of the meal should be prepared before you begin this recipe.

3½ pounds bay scallops
1½ teaspoons salt
½ teaspoon ground black pepper
½ cup unbleached white flour
9 tablespoons clarified butter
4 leeks, white parts only, cut into thin strips
½ cup peeled and finely chopped shallots
1 cup dry white wine
1 cup Crème Fraîche
2 tablespoons chopped dill (for garnish)

Mix the scallops with the salt, pepper, and flour until they are well coated. Set aside.

Melt 3 tablespoons of the clarified butter in a heavy saucepan. Add the leeks and sauté over very low heat, stirring constantly for about 2 minutes. Transfer to a large, warmed serving dish. Keep it warm.

In the same pan, melt 3 more tablespoons clarified butter. Add half the scallops and sauté over high heat for 3 to 4 minutes. Spoon them over the leeks. Repeat this procedure with the rest of the scallops.

Melt the remaining 3 tablespoons clarified butter in a small, heavy saucepan. Add the shallots and sauté over low heat for 2 minutes. Add the wine and reduce it over high heat by one-half. Add the Crème Fraîche and continue to reduce until the sauce starts to thicken, about 3 to 4 minutes. Pour over the scallops and leeks. Garnish with chopped dill.

Yields: 8 servings

Preparation time: 20 minutes

SCALLOPS WITH TOMATOES, GARLIC, AND CREAM

Tomatoes, garlic, and cream—in a rich, savory sauce, that is so quick and easy to prepare. The only suggestion I have is that you slightly undercook the scallops, since they continue to cook on your plate.

In this area of the country, bay scallops are tiny, tender, sweet, and can be eaten raw. They come into season in mid-September and disappear in mid-May, as do most of the bivalves, which thrive in the months that have an *r* in their names. Sea scallops, however, are available year-round. Neither the bay nor the sea scallops should be overcooked.

SAUCE

4 tablespoons (½ stick) butter
3 cloves garlic, peeled and minced
2 cups heavy cream
½ teaspoon salt
½ teaspoon ground black pepper
4 fresh plum tomatoes, diced, or 1 cup canned tomatoes, drained and chopped

2½ pounds fresh bay or sea scallops, halved
½ cup unbleached white flour
1½ teaspoons salt
¾ teaspoon ground black pepper
¼ cup clarified butter

To make the sauce, melt the butter, add the garlic, and sauté over low heat for 2 minutes, making sure the garlic doesn't brown. Add the cream, ½ teaspoon salt, ½ teaspoon pepper, and tomatoes. Simmer until the sauce starts to thicken, about 5 minutes.

Toss the scallops with the flour, 1½ teaspoons salt, and ¾ teaspoon of pepper, coating them well.

Melt the clarified butter in a separate large skillet. Add the scallops. Sauté for 2 minutes, stirring once or twice. You may need to do this in 2 or 3 batches, depending on the size of your skillet. Don't crowd the pan.

When they're done, transfer the scallops to the pan with the sauce. Heat through and serve.

Yields: 6 main-course servings or 10 first-course servings

Preparation time: 30 minutes

POULTRY

What is sauce for the goose may be sauce for the gander, but it is not necessarily sauce for the chicken, the duck, the turkey, or guinea hen.
—Alice B. Toklas

Suppose you suddenly had six guests coming for dinner and had nothing planned or prepared. What would you think of shopping for first?" That was a question I put to my class one day. Almost instinctively one student's response was "Chicken, of course." They all seemed to agree. "Why of course?" I asked. "Well, first of all, not everyone likes fish, and many people don't eat red meat, but everyone seems to like chicken." Everyone nodded. She was expressing the sentiments of many more people than were seated in that classroom. Many of our customers prefer serving chicken dishes when planning party dinners or large buffets. There are so many ways of preparing poultry; it seems naturally to lend itself to new ideas. For that reason, most of the poultry recipes in this collection are based on the ever-popular chicken.

When you shop for chicken, buy it whole, even if the recipe calls for chicken breasts. Debone it yourself. The livers can be made into a pâté, the giblets go into stuffing or gravy, the legs and thighs can be tomorrow's dinner, and all the other leftovers such as the back, neck, and wings can be placed in a plastic bag and frozen until you are ready to make more stock. It is indeed an economical bird.

Another consideration of mine was to include recipes that take little time to prepare and have some flair. Chicken Breasts with Black Bean Sauce takes thirty minutes from pan to plate. Chicken Breasts with Apple–Curry Sauce also takes only thirty minutes from start to finish, and what a wonderful aroma to greet your friends: curry, coriander, apples, and a hint of garlic . . . marvelous. The Chicken Breasts with Goat Cheese and Mint takes twenty minutes to assemble and twenty-five minutes to bake. And while you're preparing the rest of the dinner, the goat cheese melts around the chicken, creating its own minted savory sauce.

I have also included a very special home recipe of mine, Apples with Stuffed Prunes, which I always serve with Roast Goose during the holiday season.

At the end of that particular class, while we were finishing off the dinner we had made together, one of the students raised his glass toward the elegant Terrine of Chicken with Dill Pesto Sauce and offered a toast—"Here's to simple food beautifully prepared." I couldn't agree more.

ROAST GOOSE

From my personal files—a traditional holiday feast.

1 goose (about 10 pounds)
Salt and pepper to taste
1 large onion, peeled and chopped
2 tablespoons butter
3 cups cooked and peeled chestnuts, chopped
2 apples, peeled and sliced
1 teaspoon thyme
1 cup soft bread crumbs
1/3 cup French brandy
1 egg
Dash of cayenne pepper
2 cups beef stock
2 cups dry white wine

SAUCE

4 tablespoons (1/2 stick) butter
1/4 cup unbleached white flour
3 cups roasting juices
1/4 cup port wine
Salt and pepper to taste

Preheat the oven to 450°F.

Rinse and dry the goose, inside and out. Sprinkle the cavity and skin with salt and pepper. Sauté the onion in the butter until soft. Add the chestnuts, apples, thyme, salt, pepper, bread crumbs, brandy, egg, and cayenne. Stuff this mixture into the cavity of the goose. Tie the legs and wings and prick the skin all over with a fork. Roast for 20 to 30 minutes, or until the goose is golden brown. Heat the beef stock and wine and add to the roasting pan. Reduce the oven temperature to 325°F and continue roasting until done, about 2 hours more. Baste 3 or 4 times during roasting.

To make the sauce, melt the butter in a heavy saucepan. Add the flour and cook the roux for 1 minute, then remove from the heat. Add the roasting juices and bring to a boil, stirring constantly. Add the port wine, season with salt and pepper, and serve with the goose.

Yields: 6 servings

Preparation time: 3 hours

APPLES WITH STUFFED PRUNES

Steep 6 large pitted prunes in ½ cup of port wine and ½ cup of sugar for 10 minutes. Set aside. Sauté 3 goose livers in 1 tablespoon of butter until just done. Cool. Mash the livers with a fork, adding 1 tablespoon of heavy cream and 2 tablespoons of the prune poaching liquid. Blend until creamy. Add salt and pepper to taste, then set aside. Poach 3 large tart apples that have been peeled, halved, and cored in 1 cup of white wine and ½ cup of sugar until the apples are just tender. Stuff the goose liver mixture into the prunes and set 1 prune in each apple half. Place them in an 8-by-11-inch casserole, drizzle them with the rest of the apple poaching liquid, and bake for 15 minutes inside a preheated 325°F oven.

TERRINE OF CHICKEN WITH DILL PESTO SAUCE

Almost a pâté yet very light, this can be sliced for lunch, served as a first course or as part of a cold buffet.

The dill pesto sauce also goes very well with poached seafood, drizzled over sliced tomatoes, or over sautéed veal scallops. All in all, it's a great summertime sauce to have in your refrigerator.

MOUSSE

3½ pounds chicken cutlets, trimmed
1 egg plus 1 egg white
2 teaspoons salt
2 teaspoons ground black pepper
¼ cup peeled and minced shallots
½ teaspoon ground nutmeg
2 tablespoons fresh thyme or 2 teaspoons dried
3 tablespoons cognac
1 cup heavy cream

1 cup boiled ham, diced into ¾-inch pieces
¼ cup shelled pistachio nuts

SAUCE

1 cup olive oil
6 cloves garlic, peeled
3 cups fresh dill, coarsely chopped, omitting hard stems
¼ cup terrine juices, or strong chicken stock

Preheat the oven to 350°F.

To make the mousse, place the chicken meat into the bowl of a food processor, reserving one whole breast. Add the egg and egg white, salt, pepper, shallots, nutmeg, thyme, and cognac. With the metal blade in place, process for 1 minute. With the motor running, pour in the cream. Process the mixture to the consistency of a mousse, about 20 seconds.

Dice the reserved chicken breast into ¾-inch cubes. Place it in a mixing bowl. Add the ham, pistachio nuts, and chicken mousse and mix well.

Fill a buttered loaf pan or pâté terrine with the chicken mixture. Place a piece of buttered parchment paper, buttered side down, against the top of the chicken mixture. Set the terrine in a larger roasting pan. Pour enough hot water in the roasting pan to come halfway up the outside of the terrine. Bake for 1½ hours. Remove from the water bath and let set for 15 minutes. Drain off and reserve ¼ cup terrine juices for the sauce.

To make the sauce, place the olive oil, garlic, and

dill in a food processor bowl, fitted with a steel blade. Whirl until creamy. Add the terrine juices. Mix well. Serve with the sliced terrine.

Yields: 6 to 8 servings

Preparation time: 2 hours

CHICKEN BREASTS WITH GOAT CHEESE AND MINT

I like using Bucheron cheese with this recipe because it stands up to the mint. While the chicken rolls are baking, the cheese slowly melts and makes its own rich, creamy sauce.

FILLING

¾ cup (1½ sticks) butter, softened
½ pound Bucheron goat cheese, at room temperature
½ cup fresh mint leaves, finely chopped
1 tablespoon fresh thyme or 1 teaspoon dried
⅓ cup peeled and minced shallots
½ teaspoon ground black pepper

6 chicken breasts, skinned and boned, cut in half and pounded thin
1 teaspoon salt
1 teaspoon ground black pepper
½ cup unbleached white flour
¼ cup clarified butter
½ cup fresh mint leaves (for garnish)

Preheat the oven to 400°F.

To make the filling, mix all the ingredients in a medium bowl until creamy and well blended. Set aside.

Sprinkle the chicken breast pieces with salt and pepper. Divide the filling among the 12 pieces. Spread it to about ½ inch from the edges. Roll each breast and tie with a string. Dust the chicken rolls with the flour. Heat the clarified butter in a large skillet. Brown the chicken rolls over medium heat. Transfer them to a buttered casserole. Bake for 25 minutes. Place on a serving platter and pour the sauce over them. Sprinkle with the mint leaves.

Yields: 6 servings

Preparation time: 45 minutes

CHICKEN WITH PRUNES AND ONIONS

This meal can be prepared ahead of time, covered, and refrigerated for up to 2 days. When needed, all you do is bake it in a preheated 350°F oven for 35 to 40 minutes, or until it's heated through.

Steeped in a red wine sauce, flavored with Canadian bacon, fresh herbs, and onions, sweetened with prunes, and garnished with crisp green parsley, this traditionally European combination makes an exceptional meal around the holiday season when served with either Spaetzle or Coriander Brown Rice.

1 pound pitted prunes
3 cups Burgundy red wine
3 tablespoons butter
½ teaspoon sugar
1½ pounds small white onions, peeled
½ pound Canadian bacon, cut into 1-inch strips
6 tablespoons clarified butter
Two 3-pound chickens, cut into serving-sized pieces
Salt and pepper to taste
1½ cups peeled and finely chopped onion
2 cloves garlic, peeled and minced
1 cup reserved prune-cooking liquid
2 cups chicken stock
2 tablespoons fresh thyme or 1½ teaspoons dried
1 tablespoon fresh sage or 1 teaspoon dried
1 large bay leaf, broken in half
2 tablespoons unbleached white flour, mixed with 3 tablespoons of the prune-cooking liquid
2 tablespoons chopped parsley (for garnish)

Combine the prunes and wine in a medium saucepan and bring to a boil. Simmer for 15 minutes. Remove from the heat and set aside.

Heat the butter in a large sauté pan. Add the sugar and whole white onions and sauté for 8 to 10 minutes, stirring often, until the onions are nicely browned. Remove from heat and set aside.

Sauté the Canadian bacon in 2 tablespoons of the clarified butter for about 3 minutes in a large pan. Transfer to a plate and set aside. Heat the remaining clarified butter in the same pan. Sprinkle the chicken pieces with salt and pepper, place them in the pan, and brown them on both sides, then transfer the pieces to a platter.

In the same pan, sauté the chopped onion and

garlic for about a minute or so. Add 1 cup of the prune-cooking liquid, the chicken stock, thyme, sage, and bay leaf. Place the chicken pieces back in the pan and simmer for about 25 minutes. Transfer the chicken pieces to a deep ovenproof serving platter.

Meanwhile, preheat the oven to 350°F.

Thicken the sauce remaining in the pan with the flour mixed with prune-cooking liquid. Bring the sauce to a boil and correct the seasoning. Pour the sauce over the chicken, then scatter the prunes, onions, and Canadian bacon over the top. Set the platter in the oven for 10 minutes. Sprinkle with parsley and serve.

Yields: 6 to 8 servings

Preparation time: 1 hour 15 minutes

If you're ever tired of serving stuffed turkey during the holiday season, please try this recipe.

CHICKEN BREASTS FILLED WITH SAUSAGE AND PINE NUTS

The apple-flavored sauce is the color of cooked mushrooms in this savory dish of stuffed chicken breasts.

FILLING

3 tablespoons butter
½ cup peeled and finely chopped onion
¼ cup finely chopped fennel
½ pound sweet sausage meat
½ pound mushrooms, minced
¼ teaspoon hot red pepper flakes
½ teaspoon salt
2 tablespoons pine nuts
4 ounces cream cheese

6 whole chicken breasts, boned but skin left on
½ teaspoon salt
½ teaspoon ground black pepper
4 tablespoons (½ stick) butter, melted

SAUCE

2 tablespoons Calvados
¼ cup peeled and minced shallots
½ cup chicken stock
1 cup Crème Fraîche

Chopped chives (for garnish)

Preheat the oven to 400°F.

To make the filling, heat the 3 tablespoons butter in a sauté pan. Add the onion and fennel and sauté for about 2 minutes. Add the sausage meat and sauté over medium heat 5 to 7 minutes, until the meat is just done. Add the mushrooms and sauté over high heat, about 3 minutes, to reduce the liquid. Remove from heat. Add the hot red pepper flakes, salt, pine nuts, and cream cheese. Mix well and set aside.

Cut the chicken breasts in half. Pound each to ¼-inch thickness. Sprinkle with salt and pepper. Divide the filling evenly among the 12 breast pieces. Roll each breast, encasing the filling, and secure it with a toothpick. Place the rolls in a buttered roasting pan, and brush each one with melted butter. Bake for 25 minutes, or until golden brown.

To make the sauce, transfer the breasts to a serving platter. Discard the excess fat from the pan. Pour the Calvados into the pan. Over a medium heat, quickly scrape off all the brown bits at the bottom of the pan. Add the shallots and sauté for 1 minute, stirring well, then add the chicken stock and Crème Fraîche. Stir. Reduce the sauce until it just begins to thicken, no more than 2 minutes. Pour the sauce over the chicken rolls, garnish with the chives, and serve.

Yields: 6 to 8 servings
Preparation time: 45 minutes

CHICKEN BREASTS WITH MORELS

Morels vary in color from tan to a rich brown, and they resemble tiny pine cones. Since they seem only to appear for a brief 2-week period, from February in some southern states through late May in some northern states, we always buy them dried. They are a strongly flavored mushroom and are wonderful for almost any sauce.

1 ounce morels, soaked for 30 minutes in hot water
3 whole chicken breasts, skinned and boned
¼ cup unbleached white flour
1 teaspoon salt
¾ teaspoon ground black pepper
¼ cup clarified butter
⅓ cup peeled and minced shallots
1 tablespoon peeled and minced garlic
1 cup Madeira wine
1 cup Crème Fraîche
1 cup heavy cream
2 tablespoons lemon juice

Preheat the oven to 375°F.

Drain the morels and dry them with paper towels. Set aside. Cut the chicken breasts in half. Dust with the flour, then sprinkle with the salt and pepper.

Melt half the clarified butter in a large sauté pan. Place the chicken breasts in the pan and sauté over over medium heat until they are browned on both sides. Remove the chicken to an ovenproof casserole. Add the rest of the butter to the sauté pan along with the shallots, garlic, and morels. Sauté over medium heat for 2 minutes, tossing and stirring constantly. Pour the Madeira wine into the pan. Reduce the liquid to half its amount over high heat. Add the Crème Fraîche, heavy cream, and lemon juice. Reduce the sauce until it starts to thicken, about 3 minutes. Pour the sauce over the chicken. Bake for 12 minutes or until the dish is heated through.

Yields: 6 servings
Preparation time: 40 minutes

CHICKEN BREASTS WITH APPLE–CURRY SAUCE

A very special favorite of mine. Sweet, tart, and spicy, this spunky sauce goes so well with chicken. Serve it over plain white rice.

¼ cup clarified butter
6 chicken breasts, skinned, boned, and halved

SAUCE

4 tablespoons (½ stick) butter
1½ cups peeled and finely chopped onion
2 cloves garlic, peeled and minced
1½ cups peeled, cored, and finely chopped tart apples
3 tablespoons unbleached white flour
1½ tablespoons curry powder
½ teaspoon ground cardamom
1 teaspoon ground coriander
¾ teaspoon salt
½ teaspoon ground black pepper
3 cups chicken stock
2 teaspoons grated lime rind
1 tablespoon lime juice
½ cup mango chutney, finely chopped

Preheat the oven to 200°F.

Heat the clarified butter in a large sauté pan and sauté the chicken breasts on both sides until browned. Cover the pan. Heat the chicken breasts over low heat for 5 minutes. Transfer them to a platter. Keep warm in the oven while you're making the sauce.

To make the sauce, melt the butter in the sauté pan. Add the onion and sauté over low heat until transparent. Add the garlic and apples and sauté for 2 minutes. Add the flour, curry powder, cardamom, coriander, salt, and pepper. Stir to mix well. Add the chicken stock, lime rind, lime juice, and chutney. Bring the sauce to a boil, stirring constantly. Pour around the chicken and serve.

Yields: 6 servings
Preparation time: 30 minutes

CHICKEN CUTLETS PARMESAN WITH TOMATO CHILI SAUCE

This is a very convenient dish to prepare. You can sauté the chicken breasts ahead of time and make the sauce later. The cutlets can be served at room temperature or heated through.

4 whole chicken breasts, skinned, boned, and halved
¾ cup unbleached white flour
1½ teaspoons salt
1 teaspoon ground black pepper
3 eggs, beaten well
2 tablespoons heavy cream
¾ cup freshly grated Parmesan cheese
¾ cup dry bread crumbs
½ cup olive oil

SAUCE

2 cups peeled and minced fresh tomatoes or one 18-ounce can Italian plum tomatoes, drained and minced
½ cup peeled and minced onion
2 pickled hot jalapeño peppers, halved, seeded, and minced
½ green pepper, seeded and minced
1 teaspoon salt

Italian parsley sprigs (for garnish)

Place the chicken cutlets, smooth side down, on wax paper, and pat down with your hands. Cover with a second piece of wax paper. Flatten the cutlets with a meat pounder until they are ¼-inch thick. Combine the flour, salt, and pepper on another piece of wax paper. Whisk the eggs and cream in a shallow bowl or soup plate. Combine the Parmesan cheese and bread crumbs on another piece of wax paper.

Dip each chicken cutlet first into the flour, then into the egg mixture, and finally into the cheese and crumb mixture, coating both sides. Place on a large plate and refrigerate for 30 minutes.

To make the sauce, place all the sauce ingredients in a mixing bowl and stir to blend well. Refrigerate for at least 30 minutes.

Heat the olive oil in a large skillet. Sauté the cutlets for 1 minute on each side over a medium heat, then transfer to a warm platter. Garnish with parsley and serve with the sauce on the side.

Yields: 6 servings
Preparation time: 45 minutes

LEMON CHICKEN BREASTS WITH SHIITAKE MUSHROOMS

A lemony sauce, accented by a touch of garlic, mustard, and brown sugar. Add to that the delicate fragrance of Shiitake mushrooms and you have an elegant meal. Assemble this recipe the night before in order to give the chicken pieces time to marinate. It takes about thirty minutes to prepare.

6 chicken breasts, skinned, boned, and halved
1/3 cup olive oil
2/3 cup lemon juice
1 tablespoon Dijon mustard
1/2 teaspoon ground black pepper
1/2 teaspoon salt
2 medium onions, peeled and chopped
2 cloves garlic, peeled and chopped
2 tablespoons brown sugar
1/4 cup clarified butter
1 ounce Shiitake mushrooms, soaked in warm water for 30 minutes

SAUCE

1/3 cup peeled, chopped shallots
1 1/2 cups chicken stock
1 tablespoon cornstarch
2 tablespoons lemon juice

Lemon zest (for garnish)
1 tablespoon chopped parsley (for garnish)

Arrange the chicken breasts over the bottom of either a glass or an earthenware casserole. Mix the olive oil, lemon juice, mustard, pepper, and salt in the bowl of a food processor, fitted with a steel blade. Add the onion, garlic; and brown sugar and puree until smooth. Pour over the chicken and marinate overnight in the refrigerator.

Remove the chicken from the marinade, saving the marinade for the sauce. Pat the chicken dry and, using half the clarified butter, sauté the breasts in a large skillet over medium heat for 5 to 7 minutes until they are just done and browned on both sides. Transfer them to a large platter. Drain the mushrooms. Add them to the pan and sauté them over a medium heat for 2 to 3 minutes. Transfer them to the platter with the chicken.

To make the sauce, in the same skillet, sauté the shallots for 2 minutes over medium heat. Add the chicken stock and half the marinade and bring to a boil, reducing the sauce for about 3 minutes. Mix the cornstarch with the lemon juice and add it to the sauce, stirring constantly, over a low heat. Strain the sauce and pour it over the chicken with Shiitake mushrooms. Garnish with the lemon zest and chopped parsley.

Yields: 6 to 7 servings

Preparation time: about 30 minutes (excluding marinating time)

Shiitake mushrooms are dark brown, velvety, and have circular caps. They are grown in cut logs of the oaklike *shii* tree, which lends its light aroma to the mushroom.

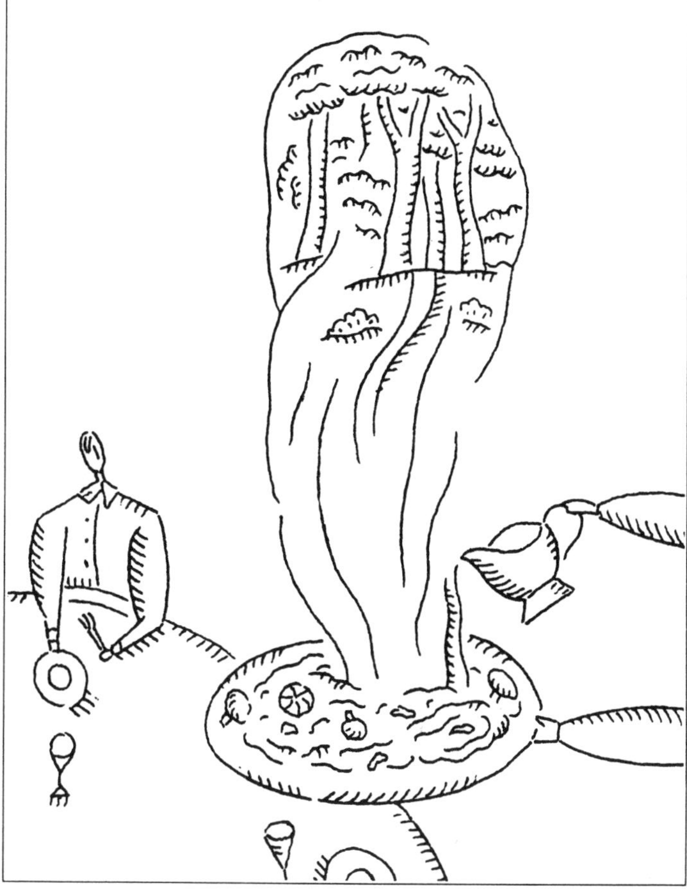

Fermented beans can be purchased in any Oriental food store. Many grocery stores carry this item as well.

CHICKEN BREASTS WITH BLACK BEAN SAUCE

Tahini gives this sauce a lot of body. The chicken, cut into strips, is served warm, with the thick, chilled sauce on the side. An ideal meal with sautéed snow peas, it also makes an excellent addition to any buffet.

6 chicken breasts, skinned and boned
3/4 cup unbleached white flour
1 teaspoon salt
1 teaspoon ground black pepper
1/2 teaspoon cayenne pepper
1/4 cup clarified butter
Chopped scallions, green parts only (for garnish)

SAUCE

3 tablespoons fermented black beans, rinsed
1 cup soy sauce
1/4 cup sugar
4 cloves garlic, peeled and minced
1 teaspoon ground black pepper
3/4 cup sesame tahini
Juice of 1 lemon
1 cup olive oil

Place all the sauce ingredients in the bowl of a food processor fitted with the metal blade. Process to blend, about 4 minutes. Chill.

Cut each chicken breast into 4 strips. Combine the flour, salt, pepper, and cayenne. Dust the chicken pieces with the flour mixture. Heat the clarified butter in a sauté pan. Add the chicken and sauté over medium heat until just done, about 3 minutes on each side. Transfer the chicken pieces to a platter. Sprinkle with the chopped scallion greens. Serve the chilled sauce on the side.

Yields: 6 servings
Preparation time: 30 minutes

CHICKEN, CHILIES, AND CHEESE

Browned chicken breasts in a casserole, covered by a spicy tomato sauce.

SAUCE

2 tablespoons olive oil
2 cups peeled and finely chopped onion
6 cloves garlic, peeled and minced
1 cup finely chopped fresh fennel or 1 teaspoon dried
1 green pepper, seeded and finely chopped
One 4-ounce can green chili peppers, drained and diced
2 fresh green jalapeño peppers
3 cups peeled and chopped fresh tomatoes or one 28-ounce can tomatoes, crushed
One 6-ounce can tomato paste
1 cup water
1 bay leaf
½ cup chopped fresh basil or 1½ teaspoons dried
1 teaspoon salt

2 tablespoons clarified butter
6 chicken breasts, halved
¾ pound feta cheese, crumbled
¼ cup finely chopped parsley (for garnish)

It's wise to make the sauce first. Heat oil in a heavy saucepan, large enough to accommodate all the ingredients. Sauté onion over low heat for about 5 minutes, or until transparent, not browned. Add the garlic, fennel, green pepper, and diced chili peppers. Cut the jalapeño peppers in half, discard the seeds, and add them to the sauce. Add the chopped or crushed tomatoes, tomato paste, and water, and stir to dissolve the paste. Add bay leaf, basil, and salt, and bring to a boil. Simmer for 30 minutes. Meanwhile, preheat the oven to 350°F.

Heat the clarified butter in a large skillet and sauté the chicken breasts over medium heat on both sides until browned. This should take 4 to 5 minutes. Spoon half of the sauce into an ovenproof casserole. Add the browned chicken breasts and spoon the rest of the sauce over the pieces. Sprinkle with the feta cheese. Bake for 35 minutes. Garnish with the parsley and serve.

Yields: 6 to 8 servings
Preparation time: 1 hour 30 minutes

You can make a double batch and freeze one of the pies. If you take it directly from the freezer, bake it for at least an hour.

CHICKEN PIE

An old-fashioned standby that is a very big favorite at Loaves and Fishes.

PASTRY

2 cups unbleached white flour
½ teaspoon salt
¼ teaspoon ground black pepper
6 tablespoons butter, chilled and cut into small pieces
6 tablespoons margarine, cut into small pieces
1 tablespoon lemon juice
¼ cup cold water

FILLING

3 pounds chicken cutlets
3 carrots, peeled and diced
¾ cup (1½ sticks) butter
2 medium onions, peeled and chopped
¾ cup unbleached white flour
1½ teaspoons salt
¾ teaspoon paprika
4 cups chicken stock
1 teaspoon Worcestershire sauce
1 cup fresh shelled peas or one 10-ounce package frozen, thawed
½ cup chopped parsley

1 egg yolk
1 tablespoon heavy cream

To make the pastry, place the flour, salt, pepper, butter, and shortening in the bowl of a food processor, fitted with the metal blade, and pulse 5 times. Add the lemon juice and water and turn on the machine for 3 seconds. Using your hands, scrape the dough onto a floured surface and work it together into a smooth ball. Cover with plastic wrap and chill for 30 minutes.

Meanwhile, preheat the oven to 375°F.

To make the filling, place the chicken cutlets in boiling water and simmer for 7 to 8 minutes. Drain. When they are cool enough to handle, cut into bite-sized pieces and set aside.

Place the carrots in boiling water and simmer for 4 minutes. Drain and set aside.

Heat the butter in a large skillet. Add the onion

and sauté until transparent. Add the flour and sauté for 3 minutes, over medium heat, stirring constantly. Add the salt and paprika. Mix well. Add the chicken stock gradually while stirring and bring to a boil. Add the Worcestershire sauce, peas, parsley, poached chicken pieces, and the carrots. Mix well. Transfer to a casserole.

Roll out the pastry dough 1-inch larger all around than the area of your casserole. Place the dough on top of the chicken filling and flute the edges. Cut small slits in for places to let the steam escape while baking. Beat the egg yolk with the heavy cream and brush the top of the pastry with the mixture. Bake 40 minutes.

Yields: 6 to 8 servings
Preparation time: 1 hour 30 minutes

TARRAGON-ROASTED GAME HENS

The tarragon, garlic, and butter mixture not only crisps these succulent birds but adds body and a firm taste to their natural juices.

Salt and pepper to taste
6 small hens, halved
½ cup (1 stick) butter, melted
2 tablespoons tarragon vinegar
½ cup fresh tarragon leaves, chopped
2 cloves garlic, peeled and minced
Tarragon sprigs (for garnish)

If fresh tarragon is unavailable, substitute tarragon leaves in vinegar (imported from France), using ½ cup, drained.

Preheat the oven to 425°F.

Salt and pepper the hens and place them on a large buttered baking sheet, skin side up. Mix together the melted butter, vinegar, tarragon leaves, and garlic. Brush the hens with half the mixture. Roast them for 20 minutes.

Divide the rest of the butter–tarragon mixture over the hens and roast for 20 minutes more. Place the hens on a warm serving platter and pour the pan juices over them. Garnish with fresh tarragon sprigs.

Yields: 6 servings
Preparation time: 50 minutes

GLAZED DUCK

Here's a simple, foolproof way to cook a wonderful duck dinner. This is delicious served cold as well as hot, or even at room temperature.

Three 4½-pound ducks
Salt and ground black pepper
2 oranges
½ cup red currant jelly
½ cup Marsala wine
2 teaspoons Dijon mustard
1 tablespoon red wine vinegar
1 teaspoon salt
1 teaspoon ground black pepper
¼ teaspoon cayenne pepper
1¾ cups chicken stock
2 tablespoons cornstarch

Preheat the oven to 375°F.

Cut the ducks in half. Remove the center backbone, reserving for future use in making stock. Sprinkle a little salt and pepper on the inside of the duck halves. Place them in 1 or 2 shallow roasting pans, skin side up. Roast for 30 minutes.

Zest the rind of an orange into a bowl. Peel both oranges, cut the flesh into small pieces, and place these in the bowl of a food processor with the metal blade in place. Add the currant jelly, Marsala, mustard, vinegar, 1 teaspoon salt, 1 teaspoon pepper, and cayenne. Puree until fine and pour into the bowl that contains the orange zest.

Remove the ducks from the oven and drain off all the fat. Increase the oven temperature to 400°F. Baste the ducks with the orange sauce. Roast for 15 minutes more. Transfer the ducks to a large heatproof platter and place them in the turned-off oven to stay warm.

Pour 1½ cups of the chicken stock into the roasting pan. Scrape up all the brown bits from the bottom. Strain the stock into a medium pan and bring the stock to a boil. Mix the cornstarch with the remaining ¼ cup stock and add this to the pan. Stirring constantly, bring the stock to a boil. Pour into a sauceboat and serve with the duck.

Yields: 6 servings

Preparation time: 1 hour 20 minutes

SAUTÉED BREAST OF DUCK

I had this in Paris for the first time, and it is a very special meal. The duck meat should be pink, so don't overcook it or you might risk having it turn tough. Serve with a fresh, light red wine.

For this recipe I prefer the Muscovy duck, which has less fat and more meat than other domesticated ducks.

3 ducks, averaging 4 to 4½ pounds each
¾ teaspoon salt
½ teaspoon ground black pepper
¼ cup clarified butter

SAUCE

¾ cup red wine vinegar
½ cup peeled and minced shallots
½ cup chicken stock
¾ cup (1½ sticks) butter
½ teaspoon salt
½ teaspoon ground black pepper
¼ cup minced parsley

Cut the ducks in half. Carefully trim out the breast halves. Trim away all the skin and fat. Save the rest of the duck for making stock. Sprinkle the 6 breast halves with the salt and pepper.

Heat the clarified butter in a large skillet. Sauté the breasts for 2 minutes on each side, over medium heat. Thinly slice each duck breast on the diagonal and transfer slices to dinner plates. Keep the plates warm while you're preparing the sauce.

To make the sauce, pour the vinegar into the skillet. Add the shallots and simmer over high heat until the liquid is reduced to about 2 tablespoons. Add the chicken stock and bring to a boil. Add the butter, one-quarter at a time, stirring constantly over medium heat. Add the salt, pepper, and parsley. Stir, then spoon a little sauce over each sliced duck breast, and serve.

Yields: 6 servings
Preparation time: 30 minutes

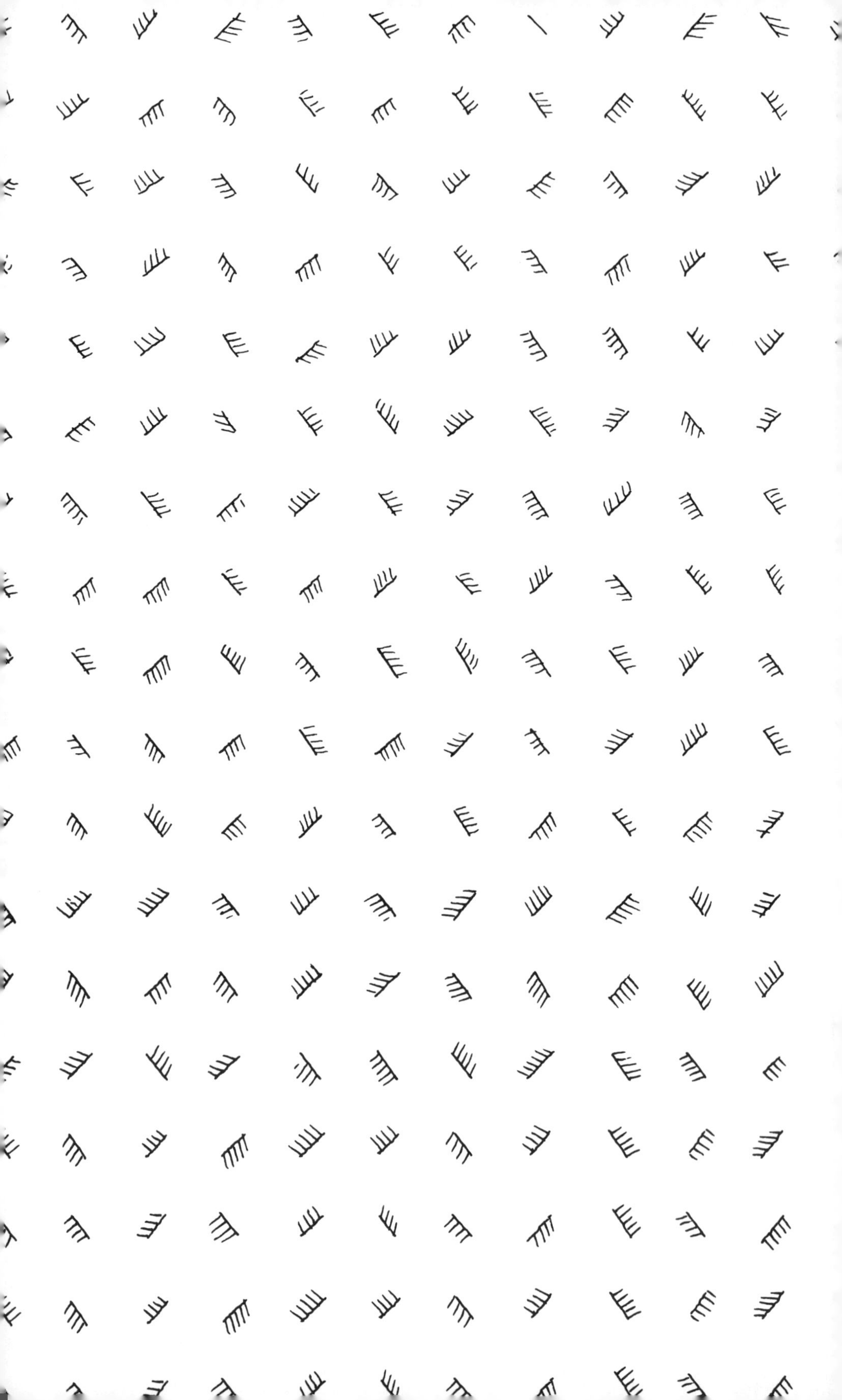

MEATS

Upon what meat doth
this our Caesar feed,
That he is grown so
great.
—Shakespeare,
Julius Caesar

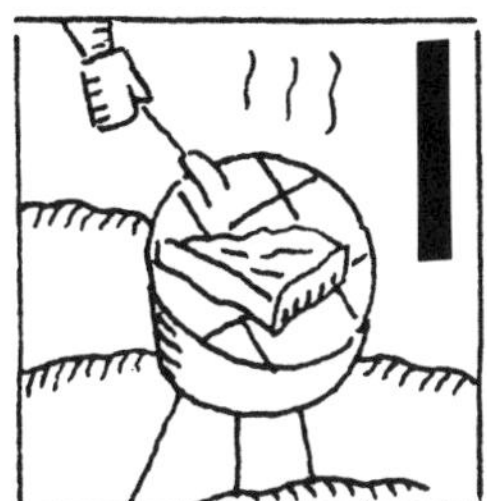

I am a proponent of the "fast cooking" approach to meats. This includes sautéing, grilling, and broiling. In testing for doneness, press your finger against the top of the meat; if it "sinks" in, the meat is probably still blue and underdone. If there is no resistance, if the meat doesn't bounce back at all, it is probably overcooked. But, if your finger meets with a slight resistance, the meat will be perfectly cooked: rosy pink and moist on the inside and ready for the plate.

Since I have enough recipes to fill several books, I decided to keep within the theme of this cookbook and present a variety of meat dishes, all favorites at Loaves and Fishes, that are easy to prepare and might introduce some daring and innovative ideas to my readers.

VEAL ROAST FILLED WITH SPINACH AND ROQUEFORT

You can prepare this roast up to three days ahead of time, which makes it an ideal menu choice when you're planning a dinner party or a large buffet.

4 pounds boneless rump of veal
12 ounces fresh spinach or one 10-ounce package frozen spinach, thawed
1 cup water
4 tablespoons (½ stick) butter, softened
½ pound Roquefort cheese
1 teaspoon ground black pepper
1 tablespoon dry sherry
3 strips smoked bacon
1 cup dry white wine
1 cup chicken stock
1 clove garlic, peeled and quartered
1 medium onion, peeled and quartered
1 carrot, scraped and sliced
2 tablespoons unbleached white flour mixed with ¼ cup chicken stock

If Roquefort seems too strong for your taste, try some nice English Stilton, or a blue cheese. Also, you can substitute watercress, arugula, or lettuce for the spinach.

LEMON SAUCE

1 egg
¼ teaspoon salt
¼ teaspoon ground black pepper
2 teaspoons Dijon mustard
3 tablespoons lemon juice
1 cup safflower oil
2 tablespoons heavy cream

Preheat the oven to 375°F.

Trim the veal of all fat and tissue and set aside.

Place the spinach leaves in a large pot. Add the water. Steam the spinach over high heat until the leaves are wilted. Drain and press out all the water. If using frozen spinach, drain and remove all the excess liquid. Place the spinach in the bowl of a food processor with a metal blade in place, along with the butter, Roquefort, pepper, and sherry. Puree the mixture until creamy, about 15 seconds.

Using the tip of a small, sharp knife, pierce deep holes all over the meat. Fill each hole with some of the spinach–Roquefort mixture, pushing it down with

Either serve this hot with a rich gravy made from stock and the roast's pan juices, or serve it cold, thinly sliced, with a bold lemon sauce on the side. It goes wonderfully with buttered noodles or fettucine.

your fingers. Tie the meat to hold it firmly together.

Place the veal in a large roasting pan. Cut the bacon strips in half and drape them over the meat. Add the wine, stock, garlic, onion, and carrot to the pan. Roast the meat for 1 hour. Cover the pan with foil and roast for 30 minutes more. To serve the roast hot, remove it from the pan and let it rest for 10 minutes. Remove the string, slice the roast, and arrange the pieces on a large serving platter.

To make a sauce for the hot veal roast, strain all the pan juices into a saucepan. Reduce it until you have two-thirds of it left. Thicken the sauce by adding the flour–chicken stock mixture, stirring constantly. Let it come to a full boil. Pour a little of it over the meat and serve the rest on the side.

To serve the roast cold, take the roast from the pan, cool for 30 minutes, then wrap it in foil. Chill for 6 hours or overnight. Remove the string and thinly slice the roast, arranging the pieces on a platter. Serve with lemon sauce on the side.

To make lemon sauce, drop the egg into a blender. Add the salt, pepper, mustard, lemon juice, and half the safflower oil. Blend at medium speed for 10 seconds. With the motor running, add the rest of the oil in a stream. Add the cream. Blend until the sauce has the consistency of whipped cream. This should take about 30 seconds. Serve the sauce on the side.

Yields: 6 to 8 servings
Preparation time: 2 hours

VEAL POCKETS IN MUSHROOM SAUCE

The veal, ham, shallots, garlic, and herbs contribute their individual flavors to create this all-season favorite.

8 veal scallops, pounded thin
Salt and pepper to taste

FILLING

2 tablespoons butter
2 tablespoons olive oil
3 large shallots, peeled and chopped fine
2 cloves garlic, peeled and minced
1 pound ground veal
¼ pound lean ham, chopped fine
1 egg
6 tablespoons dry bread crumbs
2 tablespoons water
1 tablespoon fresh thyme or 1 teaspoon dried
½ teaspoon ground black pepper
½ teaspoon salt

2 tablespoons butter
2 tablespoons olive oil
6 ounces mushrooms, thinly sliced
1 cup dry white wine
1 cup strong chicken stock
½ cup heavy cream
Chopped parsley (for garnish)

Lightly sprinkle the veal with salt and pepper.

To make the filling, heat the butter and olive oil in a sauté pan. Add the shallots and sauté until golden. Add the garlic, stir to mix, and remove from the heat.

Place the ground veal, ham, egg, bread crumbs, water, thyme, pepper, and salt in a bowl. Add the sautéed shallots and garlic. Thoroughly combine the ingredients with your hands.

Spoon some of the filling onto a veal scallop. Fold the veal from both ends to form a pocket and tie with string. Continue filling and tying the rest of the scallops. Sauté the pockets in butter and oil over medium heat until they are nicely browned on all

This entire meal can be prepared 3 days ahead of time. It goes beautifully with orzo pilaf, a fresh green salad with a dash of vinaigrette, and, for dessert, Blueberry Pie.

sides, 8 to 10 minutes. Add the mushrooms and continue sautéeing for 1 minute. Add the wine and the chicken stock. Bring to a boil, then simmer over low heat for 35 minutes. Transfer the pockets to a serving platter. Remove the strings and cut each pocket in half. Add the cream to the sauce. Over high heat, reduce to about 1 cup. Pour the sauce over the veal pockets, sprinkle with chopped parsley, and serve.

Yields: 8 servings
Preparation time: 1 hour 15 minutes

VEAL SCALLOPS WITH GOAT CHEESE AND OREGANO

This elegant dish takes only fifteen minutes to prepare. I usually serve it with Buttered Spinach Fettuccine and Sautéed Cherry Tomatoes with Fresh Dill.

2½ pounds veal scallops
1 tablespoon salt
2 teaspoons ground black pepper
½ cup unbleached white flour
½ cup clarified butter
2 tablespoons peeled and minced garlic
½ cup beef stock
¾ cup sour cream
3 ounces mild fresh goat cheese, such as Montrachet
2 tablespoons minced fresh oregano

Preheat the oven to 200°F.

Sprinkle each scallop with a little salt and pepper. Dip them in the flour. Heat the butter in a large skillet. Quickly brown the veal on both sides over high heat for about 1 minute on each side. Place on a serving platter and keep warm in the oven while you are making the sauce.

Add the garlic to the skillet. Sauté for 5 seconds, tossing over medium heat. Add the beef stock and simmer over high heat for 1 minute. Lower the heat, then add the sour cream, goat cheese, and oregano. Stir until smooth and creamy, 4 to 5 minutes. Pour the sauce around the veal scallops and serve.

Yields: 6 servings
Preparation time: 15 minutes

VEAL CHOPS WITH SPINACH CREAM

Baby Carrots with Ginger is a nice accompaniment for this meal, followed by Raspberry–Walnut Pie.

A very good way to treat the delicate veal chop. A bit of bite from some fine cognac, a taste of shallots, and garlic in a creamy sauce flecked with leaves of fresh spinach.

3 tablespoons clarified butter
Salt and pepper to taste
6 veal chops, each 1½ inches thick

SAUCE

3 tablespoons cognac
⅔ cup peeled and minced shallots
3 cloves garlic, peeled and minced
3 cups finely chopped fresh spinach
1⅓ cups heavy cream
¼ teaspoon salt
¼ teaspoon ground black pepper

Feel free to substitute watercress, arugula, or fresh basil leaves for the spinach. And remember not to overdo the veal chops, they ought to be just done, yet done through.

Heat the clarified butter in a large skillet. Lightly salt and pepper the veal chops. Place them in the hot butter and sauté over medium heat for about 12 minutes on each side. Remove the chops to a warm platter and cover to keep them warm while making the sauce.

To make the sauce, pour the cognac into the skillet and ignite. After the flames subside, add the shallots and garlic, and sauté, tossing and stirring a few seconds. Add the spinach, cream, salt, and pepper. Let the sauce come to a full boil. Reduce the sauce for a minute, scraping and stirring up all the brown bits from the bottom. To serve, place a veal chop on each plate. Spoon some of the sauce and spinach over it.

Yields: 6 servings
Preparation time: 35 minutes

SAUSAGE AND DUCK CASSEROLE

These two meats complement each other beautifully. The duck meat stays very moist, absorbing the peppery flavoring of the hot sausages. In winter, when the snow is flying, I serve this to my friends, poured over white beans that have been boiled in herbs.

1/4 pound bacon strips, halved
2 ducks, cut into 6 pieces each, skinned and all fat removed
1 tablespoon salt
2 teaspoons ground black pepper
2 pounds hot Italian or Spanish sausage links
3 cups peeled and minced onion
1/4 cup peeled and minced garlic
3 cups chicken stock
1/2 cup red Burgundy wine
1/4 cup tomato paste
3 sprigs fresh thyme or 3/4 teaspoon dried
1 bay leaf
1 stalk celery
3 sprigs parsley
2 tablespoons chopped parsley (for garnish)

Preheat the oven to 350°F.

Sauté the bacon in a large skillet until crisp. Transfer to a plate and reserve. Discard all but 3 tablespoons of the bacon fat. Rub the duck pieces all over with the salt and pepper. Brown in a buttered ovenproof casserole, over medium-high heat for 10 to 12 minutes. Brown the sausages and add them to the casserole. Place the onion in the skillet. Sauté for 5 minutes over low heat, stirring now and then. Add the garlic, chicken stock, wine, and tomato paste. Bring to a boil. Scrape up all the brown bits from the bottom. Stir in the thyme, bay leaf, celery, and parsley sprigs. Pour the sauce over the meat in the casserole. Scatter the bacon on top. Cover and bake for 1 hour 30 minutes.

To serve, arrange the duck and sausage pieces on a deep serving platter. Strain the sauce and pour it over the meat. Sprinkle with parsley.

Yields: 6 servings
Preparation time: 2 hours

This can also be served at room temperature on hot days, with a green salad dressed in a lemon sauce. The casserole can also be made up to 3 days ahead of time and reheated in a 350°F oven for 30 minutes.

I have successfully substituted sautéed pears instead of apples and I always serve the roast with browned, oven-roasted potatoes.

ROAST PORK LOIN WITH APPLES AND HORSERADISH

A "country" recipe that can be served either hot or cold.

One 4-pound pork loin, tied
2 cloves garlic, peeled
1 tablespoon salt
1 tablespoon fresh thyme or 1 teaspoon dried
¼ cup Dijon mustard

SAUCE

¾ cup peeled fresh horseradish, cut into 1-inch pieces
¼ teaspoon cayenne pepper
½ teaspoon salt
8 ounces cream cheese
1¼ cups sour cream
½ cup peeled and minced scallions

6 tablespoons (¾ stick) butter
3 tart apples, peeled, cored, and cut into eighths
6 sprigs parsley (for garnish)

Preheat the oven to 425°F.

Place the loin of pork in a buttered baking dish. Mash the garlic, salt, and thyme into a paste. Mix in the mustard. Brush the mixture all over the pork loin. Roast, uncovered, for 1 hour and 20 minutes. Remove from the oven. Cover with foil and let rest for 15 minutes to settle the juices.

Meanwhile, to make the sauce, place the horseradish in the bowl of a food processor with the metal blade in place. Process until fine. Add the cayenne, salt, cream cheese, and sour cream and process until smooth, 10 to 15 seconds. Transfer the sauce to a bowl and stir in the scallions. Chill until ready to use.

Melt the butter in a large skillet. Add the apples and sauté for 7 or 8 minutes over medium-high heat, stirring occasionally.

To serve, slice the roast loin of pork and arrange it on a large platter. Surround it with the sautéed apples. Pour the pan juices over the pork. Garnish with parsley and serve with the sauce on the side.

Yields: 6 to 8 servings
Preparation time: 2 hours

CALVES' LIVER WITH TARRAGON BUTTER SAUCE

One of the keys to the success of this dish is that the calves' liver be slightly pink inside. Sauté it lightly, and it becomes so tender, it practically melts in your mouth. The tart sauce enriched with white wine, shallots, and tarragon is a perfect complement to this flavorful meat.

When shopping for calves' liver always buy it fresh, and be sure that it is much paler in color than beef liver.

2½ pounds calves' liver, cut into 6 slices, each ⅝ inch thick
½ cup unbleached white flour
1 tablespoon salt
1 teaspoon ground black pepper
6 tablespoons clarified butter

TARRAGON BUTTER SAUCE
⅓ cup white wine vinegar
⅓ cup dry white wine
¼ cup peeled and minced shallots
1 cup (2 sticks) butter
½ teaspoon salt
½ teaspoon ground black pepper
2 tablespoons minced tarragon

6 sprigs tarragon (for garnish)

Dust both sides of the liver slices with flour, then sprinkle them with the salt and pepper. Heat the butter in a large sauté pan. Sauté the calves' liver quickly over medium-high heat for 1½ to 2 minutes on each side, or until browned on the outside but still pink on the inside. Transfer the liver to a warm platter.

To make the sauce, place the vinegar, wine, and shallots in a medium skillet. Reduce over high heat to 2 tablespoons. Reduce the heat and swirl the butter into the vinegar–shallot mixture, 3 tablespoonfuls at a time. Add the salt, pepper, and minced tarragon. Pour the sauce over the liver. Garnish with the tarragon sprigs and serve.

Yields: 6 servings
Preparation time: 20 minutes

MARINATED STEAK WITH MADEIRA CREAM SAUCE

Madeira lends this curried, peppery cream sauce extra warmth and body. This dish is attractive, simple, and a favorite both at home and at Loaves and Fishes.

4 tablespoons (½ stick) butter, softened
¼ cup Dijon mustard
1 tablespoon curry powder
1 tablespoon Worcestershire sauce
1 teaspoon salt
1 teaspoon ground black pepper
2 boneless 2-pound steaks, such as London broil or flank steak
1 cup Madeira wine

SAUCE

2 tablespoons butter
¼ cup peeled and chopped shallots
1 clove garlic, peeled and minced
1½ cups sour cream

Chopped parsley (for garnish)

Mix the softened butter, mustard, curry powder, Worcestershire sauce, salt, and pepper until blended. Slather this creamy mixture on the steak, spreading it over the sides, too. Place the steak in a noncorrosive dish. Pour the Madeira over the steak. Refrigerate for 8 hours or more.

Preheat the broiler to high heat.

Reserving the marinade, transfer the meat to a broiler pan and broil for 3 minutes on each side. Transfer the steaks to a warm platter. Keep warm.

To make the sauce, melt 2 tablespoons butter in a small, heavy saucepan. Add the shallots and garlic and sauté over low heat for about 3 minutes until transparent. Add the sour cream and stir to blend.

Add the Madeira marinade to the broiler pan and scrape up all the brown bits. Pour this into the shallots and sour cream mixture. Heat the sauce, stirring constantly, until hot, but not boiling.

Transfer the meat to a cutting board. Slice thinly on the diagonal. Transfer back to the serving platter, pour the sauce over the steak, and garnish with chopped parsley.

Yields: 8 servings

Preparation time: 15 minutes (excluding marinating time)

SAUTÉED STEAKS WITH BASIL HOLLANDAISE

Prime tender steaks, sautéed until medium rare, then bathed in fresh, buttery hollandaise and flavored with pungent fresh basil leaves.

6 center-cut tenderloin steaks, each about 1¾ inches thick
1½ teaspoons salt
1 teaspoon pepper
6 tablespoons clarified butter

BASIL HOLLANDAISE SAUCE

5 egg yolks
3 tablespoons lemon juice
½ teaspoon salt
½ teaspoon ground black pepper
¾ cup (1½ sticks) butter, melted and sizzling hot
2 tablespoons finely chopped basil

Preheat the oven to 175°F.

Sprinkle the steaks with the salt and pepper. Melt the clarified butter in a large skillet and sauté the steaks for about 4 minutes on each side over medium-high heat until desired doneness. Transfer to warm dinner plates and place them in the warm oven while you prepare the sauce.

To make the basil hollandaise sauce, blend the egg yolks, lemon juice, salt, and pepper in a blender for 12 seconds. With the motor running, add the hot butter slowly in a thin stream. Add the basil. Turn the motor on, then off, to mix it. Pour a little of the hollandaise over part of each steak and on the plate.

Yields: 6 servings

Preparation time: 20 minutes

A BLENDER HOLLANDAISE

The beauty of this recipe is that the hollandaise can rest in the blender while you're preparing the steaks. If you haven't had success in the past, don't be discouraged or intimidated; it's only a question of practice. For example if the eggs are too large for the proportions given, just add a tablespoon of cream or lemon juice. More important, the butter has to be the right temperature, that is, hot, yet not hot enough to curdle the eggs. If you find this happening in the first batch, don't despair: Throw it away and try again. You'll get the hang of it and never have to waste a blender full of ingredients again. You'll have the technique of making perfect hollandaise right at your fingertips.

This stew can be made 3 days in advance, then reheated in a 350°F oven for 40 minutes. I usually serve it with Barley Pilaf followed by a crisp green salad and a platter of assorted cheeses. For dessert I find that fresh Raspberry Ice Cream and a plate of Madeleines are a perfect finale to this hearty dinner.

BEEF STEW WITH SUN-DRIED TOMATOES

A stew rich with wine, pungent with sun-dried tomatoes, and perfect for cool evenings.

1/4 pound lean bacon strips, cut into 1-inch pieces
4 pounds stewing beef, cut into 1 1/2-inch chunks
3 cups peeled and finely chopped onion
2 tablespoons peeled and minced garlic (about 4 large cloves)
1/4 cup unbleached white flour
3 1/2 cups red Burgundy wine
2 1/2 cups chicken stock
1/2 cup sun-dried tomatoes
1 tablespoon chopped fresh thyme or 1 teaspoon dried
2 bay leaves, broken in half
1 1/4 teaspoons salt
1 teaspoon ground black pepper
32 small white onions, skins left on
2 tablespoons butter
1 pound small mushrooms, stems removed
Thyme sprigs (for garnish)

Preheat the oven to 350°F.

Brown the bacon in a large sauté pan. Transfer to a plate and set aside. Discard all but 3 tablespoons of the bacon fat. Add half the beef to the fat in the sauté pan. Brown over medium-high heat. Transfer the browned meat to a large casserole and repeat this procedure with the remaining meat.

Place the onion and garlic in the same pan. Brown, over medium heat, stirring a few times. Add the flour and stir until blended with the onions. Add the wine, stock, and tomatoes. Stir to scrape up all the brown bits from the bottom of the pan. Add the thyme, bay leaves, salt, and pepper. Bring the liquid to a boil. Then pour it over the meat in the casserole. Bake the stew, covered, for 2 1/2 hours.

When the stew is almost ready, place the small unpeeled white onions in a saucepan, cover with water, and bring to a boil. Boil for 2 minutes and drain. When they are cool enough to handle, remove their skins and set aside.

Melt the butter in a skillet and sauté the mushroom caps over high heat until lightly browned and heated through, about 3 to 4 minutes.

To serve, add the bacon, onions, and mushrooms to the stew. Stir carefully to mix them in. Garnish with thyme sprigs.

Yields: 6 to 8 servings
Preparation time: 3 hours

ROAST FILLET OF BEEF WITH ROQUEFORT SAUCE

A robust sauce, spiked with white wine and flavored with the rich taste of Roquefort cheese.

Stilton or blue cheese can easily be substituted in this recipe, and leftover fillet can be incorporated in a red meat salad.

One 4½- to 5-pound fillet of beef, trimmed and tied with cotton string
3 cloves garlic, peeled
4 tablespoons (½ stick) butter
¾ teaspoon ground black pepper
1 teaspoon salt

ROQUEFORT SAUCE

1½ cups dry white wine
3 cups heavy cream
½ pound Roquefort cheese, crumbled
½ teaspoon ground black pepper

Any leftover is excellent served cold with a little Mustard Sauce:
Mix 1 cup Dijon mustard with 1 cup sour cream. Add ½ cup heavy cream, 1 tablespoon white wine vinegar, 1 teaspoon ground cumin, ¼ teaspoon salt, ¼ teaspoon ground black pepper, and ½ teaspoon sugar. Stir well.
Yields: 2½ cups

Preheat the oven to 500°F.

Place the fillet in a buttered roasting pan. Mash the garlic, butter, pepper, and salt into a paste. Rub the mixture over the meat. Roast the fillet, uncovered, for 22 minutes. Remove from the oven. Cover the roast tightly with foil. Let it rest in a warm place for 20 minutes. The fillet will be rare in the thickest part and medium in the thinner part. Remove the string and slice into ½-inch slices.

To make the Roquefort sauce, heat the wine in a heavy saucepan over high heat for about 15 minutes, or until it is reduced to ¼ cup. Add the cream and reduce to about 2 cups. Add the Roquefort and pepper. Simmer, stirring constantly, until the cheese has dissolved and the sauce starts to thicken. Serve with the fillet slices.

Yields: 6 to 8 servings
Preparation time: 1 hour

Mustard's no good without roast beef.
—Chico Marx

BEEF ROULADEN

Rouladen are excellent made ahead of time and reheated in the sauce in a 350°F oven for 40 minutes.

There are countless ways to make rouladen. It seems to change from area to area in France. Some restaurants use lots of mustard, others serve it with pickles instead of capers, but this one is my favorite. With its good rich sauce and its enticingly piquant filling, this would be marvelous over spaetzle with red cabbage as a side dish and accompanied by a good Burgundy.

4 pounds short loin of beef, cut into sixteen ¼-inch slices (have your butcher do the slicing)
Salt and pepper to taste
½ pound lean bacon, diced
6 tablespoons capers, drained
One 2-ounce can flat anchovy fillets
6 tablespoons clarified butter
3 cups peeled and diced onion
3 cloves garlic, peeled and minced
1 bay leaf
3 cups beef stock
1½ cups dry white wine
2 tablespoons minced fresh thyme or 2 teaspoons dried
½ teaspoon ground black pepper
½ cup heavy cream
3 tablespoons flour kneaded into 3 tablespoons softened butter
3 tablespoons chopped parsley (for garnish)

This special beef stew will last for up to 4 days in the refrigerator or can be stored in the freezer for up to 2 months.

Lightly sprinkle each slice of beef with salt and pepper. Divide the bacon, capers, and anchovy fillets evenly among the 16 slices. Roll each slice and tie with cotton string. Heat the clarified butter in a heavy sauté pan. Brown the rouladen over medium high heat on all sides and transfer to a plate. Place the onion, garlic, and bay leaf in the same pan and sauté over low heat until brown, about 5 minutes. Add the beef stock, wine, thyme, and pepper. Place the rouladen in the sauce and simmer, covered, for 2 hours.

Transfer the rouladen to a warm platter. Remove the strings. Add the cream and flour–butter mixture to the sauce and bring to a boil, stirring constantly. Strain into a sauceboat. Pour a little of the sauce over the rouladen, and serve the rest on the side. Garnish with the chopped parsley.

Yields: 8 servings
Preparation time: 2 hours 30 minutes

MOROCCAN LAMB STEW

This flavorsome stew, richly aromatic, sweet, and savory is perfect with couscous or toasted pita bread. We've served this with a dessert of Pecan–Cranberry Pie.

3 tablespoons olive oil
2 tablespoons butter
3½ pounds lamb from the leg, cut into 1½-inch cubes
4 cups peeled and finely chopped onion
6 cloves garlic, peeled and minced
2 tablespoons unbleached white flour
3 cups peeled and chopped fresh tomatoes or one 28-ounce can plum tomatoes, drained and chopped
1 cup chicken stock
1 teaspoon ground cumin
½ tablespoon chopped fresh coriander or ½ teaspoon dried
One 3-inch stick cinnamon
½ teaspoon ground cardamom
½ teaspoon cayenne pepper
2 teaspoons salt
1 cup golden raisins

A very good dish to prepare ahead of time, this stores up to 3 days in the refrigerator.

Preheat the oven to 350°F.

Heat the oil and butter in a large sauté pan, and brown the lamb on all sides over medium-high heat. Do this in two batches. Transfer the lamb to an ovenproof casserole.

Place the onion and garlic in the same pan and sauté until they turn light brown, 4 to 5 minutes. Add the flour and stir it in, then add the tomatoes and the chicken stock. Bring the mixture to a boil. Scrape up all the brown bits from the bottom of the pan. Remove the pan from the heat and add the rest of the ingredients. Stir to mix.

Pour the sauce over the lamb. Cover the casserole dish with foil and bake for 2 hours.

Yields: 6 servings

Preparation time: 2 hours 45 minutes

Leftover lamb can be sliced smaller and made into Lamb, Mint, and Spinach Salad.

GRILLED MARINATED LEG OF LAMB

Simple and delicious, this classic marinade is given extra snap by the oyster sauce. It is a luxurious dish whether broiled or grilled outdoors. Serve with Lemon Potatoes and a green vegetable.

One 6- to 7-pound leg of lamb, boned and butterflied

MARINADE

3 cloves garlic, peeled and minced
½ cup soy sauce
1 tablespoon white wine vinegar
1 tablespoon oyster sauce
¼ teaspoon ground black pepper
2 tablespoons peanut oil
2 tablespoons chopped fresh rosemary or 2 teaspoons dried, crushed

Rosemary sprigs (for garnish)

Place the lamb in a large glass dish. Combine the marinade ingredients in a small bowl. Pour over the lamb. Marinate for 30 minutes.

Cook the lamb on an outdoor grill or under a preheated broiler for 10 to 12 minutes on each side. Slice on the diagonal and arrange on a warm platter. Heat the remaining marinade and pour it over the lamb. Garnish with fresh rosemary sprigs.

Yields: 8 servings

Preparation time: 1 hour (including marinating time)

RACK OF LAMB WITH FRESH MINT

These chops freshly cut from a roasted rack of lamb are juicy pink in the center and crisp on the outside. I serve this dish with Broccoli with Parmesan Sauce and oven-roasted potatoes. Garnish with fresh mint leaves. Chocolate Rum Cake would be a satisfying finish to this beautiful meal.

½ cup Dijon mustard
3 tablespoons soy sauce
4 cloves garlic, peeled and minced
½ cup fresh mint leaves, chopped
2 racks of lamb, trimmed
Mint sprigs (for garnish)

Preheat the oven to 475°F.

Mash the mustard, soy sauce, garlic, and mint into a paste. Coat the lamb completely with this mixture and let it marinate at room temperature for 30 minutes. Place the meat in a large shallow roasting pan. Roast for 20 minutes and remove from the oven. Cover with foil and let the racks rest for 15 minutes.

Cut the racks into chops, arrange on a warm platter, and garnish with fresh mint sprigs. Spoon any pan juices over the meat.

Yields: 6 servings

Preparation time: 1 hour (including marinating time)

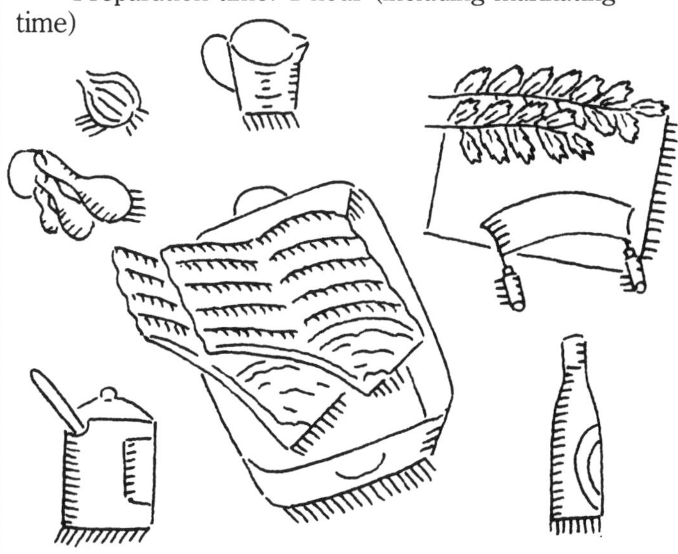

Can we ever have enough of a good thing?
—Miguel de Cervantes

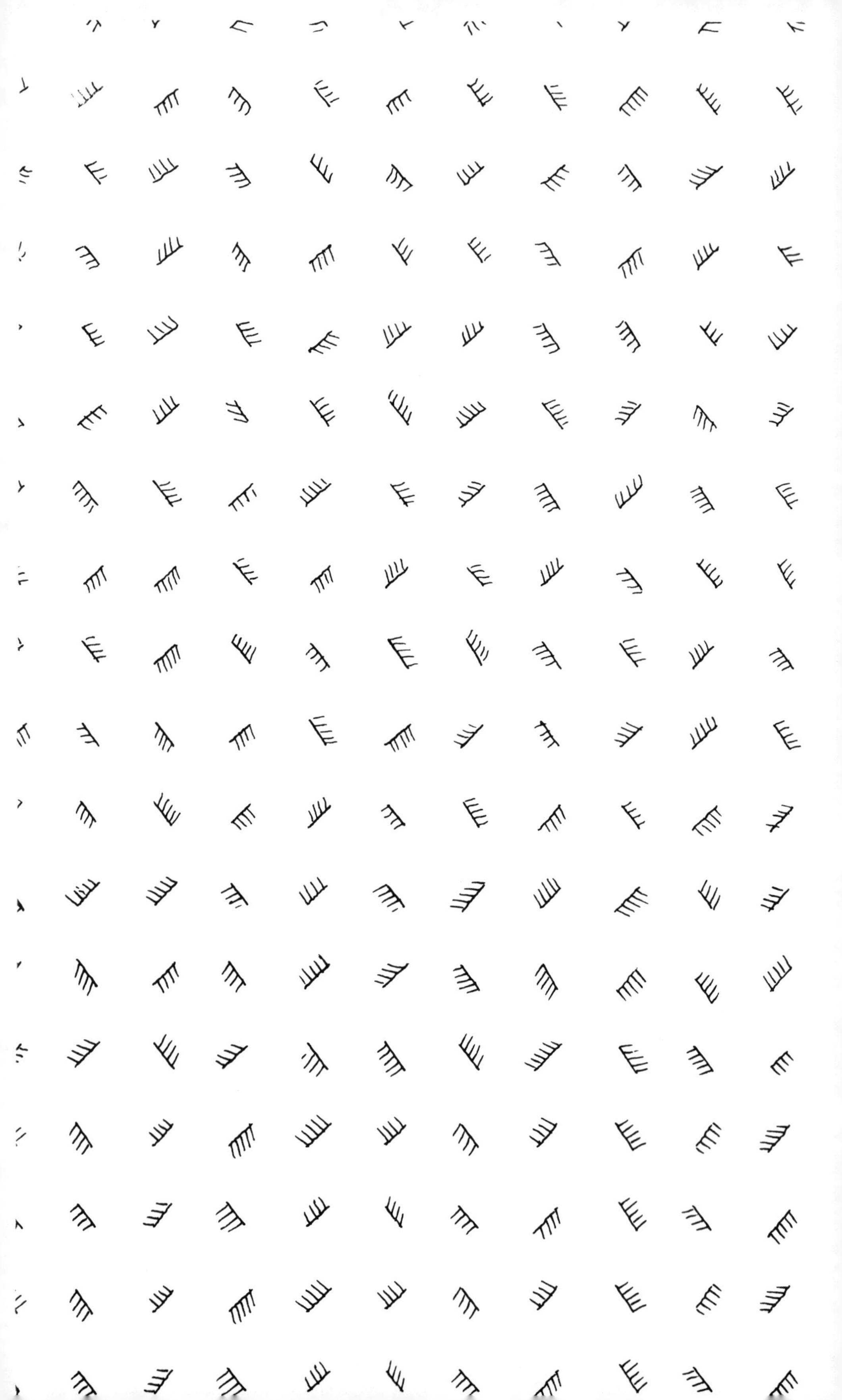

PASTAS, RICE, AND GRAINS

Pasta?
Basta.
Scungilli?
Not really.
Calamari?
I'm sorry.
Espresso?
I guess so.
—Peter Stone

Pastas, grains, and rice often serve to balance a meal. They are thought to be the perfect alternatives to potatoes or other starchy vegetables. All three are nutritious, have different textures, are simple to prepare, and best of all, they provide the cook with perfect ways to introduce different sauces to the plate.

Lately there's been a growing interest in homemade pastas. Some stores have created special counters that turn out fresh pasta daily—spinach pastas, whole wheat pastas, tomato pastas, and so forth. Contrary to popular opinion, dried pastas are not inferior to the freshly made ones. The texture is different, that's true; a dried pasta will give you a more toothsome meal, but the main difference is in the preparation time. Freshly made pasta takes less time to cook and should be watched so that it isn't overdone. Pastas are so adaptable; we see pasta salads, pasta dinners, pasta mixed with every conceivable vegetable, every sort of meat, poultry, and fish. Even pastas mixed with pasta! At Loaves and Fishes we have a popular pasta dish that combines fusilli with ziti and spaghettini, covered in our favorite sauce.

Risotto and rice, like pasta, don't need a lot of fuss to turn them into a suitable side dish or an ideal accompaniment to a meal. Just a little hot butter, some salt and pepper to taste, perhaps some herb oil or, as with a pasta side dish, a liberal sprinkling of freshly grated cheese.

It's very important to keep pastas, grains, and rice in your Essential Pantry because of their many uses and because of their long shelf life. They sometimes serve as just the right addition you need to give your dinner that extra bit of style.

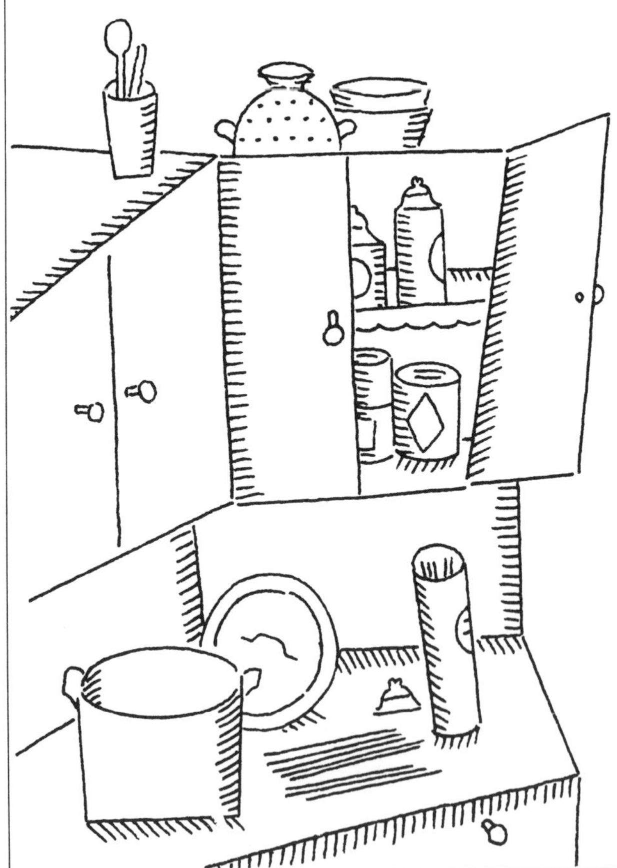

SCALLION CAPELLINI

I sometimes serve this with a tablespoon of caviar sprinkled over each plate; it's magnificent. I've also served it with julienne strips of smoked fish placed over the top.

1 pound capellini
1 cup olive oil
1/4 cup white wine vinegar
1 teaspoon peeled and minced garlic
12 scallions, trimmed and cut into 1-inch pieces
1 1/2 teaspoons salt
1 teaspoon ground black pepper
1/4 teaspoon cayenne pepper
3/4 cup heavy cream

Break the capellini in half and drop it into 4 quarts of boiling water. Simmer for about 6 to 8 minutes, or until al dente. Drain. Pour the noodles into a large bowl.

Place all the remaining ingredients except the cream in the bowl of a food processor fitted with a metal blade. Process for 30 seconds. With the motor running, slowly add the cream. Pour the sauce over the capellini. Toss to mix well. Cover and marinate for 1 hour, or for up to 12 hours.

Yields: 6 to 8 servings

Preparation time: 20 minutes (excluding marinating time)

Capellini is a thin spaghetti. You could substitute vermicelli, angel hair pasta, or spaghettini.

The choice of additions for risotto are almost limitless. Fresh tomatoes cut into chunks, sautéed vegetables, or shellfish all work very well. You can change the cheese to Gruyère, Romano, or whatever you have on hand, but be generous!

RISOTTO WITH AVOCADO

4 tablespoons (½ stick) butter
1½ cups peeled and diced shallots
1¾ cups Italian short-grain rice
2 cups chicken stock
2½ cups dry white wine
1 teaspoon salt
½ teaspoon ground black pepper
¾ cup freshly grated Parmesan cheese

GARNISHES

2 ripe avocados, peeled and diced into 1-inch pieces
Juice and grated rind of 1 lemon

Heat the butter in a heavy saucepan. Add the shallots and rice and sauté over a low heat for 7 minutes, stirring occasionally. Add the chicken stock, wine, salt, and pepper. Bring to a boil. Simmer, covered, for 18 minutes. Add the Parmesan cheese and stir well to mix. Remove from the heat. Fold in the avocado, lemon juice, and rind. Pour into a warm casserole and serve.

Yields: 6 servings
Preparation time: 30 minutes

WILD RICE WITH LEEKS

At Loaves and Fishes this special side dish is most often served with duck or chicken dinners. I find it complements veal and beef just as much. An interesting and delicious alternative to potatoes.

4 tablespoons (½ stick) butter
5 small leeks, white parts only, chopped
1½ cups wild rice
3 cups chicken stock
¾ teaspoon salt
¾ teaspoon ground black pepper
½ cup slivered almonds, toasted

Melt the butter in a heavy saucepan. Add the leeks and sauté for 3 minutes over low heat. Add the rice, chicken stock, salt, and pepper. Bring to a boil. Cover and simmer for about 30 minutes. To test for doneness, the rice should be firm to the bite. Fold in the almonds and serve.

Yields: 6 servings
Preparation time: 40 minutes

CORIANDER BROWN RICE

Coriander and cardamom add great taste to this earthy rice dish. It goes well with Beef Rouladen, Moroccan Lamb Stew, and other hearty meat dishes.

1½ cups brown rice
3½ cups water
¾ teaspoon salt
½ teaspoon ground black pepper
1 teaspoon ground coriander
½ teaspoon ground cardamom
3 tablespoons butter

Place the rice and water in a heavy saucepan. Add the salt, pepper, coriander, and cardamom. Cover and bring to a boil, stirring only once. Reduce heat and simmer for 45 minutes. Remove from heat. Add the butter and mix it in well. The rice will stay hot with the lid on for about 10 to 15 minutes.

Yields: 6 to 8 servings
Preparation time: 45 minutes

CRACKED WHEAT WITH VEGETABLES AND FRESH MINT

A splendid side dish for summer entertaining, served with chicken, fish, or veal.

1½ cups bulgur (processed cracked wheat)
¾ cup lemon juice
⅓ olive oil
1½ cups peeled and finely chopped red onion
2 cups peeled, seeded, and finely chopped cucumber
2 cups snow peas, cut in thirds
1 green pepper, finely chopped
1 cup minced parsley
1 teaspoon salt
¾ teaspoon ground black pepper
2 cups minced mint
Green leafy lettuce (for garnish)

Place the bulgur in a small bowl, cover with cold water, and let it soak for 20 minutes. Drain, pressing hard against the wheat to remove as much liquid as possible. Place the drained bulgur in a large bowl. Add all the remaining ingredients and mix thoroughly. Chill for 1 hour or up to 24 hours. Serve surrounded by fresh green lettuce leaves.

Yields: 6 servings

Preparation time: 30 minutes (excluding refrigeration time)

BARLEY PILAF

Pour hot water over the barley. Let it soak overnight, and the cooking time will be only 35 to 40 minutes.

1¼ cups pearl barley, soaked in hot water overnight
3 tablespoons olive oil
1 cup peeled and minced onion
1 teaspoon salt
½ teaspoon ground black pepper
3½ cups beef stock
2 tablespoons chopped parsley
½ teaspoon freshly grated nutmeg

Drain the barley, then sauté it in the olive oil for about 5 minutes over medium-high heat with the onion. Add the salt, pepper, and beef stock. Cover and bring to a boil. Simmer for 35 to 40 minutes or until the barley is just done. Don't overcook it or it will lose its nutty flavor. Add the parsley and nutmeg. Toss lightly and serve.

Yields: 6 servings

Preparation time: 45 minutes (excluding soaking time)

COUSCOUS WITH ALMONDS

This makes a wonderful complement to spicy dishes.

Serve couscous as a side dish with Tarragon-Roasted Game Hens or Moroccan Lamb Stew.

4 tablespoons (½ stick) butter
1 medium onion, peeled and chopped
1½ cups couscous
3 cups chicken stock
½ teaspoon salt
½ teaspoon ground black pepper
½ cup slivered almonds, toasted

Melt the butter in a medium saucepan. Add the onion and sauté for 2 minutes over medium heat. Add the couscous, chicken stock, salt, and pepper and bring to a boil. Simmer for 2 minutes. Cover the pan and remove from the heat. Let it stand for 10 minutes. Add the toasted almonds. Fluff the couscous with a fork and serve.

Yields: 6 servings

Preparation time: 15 minutes

VEGETARIAN LASAGNA

Loaves and Fishes most popular freezer item. We make three times this recipe each week, pack it into 4-by-7-inch casseroles, cover, and freeze them. Before the week is ended, they are gone.

SAUCE

1 tablespoon olive oil
1½ cups peeled and finely chopped onion
1 green pepper, seeded and diced
1 clove garlic, peeled and minced
3 cups peeled and mashed fresh tomatoes or one 28-ounce can crushed tomatoes
1 6-ounce can tomato paste
1 cup water
1 bay leaf, broken in half
1½ tablespoons fresh basil or 1½ teaspoons dried
1½ tablespoons fresh fennel or 1½ teaspoons dried
½ teaspoon ground black pepper
1 teaspoon salt

VEGETABLES

2 tablespoons olive oil
1½ cups peeled and chopped onion
3 cloves garlic, peeled and minced
1 pound mushrooms, thinly sliced
1 pound small zucchini, thinly sliced
1 tablespoon fresh rosemary or 1 teaspoon dried
1 tablespoon fresh oregano or 1 teaspoon dried
1 teaspoon salt
½ teaspoon ground black pepper

FILLING

1 pound ricotta cheese
1 pound mozzarella cheese, grated
2 eggs
¼ teaspoon pepper
¼ cup finely chopped parsley
1 pound lasagna, cooked according to package directions
½ cup grated Parmesan cheese

Chopped parsley (for garnish)

To make the sauce, heat the olive oil. Add the onion, green pepper, and garlic. Sauté for about 5 minutes over low heat. Add the tomatoes, tomato paste, water, bay leaf, basil, fennel, pepper, and salt. Bring the sauce to a boil and simmer for 45 minutes. Remove from the heat.

To prepare the vegetables, heat the olive oil and sauté the onion and garlic over low heat until the onions become transparent. This should take about 5 minutes. Stir in the mushrooms and zucchini. Add the rosemary, oregano, salt, and pepper. Sauté the vegetables for about 5 minutes over high heat, stirring twice.

To make the filling, mix the ricotta, mozzarella, eggs, pepper, and parsley together in a medium bowl.

Preheat the oven to 375°F.

Using either a very large casserole or 2 medium ones, assemble by layering the sauce, noodles, vegetables, and cheese until they are all used up, ending with the sauce. Sprinkle the casserole with the Parmesan and bake for about 45 minutes. Garnish with parsley and serve.

Yields: 12 or more servings

Preparation time: 2 hours

You can vary this simple side dish by adding one of the following: 1 tablespoon poppy seed, 1/4 cup toasted pine nuts, or 1 tablespoon caraway seed.

BUTTERED SPINACH FETTUCCINE

A perfect complement to chicken and veal.

1 pound fresh spinach fettuccine
4 tablespoons (1/2 stick) butter
1 teaspoon salt
3/4 teaspoon ground black pepper
2 tablespoons minced fresh oregano

Bring 4 quarts water to a boil. Add the fettuccine. Simmer for 1 to 2 minutes and test for doneness. Drain. Pour the pasta back into the pot. Add the butter, salt, pepper, and oregano. Shake the pot to mix all ingredients well. Pour into a warm bowl and serve.

Yields: 6 servings
Preparation time: 10 minutes

SPAETZLE

These buttered light noodles are delicious with any roasted meats.

1 cup plus 2 tablespoons water
3 eggs
2 1/2 cups unbleached flour
1/2 teaspoon salt
3 tablespoons butter
Salt and pepper to taste

Place the water, eggs, flour, and salt in the bowl of an electric mixer. Beat at medium speed for about 3 minutes, or until the batter is smooth and some bubbles appear. Let the batter rest at room temperature for 30 minutes.

Using a large saucepan bring 3 quarts water to a boil. Pour half the batter through a spaetzle maker (if you don't have a spaetzle maker, use a colander) into the boiling water. The spaetzle will sink to the bottom. When they rise to the top, scoop them out with a slotted spoon and transfer them to a serving bowl. Repeat this procedure with the rest of the batter. Add the butter, salt, and pepper and serve.

Yields: 6 servings
Preparation time: 45 minutes

PASTA WITH HAM, VEGETABLES, AND CREAM

Many years ago, we ate at Mama Gina's in Florence. It was my first time there, and for lunch we were served this wonderful dish.

I vary the ingredients in this recipe from time to time, using goat cheese and asparagus instead of the broccoli, pepper, and Parmesan. You can try experimenting with this recipe by using your own favorite cheese and vegetables.

6 tablespoons (3/4 stick) butter
6 ounces prosciutto
1½ tablespoons peeled and minced garlic
1 yellow pepper, cut into strips
4 cups broccoli florets
2 cups heavy cream
1½ teaspoons freshly ground black pepper
1½ teaspoons salt
½ cup freshly grated Parmesan cheese
1½ pounds fresh or dried angel hair pasta

Heat the butter in a large sauté pan. Add the prosciutto, garlic, pepper strips, and broccoli. Stir-fry for 5 minutes over low heat. Add the cream, pepper, salt, and Parmesan. Bring to a boil and simmer for 3 minutes.

In the meantime, cook the pasta. If using fresh pasta, boil for no more than 2 minutes. If using dried pasta, boil for about 6 minutes. Drain, then pour into a deep bowl. Pour the sauce over the pasta and serve.

Yields: 6 servings
Preparation time: 15 minutes

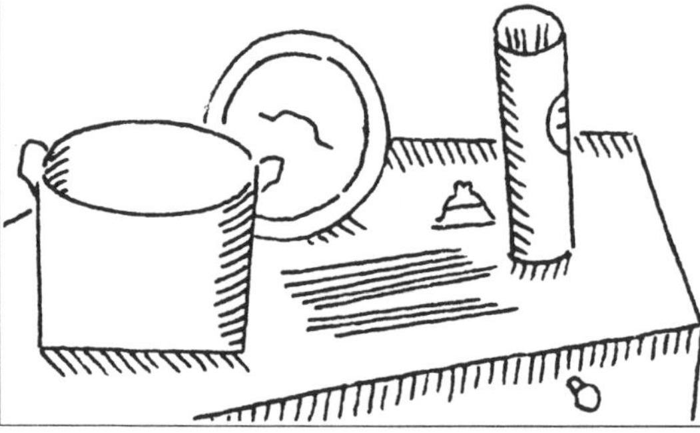

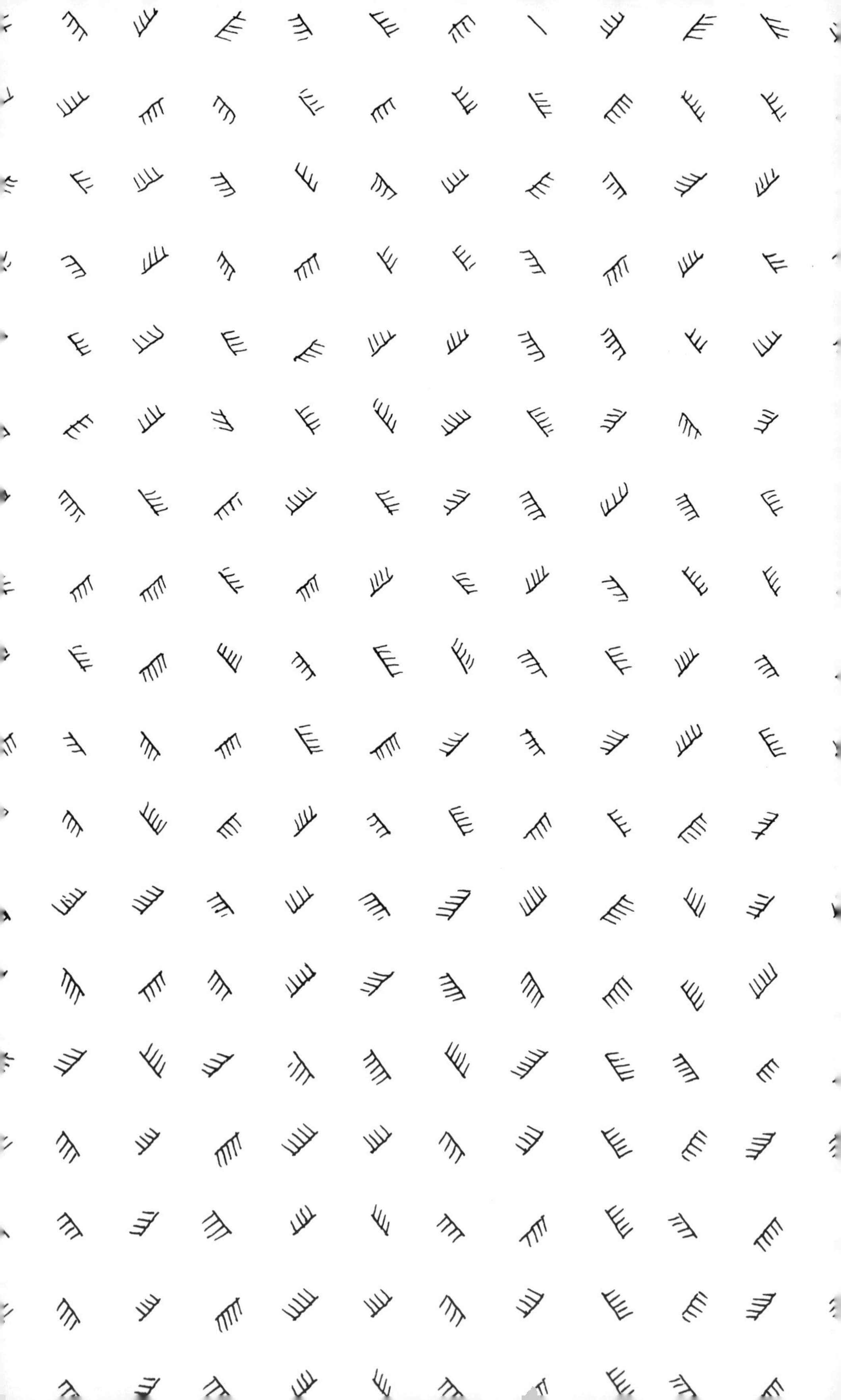

VEGETABLES

In cooking, as in all arts, simplicity is the sign of perfection.
—Curnovsky

Besides being a nutritional asset to your meal, vegetables also lend the dinner plate their individual beauty. I love the deep forest green of fresh broccoli, the bright orange-yellow of carrots, the pearly whiteness of freshly picked cauliflower surrounded by its collar of pale green, the deep wine purple of eggplants, and the list goes on. There's nothing better than examining rows of fresh vegetables to help galvanize your dinner plans, because in your mind's eye you can see how certain vegetables will look on the dinner plate. The worst thing to do, I suppose, is to plan what you're going to serve, then head out to buy that particular vegetable for a recipe you've started, only to find a few wilted leftovers at the bottom of a damp bin. I believe it's much better to shop first and let the freshness of the fruits or vegetables dictate what you will prepare.

Most people have favorite vegetables, and therefore I have included recipes that allow for a variety of choices and cooking methods: steamed, roasted, fried, sautéed, pureed, and braised. But regardless of preference, don't be afraid to experiment with new tastes. One of my greatest pleasures is learning to enjoy new, intriguing vegetables, herbs, and fruits everywhere I travel.

When buying fresh vegetables and fruit, don't have the greengrocer remove any leafy stems for you, nor should you instantly wash them when you get home. Store them just as you bought them. If a vegetable such as carrots has too much mud accumulated around the stalks, shake it off. As soon as you wash fresh produce, the process of deterioriation sets in, so do it just before you're ready to use it. More so than any other food, in the case of vegetables, freshest is best.

BAKED SPINACH AND ZUCCHINI

This recipe is a perfect accompaniment to any sautéed fish or meat dish. It is also delicious served at room temperature.

2 tablespoons clarified butter
6 scallions, chopped
1 pound small zucchini, sliced into ¼-inch rounds
3 cloves garlic, peeled and minced
1½ pounds fresh spinach, steamed, or two 10-ounce packages chopped frozen spinach, thawed
¼ teaspoon ground nutmeg
¼ cup chopped fresh basil or 1 teaspoon dried
¼ cup chopped parsley
2 tablespoons lemon juice
1 teaspoon salt
¾ teaspoon ground black pepper
1 cup cooked rice
2 tablespoons butter, melted
4 eggs
¾ cup heavy cream
¼ cup grated Parmesan cheese

Preheat the oven to 350°F.

Melt the clarified butter in a heavy sauté pan. Add the scallions, zucchini, and garlic. Sauté for 2 minutes over medium-high heat and remove the pan from the heat. Press all the liquid out of the spinach before adding it to the zucchini mixture. Add the nutmeg, basil, parsley, lemon juice, salt, pepper, and rice. Stir it well. Transfer the vegetables to a buttered, ovenproof dish.

In a small bowl, blend the melted butter, eggs, cream, and cheese. Pour over the vegetables. Bake for 20 to 25 minutes, or until the eggs are set.

Yields: 6 servings
Preparation time: 45 minutes

Baked Spinach and Zucchini is excellent served for a light lunch with some good bread. Divide the filling among 6 individual 1½ cups buttered ramekins. Bake in a preheated 350°F oven for 12 to 15 minutes.

ABOUT SPINACH

When shopping for spinach, buy loose leaves and choose only those that are of medium size. Rinse the spinach under running water to remove all the sand before cooking. Don't add water to the pan, since there will be enough moisture clinging to the spinach leaves to help them steam. Another way to cook spinach is to sauté the leaves in clarified butter. The leaves remain whole, and retain that deep, healthy green.

SPINACH IN GARLIC CREAM

For variety, add two tablespoons raisins and two tablespoons pine nuts to the sauce.

3 pounds fresh spinach leaves, well rinsed
1 teaspoon salt
1 teaspoon ground black pepper
1 tablespoon peeled and minced garlic
⅓ cup heavy cream

Place the wet spinach leaves in a large pot. Cover and steam over medium heat until all the leaves are wilted (about 3 minutes). The water on the leaves is enough to steam the spinach; you should not add any water to the pot. Sprinkle with salt and pepper. Add the garlic and cream and stir to blend. Simmer for 2 minutes and serve.

Yields: 6 servings
Preparation time: 15 minutes

BRAISED ENDIVE

The slightly bitter taste of the raw endive leaf makes a perfect appetizer when filled with 1 teaspoon finely chopped chicken or seafood salad. Arrange it sunburst fashion on a round plate and serve.

This dish is very special with veal chops or grilled lamb. When served chilled it makes a wonderful first course for six.

2 tablespoons butter
½ cup chicken stock
½ cup dry white wine
12 medium endives, trimmed
½ teaspoon salt
½ teaspoon ground white pepper

Preheat the oven to 425°F.

Melt the butter in an ovenproof and flameproof pan. Stir in the chicken stock and wine. Add the endives and sprinkle them with the salt and pepper. Cover the pan and bring to a boil. Place the covered pan inside the oven. Bake for 40 minutes.

Yields: 6 servings
Preparation time: 1 hour

In Denmark and Germany, Braised Red Cabbage is a must on any holiday buffet. It is equally good prepared one day ahead of time, then reheated in a 300°F oven for 25 minutes.

BRAISED RED CABBAGE

A splendid fall and winter vegetable to serve with duck or lamb.

One 3½-pound head of red cabbage
4 tablespoons (½ stick) butter
2 cups peeled and finely chopped onion
⅓ cup red wine vinegar
1 cup red Burgundy wine
Zest of 1 orange
2 teaspoons salt
1 bay leaf
1 teaspoon ground cardamom
¼ teaspoon ground cloves
¼ teaspoon hot red pepper flakes

Remove the outer leaves of the cabbage and discard. Core the cabbage then shred it in a food processor with the slicing disk in place, or by hand. Melt the butter in a heavy sauté pan. Add the shredded cabbage. Stir in the onion, vinegar, and wine. Add the orange zest, salt, bay leaf, cardamom, cloves, and pepper flakes. Stir well to blend. Braise over low heat for 1½ hours, stirring now and then.

Yields: 6 to 8 servings

Preparation time: 1 hour 45 minutes

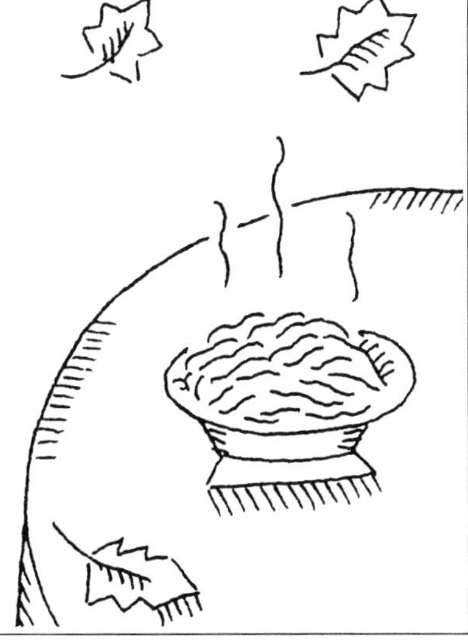

Young new potatoes are taken from the earth before maturity. Try to select all you need in about the same size so that they're all done at the same time when roasting, steaming, or boiling.

DANISH ROASTED NEW POTATOES

Delicious with roast beef, pan-fried, or broiled fish, or as part of a buffet.

20 small red or white new potatoes
½ cup (1 stick) butter
1 teaspoon salt
¼ teaspoon ground black pepper
¼ cup finely chopped dill

Scrub and dry the potatoes. Melt the butter in a heavy saucepan with a tight-fitting lid. Add the potatoes and sprinkle with the salt and pepper. Cover the pan and roast the potatoes over a medium-high heat, shaking the pan often, for about 12 minutes, or until the potatoes are just tender. Don't overcook them or they'll fall apart. Add the fresh dill. Shake the pan to distribute it evenly over the potatoes.

Yields: 6 servings
Preparation time: 18 minutes

LEMON POTATOES

The lemon juice and rind turns the simple potato into a refreshing, new side dish. It's excellent when served with fish or seafood.

18 small new potatoes
½ cup lemon juice
4 tablespoons (½ stick) butter
1 teaspoon salt
1 teaspoon ground black pepper
Rind of 1 lemon, grated
3 tablespoons finely chopped parsley

Place the new potatoes in a heavy saucepan. Add the lemon juice, butter, salt, and pepper. Bring to a boil, then simmer, covered, for 12 to 14 minutes. Drain. Sprinkle with lemon rind and parsley. Serve hot.

Yields: 6 servings
Preparation time: 20 minutes

PAN-FRIED POTATOES

Serve these with a spoonful of chives over each portion.

4 tablespoons (½ stick) butter
2 tablespoons olive oil
2½ pounds small new potatoes, thinly sliced
1 cup peeled and very thinly sliced onion
1 teaspoon salt
1 teaspoon ground black pepper
2 tablespoons minced parsley
Chopped chives (for garnish)

Heat the butter and oil in a large sauté pan. Add the potatoes, onion, salt, and pepper. Cover. Sauté for 6 minutes over medium heat. Lift the cooked vegetables from the bottom of the pan to the top. Cover and sauté for 6 minutes more. Spoon into a warm serving bowl. Sprinkle with parsley and serve.

Yields: 6 servings
Preparation time: 20 minutes

PUREE OF PEAS AND WATERCRESS

You can prepare this ahead of time, then reheat it in an earthenware casserole in a preheated 350°F oven for 30 minutes.

The addition of watercress to this recipe gives the dish a special piquant taste.

4 cups shelled peas
2 bunches watercress
4 tablespoons (½ stick) butter
1 teaspoon ground black pepper
¾ teaspoon salt

Fill a medium saucepan with water. Bring to a boil. Add the peas and return to a boil. Turn off the heat. Cut off the top 2 inches of the watercress bunches and add them to the saucepan. Cover for 5 minutes. Drain and transfer to the bowl of a food processor fitted with a metal blade. Add the butter, pepper, and salt. Process until smooth. Serve.

Yields: 6 servings
Preparation time: 15 minutes

GREEN BEANS WITH SAUTÉED SHALLOTS AND MUSHROOMS

Now that fresh green beans seem to be available to us year-round, this flavorful and colorful side dish can be served with any main dish, anytime of the year.

3 pounds green beans, trimmed
4 tablespoons (½ stick) butter
¼ cup peeled and finely chopped shallots
½ pound mushrooms, sliced
¾ teaspoon salt
¾ teaspoon ground black pepper

Bring a large pot of water to a boil. Add the beans and simmer for 2 minutes. Drain. Melt the butter in a large sauté pan. Add the shallots and sauté for 3 minutes over high heat. Add the mushrooms and sauté for 2 minutes. Add the beans. Sprinkle with salt and pepper and sauté for 3 minutes more.

Yields: 6 servings
Preparation time: 20 minutes

BROCCOLI WITH PARMESAN SAUCE

This side dish can be served with any plain roasted or grilled meats.

2 heads broccoli
2 cups water
4 tablespoons (½ stick) butter
¼ cup unbleached white flour
1 cup chicken stock
1 cup milk
¼ cup heavy cream
½ teaspoon salt
½ teaspoon ground white pepper
6 tablespoons grated Parmesan cheese

Preheat the oven to 425°F.

Cut the broccoli into florets. Place them in a saucepan with 2 cups water, cover, and bring to a boil. Remove from the heat and drain immediately. Place the broccoli in a buttered ovenproof dish.

Melt the butter in a heavy saucepan, add the flour and cook for 1 minute over low heat. Take the pan off the heat long enough to add the chicken stock, milk, heavy cream, salt, and pepper. Return it to the heat and bring to a boil, stirring constantly. Remove from the heat. Add 4 tablespoons of the Parmesan and stir to melt the cheese. Pour the sauce over the broccoli and sprinkle with the remaining Parmesan. Bake for 15 minutes.

Yields: 8 servings

Preparation time: 35 minutes

BAKED MARINATED ZUCCHINI

If you want, tomatoes can be used in place of the zucchini in this dish.

2 pounds zucchini, sliced

MARINADE

1 cup parsley
3 cloves garlic, peeled
½ cup fresh basil
1 tablespoon fresh thyme or 1 teaspoon dried
½ teaspoon ground black pepper
½ teaspoon salt
⅔ cup virgin olive oil

TOPPING

¾ pound Appenzeller or other Swiss cheese, grated
⅓ cup grated Parmesan cheese

Place the zucchini slices in a bowl. Puree the marinade ingredients in the bowl of a food processor with a metal blade and pour over the zucchini slices. Toss to coat evenly. Marinate for 30 minutes at room temperature.

Meanwhile, preheat the oven to 375°F.

Transfer the marinated zucchini to a casserole. Sprinkle with the Appenzeller and Parmesan cheeses. Bake for 25 minutes and serve.

Yields: 6 servings

Preparation time: 1 hour (including marinating time)

KARTOFFELKUCHEN (POTATO PANCAKES)

Serve these crisp, lacy-looking pancakes as a side dish with beef or pork dinners. Traditionally these are made large, about five inches in diameter. I prefer them two inches in diameter. Try them; they're fun to make and very tasty.

2 pounds baking potatoes, peeled
2 eggs, lightly beaten
1⁄3 cup sliced scallions
1⁄3 cup unbleached white flour
1⁄2 teaspoon ground black pepper
1 teaspoon salt
1⁄2 cup clarified butter

Preheat the oven to 250°F.

Grate the potatoes in a food processor. Pour them into a colander to drain, pressing hard against the solids to remove as much liquid as possible. In a medium bowl mix the potatoes, eggs, scallions, flour, pepper, and salt.

In a large skillet, heat one-third of the butter over medium-high heat until it bubbles. Set 1 tablespoon of the potato mixture in the hot pan, repeating the procedure until the pan is full, but not crowded. Press the pancakes down lightly with a spatula. Sauté for about 1½ minutes on each side. Transfer to a platter and keep warm in the oven while you repeat the procedure until all butter and batter have been used up. Serve as soon as possible.

Yields: 6 servings
Preparation time: 20 minutes

For a luxurious first course, serve these pancakes with the best black caviar and a wedge of lemon.

ASPARAGUS WITH ORANGE BUTTER

For appearance's sake, I peel the asparagus with a swivel-blade vegetable peeler, drawing the blade towards the root.

The star in the vegetable category seems to excite us again and again every season. Simply rinse and boil these elegant spears.

½ cup (1 stick) butter
Zest and juice of 1 orange
3 pounds fresh asparagus, trimmed

Melt the butter in a small saucepan. Add the zest and juice of the orange. Simmer for 3 minutes. Set aside.

Fill a large saucepan three-quarters full with water. Bring to a boil, add the asparagus, and simmer for 3 minutes. Drain. Arrange on a serving platter. Pour the orange butter over the asparagus and serve.

Yields: 6 servings
Preparation time: 20 minutes

BABY CARROTS WITH GINGER

Choose firm, smooth, bright orange-colored carrots with the tops on—they're generally fresher. I like the ones with rounded tips—they're sweeter.

The natural sweetness of carrots is enhanced by the suggestion of ginger. This is an easy-to-prepare side dish and is truly delicious served with roasted meat or chicken.

4 tablespoons (½ stick) butter
¼ cup peeled and minced ginger
1½ pounds baby carrots, scraped and trimmed
¾ teaspoon salt
¼ teaspoon ground black pepper

Melt the butter in a heavy saucepan. Add the ginger, carrots, salt, and pepper. Cover the pan and simmer the carrots for about 12 minutes, shaking the pan now and then.

Yields: 6 servings
Preparation time: 15 minutes

MUSHROOM SAUTÉ WITH MINT AND BUTTER

A luxurious treat to serve with grilled meats or poultry.

1½ pounds small white mushrooms
½ cup (1 stick) butter
1 pound chanterelles
2 tablespoons fresh mint
1 tablespoon lemon juice
½ teaspoon salt
½ teaspoon ground black pepper

In place of the chanterelles, you can use any fresh mild or woodsy mushroom, such as fresh morels, porcini, trompettes des morts, or oyster mushrooms.

Wipe the mushrooms with a damp towel. Cut off the stem ends. Heat half the butter in a large skillet. Add the chanterelles. Stir-fry for about 3 minutes over medium heat. Transfer to a warm bowl. Heat the remaining butter. Add the white mushrooms. Sauté for 5 minutes, stirring now and then. Add to the chanterelles. Sprinkle the mint, lemon juice, salt, and pepper over the mushrooms. Toss lightly and serve.

Yields: 6 servings
Preparation time: 15 minutes

CAULIFLOWER WITH SWEET GORGONZOLA SAUCE

There is a large field of cauliflower growing behind Loaves and Fishes, and as soon as the vegetables get large enough we pick some and use them in our daily vegetable salads. When the cauliflower grows a little more mature we prepare it in my favorite way, with a fresh cheese sauce. This goes perfectly with any sautéed meat dish.

1 large head cauliflower, trimmed
4 tablespoons (½ stick) butter
3 tablespoons unbleached white flour
3 cups milk
¼ pound sweet Gorgonzola cheese
2 tablespoons chopped chives (for garnish)

Place the cauliflower in a large saucepan. Add 1 inch of water. Boil, then simmer for 12 minutes. Drain and transfer to a serving dish; keep warm.

Melt the butter in a medium saucepan over low heat. Add the flour and stir for 2 minutes. While stirring, add the milk all at once. Stir until the sauce comes to a boil and thickens. Add the Gorgonzola and stir to melt and blend the cheese. Pour over the cauliflower and sprinkle with chives.

Yields: 6 servings
Preparation time: 30 minutes

GARLIC-ROASTED VEGETABLES

The beauty of this recipe is that it can easily be made and enjoyed anytime of the year. When shopping for the vegetables choose ones that are small and haven't reached their full maturity.

2 medium eggplants
3 zucchini
3 yellow squash
3 red peppers
3 yellow or green peppers
2 cloves garlic, peeled and minced
⅔ cup olive oil
2 tablespoons salt

Preheat the oven to 375°F.

Cut each eggplant lengthwise into eight strips. Place skin side down on a baking sheet or roasting pan. Cut each zucchini and squash into three pieces. Place on a second baking sheet. Cut the peppers in half and seed them. Place the cut side down on the baking sheet that holds the zucchini and squash.

Add the garlic to the olive oil and drizzle over the vegetables. Sprinkle with the salt. Bake the eggplant for 15 minutes. Bake the zucchini, squash, and peppers for 6 to 7 minutes. Arrange all the vegetables decoratively on a large platter. Serve either hot or at room temperature.

Yields: 6 servings
Preparation time: 30 minutes

It is not really an exaggeration to say that peace and happiness begin, geographically, where garlic is used in cooking.
—Marcel Boulestin

SAUTÉED CHERRY TOMATOES WITH FRESH DILL

Several vegetables can substitute for the cherry tomatoes, such as snow peas, asparagus, red or green peppers, and peeled, seeded, and sliced cucumbers. All should be sautéed until done but still crisp.

2 pounds cherry tomatoes, stemmed
4 tablespoons (½ stick) butter or olive oil
1 teaspoon salt
¾ teaspoon ground black pepper
2 tablespoons finely chopped dill

Rinse the tomatoes and pat dry with paper towels. Heat the butter or oil in a large sauté pan. Add the tomatoes and sauté for 3 minutes, or until crisply done. Sprinkle with salt, pepper, and fresh dill. Toss to mix and serve.

Yields: 6 servings
Preparation time: 10 minutes

VEGETARIAN CHILI

1 pound dried red kidney beans
2 tablespoons olive oil
1 small red onion, peeled and coarsely chopped
1 large white onion, peeled and coarsely chopped
6 cloves garlic, peeled and minced
1 green pepper, seeded and chopped
1 red pepper, seeded and chopped
2 tablespoons fresh basil or 1 teaspoon dried
1 bay leaf
1 tablespoon ground cumin
1 teaspoon cayenne pepper
2 teaspoons hot red pepper flakes
1½ tablespoons chili powder
4 cups crushed tomatoes
4 cups strong, brewed coffee
2 medium eggplants, peeled and cut into 1-inch cubes
1 cup red Burgundy wine

Pour boiling water over the kidney beans and let them soak overnight.

Next day, drain the beans and place them in a large saucepan. Fill the pan with water to 3 inches above the beans. Bring to a boil, then simmer for 30 minutes until just done. Drain and set aside.

Heat the oil in a large, heavy skillet. Add the red

and white onion and the garlic. Sauté for 5 minutes over medium heat. Add the rest of the ingredients, except for the wine and beans. Bring the chili to a boil, then simmer for 45 minutes over low heat, stirring occasionally. Add the wine and beans. Mix well and serve.

Yields: 6 to 8 servings

Preparation time: 1 hour (excluding soaking time)

KOHLRABI IN CREAM SAUCE WITH PARSLEY

This classic Schleswig-Holstein dish is perfect with any sautéed meat or fish.

Look for young, tender kohlrabi. The undersides should be smooth, not cracked and woody. Their color should be light green.

2 pounds kohlrabi, peeled and cut into ½-inch-by-2-inch sticks
2 cups water
4 tablespoons (½ stick) butter
3 tablespoons unbleached white flour
3 cups half-and-half
¼ cup finely chopped parsley
½ teaspoon salt
¾ teaspoon ground black pepper

Place the kohlrabi pieces into a saucepan, add water, bring to a boil, then simmer for 8 to 10 minutes. Drain and set aside.

Melt the butter in a heavy saucepan over medium heat. Add the flour and stir for 2 minutes. Add the half-and-half all at once, stirring constantly until the sauce thickens. Add the parsley, salt, and pepper. Stir to blend. Add the kohlrabi and simmer for 2 minutes.

Yields: 6 servings

Preparation time: 25 minutes

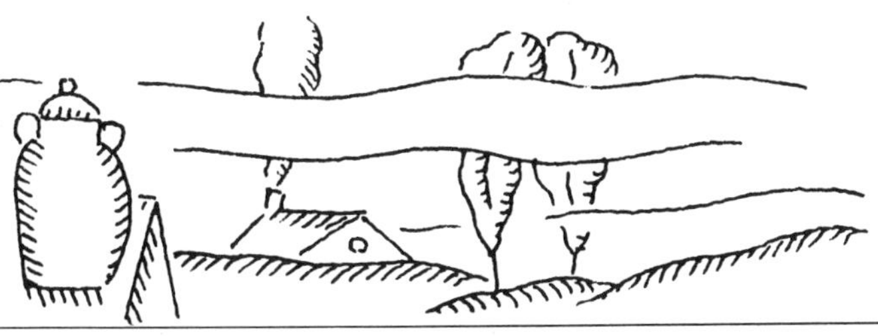

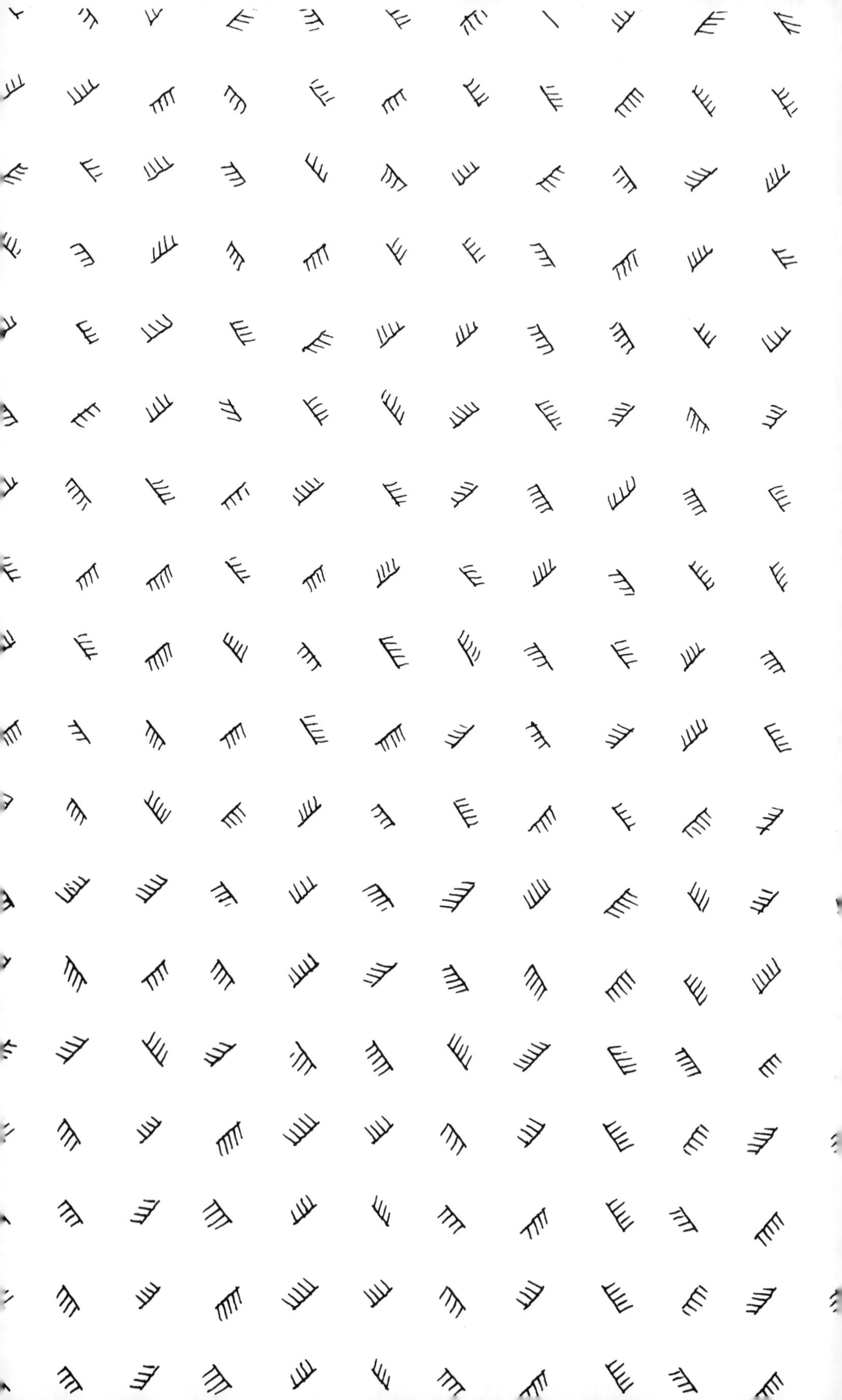

BREADS, CAKES, AND COOKIES

Werther had a love for
Charlotte
Such as words could
never utter;
Would you know how
he first met her?
She was cutting bread
and butter.
—William Makepeace
Thackeray

To me, one of the most glorious aromas in the world is that of fresh bread baking in the oven. My mother used to start her baking at dawn, and within minutes the biting chill that stole into our home during the night mellowed into a deliciously penetrating warmth.

If you've never experienced the pleasures of making your own bread, let me urge you to do so. There are simple enough guidelines to follow. Yeast dissolves best in lukewarm water and should be "fed" whatever amount of sugar or honey the recipe calls for so that it gets nourished and continues to grow.

You need a little common sense, too, when it comes to using flour. If you're baking on a humid day, chances are you will not need to use all the flour prescribed in the recipe.

You should always be guided by the consistency and texture of the dough, which should be elastic, smooth, and resilient.

Yeast shouldn't come directly in contact with egg yolks, butter, or fats. They would impede its growth.

The baking time necessary for these breads doesn't exceed an hour, yet I have suggested that you wrap them in foil and allow them to set overnight in the refrigerator, giving them a little "aging" time, which improves their taste and texture.

After French Bread you might try your hand at making Cinnamon Bread. A wonderful breakfast bread, it can be eaten plain or converted into French toast. It appears to be a real favorite with our customers. Bran–Whole Wheat Bread, Honey–Egg Bread, Cardamom–Raisin Bread, and Honey Brioche —all of them will fill your kitchen with the wholesome, rich aromas that only come with fresh home-baked bread.

Those are the only breads that require you to use yeast as an essential ingredient. The simpler breads include Buttermilk–Corn Bread, which can be made in less than an hour; or the tea breads, such as Zucchini, Raspberry, and Banana, which take less than thirty minutes to assemble.

The Macaroon Tea Cake and the Chocolate Chip Pound Cake are more substantial in texture and absolute "musts" to have stored in your refrigerator, not only for your own pleasure but also as wonderful "company cakes" for those visitors who drop in unexpectedly. The Lemon Bars, Peanut Cookies, Oatmeal Cookies, Chocolate Chip Cookies, and Mother's Kaffebrot are stored in jars near the front counter of our store. They are familiar sights and popular treats for all of our customers.

When you finally choose a recipe that tickles your fancy, read it over carefully first. Make sure you have everything you need. If the recipe calls for grated rind of lemon, grate the lemon first. If you're supposed to have eggs at room temperature and they need to be separated, do that before you start. With all the measuring and small chores out of the way, your baking time will be 100 percent pleasurable and may convince you to bake a little every day.

Eggs separate more easily when just taken from the refrigerator.

Honest bread is very well—it's the butter that makes the temptation.
—Jerrold

French loaves can be wrapped in foil and frozen for up to 2 months. When you need it, take it from the freezer and, leaving it in the foil, reheat it in a preheated 350°F oven for about 15 minutes.

FRENCH BREAD

Bread tends to take on a certain consistency and flavor depending on where it is made. A lot of it has to do with the climate and the water that's used. I believe that Italian and French breads are impossible to duplicate elsewhere. However, this is an excellent crusty loaf with ingredients similar to the real thing. My son-in-law, Michael, makes about two hundred loaves a day, and the bread sells as soon as he takes it from the oven.

2½ cups lukewarm (110°F) water
1½ tablespoons active dry yeast
2 tablespoons sugar
1½ cups semolina flour
1 tablespoon salt
5 to 5½ cups unbleached white flour
Melted butter (to grease pans)
2 egg whites, lightly beaten with 1 tablespoon water

Place the water, yeast, and sugar in a large mixing bowl. Stir a few times. Let it stand for 5 minutes and stir again until the yeast is dissolved. Add the semolina flour, salt, and 2 cups of the unbleached flour. Stir the dough vigorously with your hand until it is elastic in consistency. Add another 2½ cups flour and beat hard until all the flour is mixed in. Sprinkle the last cup of flour onto a flat surface and scrape the dough out onto that. Knead until the dough is smooth, elastic, and forms bubbles. This usually takes about 5 to 8 minutes. Return the dough to the bowl. Cover with a towel and let rise in a warm place for 1 hour.

Preheat the oven to 400°F.

Butter four French bread loaf pans. Divide the dough into four pieces. Roll each piece into a long loaf shape and place in the pan. Brush the top of the loaves with the egg white–water mixture. With a sharp knife cut four deep slits across each loaf. Let rise for about 45 minutes. Bake in the oven for 10 minutes. Reduce the heat to 350°F and bake for 25 to 30 minutes more. The breads should be nicely browned top and bottom.

Yields: 4 loaves

Preparation time: 2 hours 45 minutes

CINNAMON BREAD

We make this bread fresh every morning at Loaves and Fishes, and we never seem to make enough. They are bought from the oven, it seems, never resting on our shelves for any length of time. You, too, will want to butter a slice and have some right away. It makes excellent French toast as well.

½ cup (1 stick) butter
2 cups lukewarm (110°F) milk
1 cup plus 1 teaspoon sugar
1 tablespoon salt
1 tablespoon active dry yeast
¼ cup lukewarm (110°F) water
7½ to 8 cups unbleached white flour
2 eggs
1½ tablespoons ground cinnamon

Melt the butter over low heat. Set aside 2 tablespoons for brushing the tops of the loaves. Add the milk, ½ cup of the sugar, and the salt. Stir for about 1 minute, or until the sugar and salt are dissolved. Let cool to lukewarm. Pour into a mixing bowl.

In a separate bowl combine the yeast, lukewarm water, and 1 teaspoon of the sugar. Wait for 5 minutes for the yeast to dissolve completely.

Add 3½ cups of the flour and the eggs to the milk and butter. Beat by hand very hard for about 2 minutes. Add the yeast mixture and 2 more cups flour and beat again until the dough is smooth. Stir in another 1½ cups flour. Scrape the dough out onto a lightly floured surface and knead until smooth, about 5 to 8 minutes, adding more flour if necessary.

Place the dough in a buttered bowl, cover with a towel, and let it rise in a warm place until it has doubled in size, about 1 to 1½ hours. Punch down and divide the dough in half. With your hands pat each half into a 12-by-9-inch rectangular shape.

Mix the remaining ½ cup sugar with the cinnamon. Put aside 2 tablespoons for the topping and sprinkle the remainder over each dough rectangle. Then sprinkle each rectangle with 2 tablespoons of water.

Roll each section of prepared dough into a 9-inch long loaf, tucking the ends under. Place in buttered 9-

by-5-inch loaf pans. Brush the tops with a little melted butter and sprinkle each with the remaining cinnamon–sugar mixture. Let rise until doubled in size, about 45 minutes to 1 hour.

Meanwhile, preheat the oven to 350°F.

Bake for 45 to 50 minutes. Tap lightly; if it sounds hollow, it is done. Cool on a wire rack.

Yields: 2 loaves

Preparation time: 3 hours 20 minutes

BUTTERMILK–CORN BREAD

Here is an adaptation of an American specialty.

2 cups unbleached white flour
2 cups yellow corn meal
½ cup sugar
1½ teaspoon salt
2½ tablespoons baking powder
4 eggs
2 cups buttermilk
½ cup (1 stick) butter, melted and cooled slightly

Preheat the oven to 425°F.

Place the flour, corn meal, sugar, salt, and baking powder in the bowl of an electric mixer. Mix just to blend. Add the eggs, buttermilk, and butter. Mix at low speed until all ingredients are blended; don't overmix.

Pour the batter into a buttered 18-by-12-by-1-inch baking pan. Spread evenly. Bake for 20 minutes.

Yields: 24 pieces

Preparation time: 30 minutes

BUTTERMILK–CORN MUFFINS

Follow the same directions as for the bread, but pour the batter into buttered muffin tins. This recipe will make 18 muffins.

In the small village near our farm there were as many recipes for cardamom bread as there were bakers. Some used almonds, while others filled the bread with golden raisins and hazelnuts. You may try any of these combinations.

CARDAMOM–RAISIN BREAD

A very special recipe of my mother's.

3/4 cup (1 1/2 sticks) butter
1/2 cup milk
1/2 cup sugar
1 1/2 teaspoons salt
1 1/2 tablespoons active dry yeast
1/2 cup lukewarm (110°F) water
1/2 teaspoon sugar
2 eggs
2 teaspoons ground cardamom
3/4 cup raisins
4 1/2 cups unbleached white flour
1 egg yolk
1 tablespoon heavy cream
Sugar to taste

Melt the butter in a heavy saucepan. Add the milk and heat until lukewarm, then add the sugar and salt. Remove from the heat and stir until the sugar and salt dissolve. Pour the milk mixture into the bowl of an electric mixer. Mix the yeast, water, and sugar in a small bowl and set aside for 5 minutes.

Add the eggs, cardamom, raisins, half the flour, and the yeast mixture to the milk mixture. Mix at medium speed for 5 minutes.

Add the rest of the flour and mix at low speed for 2 minutes. Scrape the dough out onto a flat floured surface. Dust your hands with flour and knead the dough into a ball. Place it in a buttered bowl. Let it rise in a warm place until it has doubled in size, about 1 1/2 hours.

Preheat the oven to 350°F.

Divide the dough in half. Shape each piece into a round ball. Place the balls on a buttered baking sheet 8 inches apart. Combine the egg yolk with the cream. Brush over the loaves and sprinkle with the sugar. Let rise for 45 minutes more, then bake for 35 to 40 minutes. The bread is done when the crust is well-browned and the top sounds hollow when tapped with your knuckles. Cool on a wire rack.

Yields: 2 loaves

Preparation time: 3 hours 45 minutes

HONEY–EGG BREAD

A friend brought this idea back from California. Eat it plain, toast it, or make it into the best French toast imaginable, served with either a sprinkling of cinnamon sugar or a heaping of blueberry preserves.

1½ tablespoons active dry yeast
⅓ cup lukewarm (110°F) water
2 tablespoons sugar
½ cup (1 stick) butter
2 cups milk
½ cup honey
1½ tablespoons salt
3 egg yolks
6½ cups unbleached white flour
1 egg yolk, mixed with 1 tablespoon heavy cream

Place the yeast, water, and sugar in the bowl of an electric mixer. Stir a few times, then let it stand for 5 minutes until the yeast has dissolved.

Meanwhile, melt the butter over low heat. Add the milk, honey, and salt, and stir to dissolve. Let cool to 110°F and add this to the yeast water along with the 3 egg yolks and 3 cups of the flour. Mix at medium speed for 5 minutes. Add 3 more cups flour. Mix at low speed until the dough sticks together and most of the flour is blended in.

Scrape the dough out into a lightly floured surface. Sprinkle the rest of the flour over the dough. Knead until smooth; this will take about 8 minutes.

Place the dough in a mixing bowl, cover with a towel, and let it rise in a warm place for about 1 hour. Punch down and let it rise again for 30 minutes. Divide the dough in half. Shape into loaves and place in two buttered 9-by-5-inch loaf pans. Brush the tops with the egg–cream mixture. Let rise in a warm place for about 45 minutes.

Meanwhile, preheat the oven to 400°F.

Bake for 10 minutes, then reduce the oven temperature to 350°F and bake for 35 minutes more. The bread should be nicely browned and sound hollow when tapped on the top. Cool on a wire rack.

Yields: 2 loaves

Preparation time: 3 hours

The hen is an egg's way of producing another egg.
—Samuel Butler

This recipe can produce wonderful rolls. Separate the dough into 12 pieces. Shape them by hand and place on a buttered baking sheet. Brush with egg white and bake for 20 minutes. If you want to store either the bread or the rolls, they will last for about a month in the freezer.

BRAN–WHOLE WHEAT BREAD

This is my idea of a hearty loaf of bread: molasses, whole wheat, and bran.

2 cups lukewarm (110°F) water
2 tablespoons active dry yeast
⅓ cup molasses
1 cup bran
2 cups whole wheat flour
1½ tablespoons salt
¼ cup safflower oil
3¼ cups unbleached white flour
1 egg white

Mix the water, yeast, and molasses in a large mixing bowl and let rest for 5 minutes. Add the bran, whole wheat flour, salt, and safflower oil. Stir vigorously by hand for 5 minutes. Add 2¾ cups of the unbleached flour and mix well. Scrape the dough out onto a lightly floured surface and knead until it is smooth and air bubbles start to form. Use the last ½ cup flour to keep the dough from sticking while you're kneading.

Return the dough to the mixing bowl. Cover with a towel and let it rise in a warm place for about 1½ hours, or until it has doubled in size. Punch down and divide in half. Shape the dough into 2 loaves and place them in buttered 9-by-5-inch loaf pans.

Beat the egg white with a fork until frothy. Brush the loaves with it. With a sharp knife, make a few slashes in each loaf. Let rise for 45 minutes in a warm place.

Meanwhile, preheat the oven to 350°F.

Bake for 40 minutes. Breads should be rather dark brown and sound hollow when tapped on top. Cool on wire racks.

Yields: 2 loaves
Preparation time: 3 hours

Wrapped in plastic, the loaves keep up to 6 days in the refrigerator and can be frozen for up to 2 months.

HONEY BRIOCHE

Lemon rind and honey in the ingredients make this into a very special breakfast bread or a party bread. It's light and buttery. The recipe should be started a day in advance, so plan accordingly.

½ cup lukewarm (110°F) water
⅓ cup honey
2 tablespoons active dry yeast
4 eggs, at room temperature
4 cups unbleached white flour
¾ teaspoon salt
Rind of 1 lemon, grated
¾ cup (1½ sticks) butter, melted and cooled to room temperature
1 egg yolk, mixed with 1 tablespoon heavy cream

Combine the water, honey, and yeast in the bowl of an electric mixer and mix at low speed until dissolved. Let stand for 5 minutes. Add the eggs and beat well. Add half the flour, the salt, and the lemon rind. Mix at low speed for about 5 minutes. Add another 2 cups of the flour and mix to blend. Add the melted butter and mix for 2 minutes more at medium speed.

Scrape the dough out into a buttered mixing bowl. Cover with plastic wrap and refrigerate overnight.

The next day, butter two 4-cup brioche molds. After setting aside 2 pieces of dough the size of golf balls, divide the rest of the dough in half. Place these into the molds. Make a well with your fingers in the center of each brioche 2 inches in diameter and about ¾ inch deep. Roll the 2 small pieces of dough you've set aside into rounds. Place one in each well. Brush the brioche with the egg yolk–cream mixture. Let rise in a warm place for about 1½ hours.

Preheat the oven to 375°F.

Bake the brioche for about 45 minutes. Brioche should be golden brown and feel firm when pressed down lightly on the top. Cool on a wire rack.

Yields: 2 brioche

Preparation time: 2 hours 45 minutes (excluding refrigeration time)

Have you ever had an authentic cream tea, such as they serve in typical countryside restaurants in England? Scones are served warm, with a plate of butter, a dish of strawberry preserves, and a bowl of freshly whipped cream.

SCONES

Every Sunday morning we have a long line of customers waiting outside Loaves and Fishes for the scones to come out of the oven. We all know how good they are while they are still warm, buttered and slathered with a bit of fruit preserves.

4 cups unbleached white flour
⅓ cup plus 2 tablespoons sugar
2 teaspoons baking powder
1½ cups (3 sticks) butter, chilled and cut into 12 pieces
4 eggs
1¾ cup heavy cream
¾ cup raisins
1 egg yolk, mixed with 1 tablespoon heavy cream
⅓ cup sugar for topping

Preheat the oven to 350°F.

Place the flour in the bowl of an electric mixer. Add 2 tablespoons of sugar, the baking powder, and the butter, and mix until crumbly. Stop mixer to add the eggs. Then, with the motor running, add the cream and mix just to blend; do not overmix, or you will lose lightness and flakiness. Fold in the raisins by hand.

Transfer the dough to a lightly floured surface. Shape into a 12-by-18-inch rectangle, ½ inch thick. Cut into 24 triangles. Place the triangles on a lightly buttered baking sheet. Brush each scone with the egg yolk–cream mixture. Sprinkle with the remaining ⅓ cup sugar. Bake for 20 to 25 minutes.

Yields: 24 scones

Preparation time: 40 minutes

Tea breads improve with age. They should always be made a day in advance to give the flavors a chance to blend. Another marvelous advantage of tea breads is that they can be stored for up to 2 months in the freezer.

ZUCCHINI TEA BREAD

This is my updated version of an old favorite.

2 eggs
1/3 cup safflower oil
1 teaspoon lemon juice
1 teaspoon vanilla extract
1/2 cup yogurt
1/4 cup honey
1 1/4 cups whole wheat flour
3/4 teaspoon ground cinnamon
1 teaspoon baking soda
1 teaspoon baking powder
1/2 cup raisins
6 ounces zucchini, grated

Preheat the oven to 350°F.

Place the eggs, oil, lemon juice, and vanilla in the bowl of an electric mixer and mix until creamy, about 5 minutes. Add the yogurt and honey and blend in well. Add the flour, cinnamon, baking soda, and baking powder and mix until all traces of the flour have disappeared. Fold in the raisins and zucchini at low speed. Spoon the batter into a buttered 9-by-5-inch loaf pan. Bake for 50 to 60 minutes. Let cool in the pan. Remove and wrap tightly in plastic wrap.

Yields: 1 loaf

Preparation time: 1 hour 15 minutes (excluding cooling time)

BANANA TEA BREAD

When I first came to this country I had never heard of banana bread, but soon discovered that everyone I met seemed to have his or her favorite recipe for Banana Bread. Here's mine.

2 eggs
½ cup safflower oil
1 cup sugar
1 teaspoon vanilla extract
3 ripe bananas, mashed with a fork
1¼ cups unbleached white flour
1 teaspoon baking soda
½ cup walnuts, coarsely chopped

Preheat the oven to 350°F.

Combine the eggs, oil, sugar, and vanilla in the bowl of an electric mixer and mix at medium speed for about 3 minutes, or until creamy. Add the bananas and blend well. Add the flour, baking soda, and walnuts. Mix at medium speed for about 1 minute. Scrape the batter into a buttered 9-by-5-inch loaf pan. Bake until a toothpick inserted in the center comes out clean, about 55 to 60 minutes. Cool for 30 minutes. Remove from pan and cool completely on a wire rack.

Yields: 1 loaf

Preparation time: 1 hour 10 minutes (excluding cooling time)

RASPBERRY TEA BREAD

This should be made a day in advance to give it a chance to mature. It will last for up to 2 weeks in the refrigerator, or it can be frozen for up to 2 months. When you're ready to serve it, take it from the freezer, unwrap it, and let it breathe for 1 hour.

This sweet, moist tea bread is delicious when served toasted with a dish of cream cheese on the side.

One 10-ounce package frozen raspberries in light syrup, thawed
2 eggs
½ cup plus 2 tablespoons safflower oil
1 cup sugar
1½ cups unbleached white flour
1 teaspoon ground cinnamon
1 teaspoon baking soda

Preheat the oven to 350°F.

A loaf wrapped in colorful cellophane and tied with a bright ribbon becomes a perfect gift for the holiday season.

Puree the raspberries along with their syrup in your food processor fitted with a metal blade until smooth. Strain and discard the seeds.

Place the eggs, oil, and sugar in the bowl of an electric mixer. Mix at medium speed for about 3 minutes. Add the raspberry puree and blend well. Add the flour, cinnamon, and baking soda and mix the batter for about 1 minute at low speed. Scrape the dough into a buttered 9-by-5-inch loaf pan. Bake until a toothpick inserted in the center comes out clean, about 55 to 60 minutes. Cool for 30 minutes, remove from pan, and cool completely on a wire rack. Wrap tightly in plastic wrap.

Yields: 1 loaf

Preparation time: 1 hour 15 minutes (excluding cooling time)

SUPER BRAN MUFFINS

Sybille wanted to come up with a recipe for a muffin that was delicious but free of oil. She tried and tried and finally delivered a tray of these marvelous muffins for all of us to taste. They were light and moist and hearty.

½ cup (1 stick) butter, softened
2 eggs
1 cup molasses
2 cups unbleached white flour
2 cups bran
2 teaspoons baking soda
1 teaspoon salt
1½ cups yogurt
1½ cups raisins
Rind of 1 orange, grated

Preheat the oven to 375°F.

Combine the butter, eggs, and molasses in the bowl of an electric mixer, and blend well at medium speed. Add the remaining ingredients and slowly blend everything together. Don't overmix. Spoon the batter into paper-lined muffin tins. Bake for about 25 to 30 minutes. The muffins are done when a toothpick inserted in the center comes out clean. Serve warm.

Yields: 18 muffins

Preparation time: 40 minutes

CARROT MUFFINS

This is not quite a carrot cake, and not just a muffin. Enriched with eggs, walnuts, and raisins this is a substantial, nicely sweet addition to any breakfast.

2 cups sugar
1¼ cups safflower oil
4 eggs
3 cups unbleached white flour
2 teaspoons baking powder
1 teaspoon baking soda
½ teaspoon salt
2¼ cups grated carrots
1 cup walnuts, coarsely chopped
1 cup raisins

Preheat the oven to 350°F.

Place the sugar, oil, and eggs in the bowl of an electric mixer and mix at medium speed for about 2 minutes.

In a separate bowl, combine the flour, baking powder, baking soda, and salt, and add this to the sugar–egg mixture. Next add the grated carrots, walnuts, and raisins. With the mixer at low speed blend the dough until no trace of flour is left. With a spoon, scoop the dough into paper-lined muffin tins, filling them two-thirds full. Bake for about 35 to 40 minutes. The muffins are done when a toothpick inserted in the center comes out clean. Serve warm or at room temperature.

Yields: 20 muffins

Preparation time: 55 minutes

This is even better the next day. It lasts for weeks in the refrigerator and for up to 2 months when stored in the freezer.

CARROT CAKE

Many of my customers have asked me why my carrot cake is so special. Here is the answer.

2¼ cups sugar
1½ cups safflower oil
4 eggs
2½ cups unbleached white flour
2 teaspoons baking powder
2 teaspoons baking soda
½ teaspoon salt
1 tablespoon ground cinnamon
¼ teaspoon ground nutmeg
¼ teaspoon ground allspice
7 prunes, pitted and diced
1 cup walnuts, coarsely chopped
3 cups grated carrots

FROSTING

8 ounces cream cheese
4 tablespoons (½ stick) butter
2 cups confectioners' sugar
1 teaspoon vanilla extract
1 tablespoon grated lemon rind

Preheat the oven to 350°F.

Place the sugar, oil, and eggs in the bowl of an electric mixer. Beat at medium speed until smooth.

In a separate bowl, mix together the flour, baking powder, baking soda, salt, cinnamon, nutmeg, and allspice.

Add the prunes and walnuts to the oil–sugar mixture. Then add all the flour mixture. Beat at low speed for about 2 minutes. Add the carrots and mix to blend thoroughly.

Pour the batter into a buttered tube pan. Bake for 1 hour and 20 minutes, or until a toothpick inserted in the center comes out clean. Let the cake cool in the pan. Remove the cake to a cake plate.

To make the frosting, place all the ingredients in the bowl of an electric mixer. Beat at medium speed until smooth and creamy. Spread the frosting over and around the cake.

Yields: 12 to 16 servings

Preparation time: 1 hour 45 minutes (excluding cooling time)

Well-wrapped, this cake will stay fresh for up to 1 week in your refrigerator.

OMA'S APPLE CAKE

Oma was my Danish grandmother who developed this recipe and passed it down through three generations. She wouldn't have dreamed of adding Calvados, but it really does give the apples an added boost.

1 cup (2 sticks) butter
1 cup sugar
Rind of 1 lemon, grated
4 eggs
2 cups unbleached white flour
1 teaspoon baking powder
4 medium McIntosh apples
½ cup apricot jam
1 tablespoon Calvados
¼ cup slivered almonds, toasted
1 cup heavy cream

Preheat the oven to 350°F.

Cream the butter and sugar together in your electric mixer at medium speed until light and fluffy. Add the lemon rind. Add the eggs one at a time. Add the flour and baking powder and mix well. Spread half the batter in a buttered 9½-inch springform pan.

Peel, core, and cut the apples into eighths. Arrange the apples over the batter in a neat circle, filling all the spaces. Pour the rest of the batter over the apples, spreading it evenly.

Bake for about 50 minutes, or until a toothpick inserted in the center of the cake comes out clean. Let cool for 15 minutes, then remove outer ring of the springform pan.

Place the apricot jam and the Calvados in a small saucepan and melt over low heat. Brush the warm jam glaze all over the top and sides of the apple cake. Sprinkle the cake with toasted almonds. Serve at room temperature with lightly sweetened whipped cream.

Yields: 8 to 10 servings

Preparation time: 1 hour 15 minutes (excluding cooling time)

This pound cake will keep for up to 2 weeks when stored in the refrigerator.

LEMON LOAF CAKE

Serve this lemony pound cake with fresh fruit or with Crème Anglaise.

¾ cup (1½ sticks) butter, at room temperature
1 cup plus 2 tablespoons sugar
4 eggs, at room temperature
Grated rind and juice of 1 lemon
½ teaspoon vanilla extract
1½ cups unbleached white flour
½ cup cornstarch
½ teaspoon baking soda
1 teaspoon baking powder

GLAZE

Juice of 1 lemon
1 cup confectioners' sugar

Preheat the oven to 325°F.

Cream the butter and sugar together for about 5 minutes in the bowl of an electric mixer until the mixture is light in color. Add the eggs one at a time, beating well after each addition. Add the grated lemon rind and juice. Add the vanilla and mix well.

In a separate bowl, combine the flour, cornstarch, baking soda, and baking powder. Add the flour mixture all at once to the butter mixture. At low speed, blend for about 30 seconds until no trace of flour remains.

Pour the batter into a well-buttered 9-by-5-by-2-inch loaf pan. Bake for 1¼ hours, or until a toothpick inserted in the center comes out clean. Let cool for 10 minutes in the pan.

To make the glaze, mix the lemon juice with the confectioners' sugar and pour over the warm cake. Cool 20 minutes longer, then remove from the pan. Wrap the lemon loaf in foil to insure freshness.

Yields: 10 servings

Preparation time: 1 hour 30 minutes (excluding cooling time)

PEACH COFFEE CAKE

Here's a basic recipe in which you can use almost any fruit in season: blueberries, strawberries, rhubarb. It's quick and easy to prepare and should be eaten the same day.

½ cup (1 stick) butter
1½ cups light brown sugar
1 egg
1 teaspoon vanilla extract
1 cup milk
1 tablespoon lemon juice
2 cups unbleached white flour
1 teaspoon baking soda
1½ cups peeled and diced peaches
½ cup walnuts, chopped
½ cup sugar
1 teaspoon ground cinnamon

Preheat the oven to 350°F.

Using an electric mixer, cream the butter, light brown sugar, egg, and vanilla until it is light in color.

In a separate bowl combine the milk and lemon juice and pour this into the creamed mixture.

Again, separately combine the flour and baking soda and add that to the mixture. Beat at low speed, only until the flour and milk mixture are incorporated. Stir in the peaches with a wooden spoon.

Pour the batter into a buttered 9-by-13-inch sheet pan. Combine the walnuts, sugar, and cinnamon and sprinkle it over the cake. Bake for 40 to 45 minutes, or until a toothpick inserted in the center comes out clean.

Cut into squares and serve either warm or at room temperature.

Yields: 12 squares

Preparation time: 1 hour

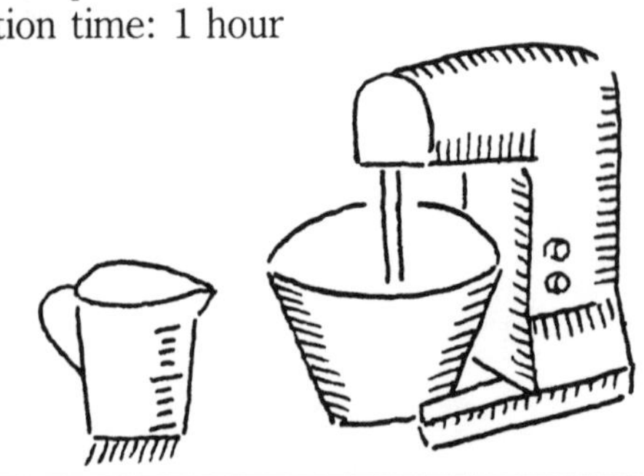

MACAROON TEA CAKE

Moist and almondy with a classic pound-cake base, this should be made a day in advance.

1¼ cups (2½ sticks) butter, at room temperature
2 cups sugar
5 eggs, at room temperature
¾ teaspoon almond extract
¾ cup milk
2¼ cups unbleached white flour
⅓ cup cornstarch
1½ cups unsweetened grated coconut
1 teaspoon baking powder
½ teaspoon baking soda
½ cup confectioners' sugar (optional)

Preheat the oven to 325°F.

Butter and flour a 9-cup bundt pan, or use any tube pan you have.

Cream the butter and sugar with an electric mixer until light in color, about 5 minutes. Add the eggs one at a time, then turn the machine to low speed and add the almond extract and milk, blending well.

In a separate bowl, mix together the flour, cornstarch, coconut, baking powder, and baking soda. Add to the butter–egg mixture all at once, mixing very well. Spoon into the bundt pan.

Bake for about 1 hour 20 minutes, or until a toothpick inserted in the center comes out clean. Let cool for about 20 minutes. Loosen the edges with a small knife. Unmold the cake onto a plate. Let cool to room temperature. Dust with confectioners' sugar, if you like, before serving.

Yields: 16 slices

Preparation time: 1 hour 40 minutes (excluding cooling time)

This cake will last for 2 weeks in the refrigerator when wrapped in foil or plastic wrap. Or you can store it for up to 2 months in the freezer.

MY MOTHER'S KAFFEBROT

My mother always served coffee at three o'clock in the afternoon and it was always accompanied by a sweet. These almond cookies are meant to be dunked in coffee.

3½ cups unbleached white flour
1⅔ cups sugar
1 teaspoon baking soda
3 eggs
1 cup (2 sticks) butter, chilled and cut into small pieces
Rind of 1 lemon, grated
¼ teaspoon almond extract
1 egg yolk, mixed with 1 tablespoon heavy cream
½ cup slivered almonds

Preheat the oven to 350°F.

Place the flour, 1⅓ cups sugar, the baking soda, eggs, butter, lemon rind, and almond extract in the bowl of a food processor fitted with a metal blade. Process until the dough masses into a ball. Scrape out onto a flat surface. Divide the dough into 4 pieces. Shape each piece into a roll 1 inch thick and 17 inches long. Place on a buttered baking sheet. Press the rolls down a bit, using a fork dipped in flour. Brush with the egg–cream mixture. Sprinkle the almonds and the remaining sugar evenly over all four rolls.

Bake for 18 minutes. Cut each roll crosswise into 1¼-inch cookies. Return the baking sheet to the turned-off oven for 30 minutes to dry.

Yields: 4 dozen cookies
Preparation time: 1 hour

If kept in an airtight cookie tin, the kaffebrot will last for up to 3 weeks.

CHOCOLATE CHIP POUND CAKE

Chocolate upon chocolate. What could be a better dessert?

5 ounces unsweetened chocolate
1⅓ cups water
2 cups unbleached white flour
2 cups sugar
1 teaspoon salt
½ cup (1 stick) butter
3 eggs
1 teaspoon vanilla extract
1½ teaspoons baking powder
¾ cup walnuts, coarsely chopped
½ cup chocolate chips

Preheat the oven to 325°F.

Combine the chocolate with the water and melt over low heat in a heavy saucepan. Let cool to room temperature. Place the flour, sugar, salt, and butter in the bowl of an electric mixer and add the melted chocolate. Mix at medium speed for about 5 minutes. Add the eggs, vanilla, and baking powder. Mix for 2 minutes more. Add the walnuts and chocolate chips and mix at low speed until blended.

Spoon the batter into a 4-by-12-inch loaf pan. Bake for 1½ hours, or until a toothpick inserted in the center comes out clean. Let the cake cool for 15 minutes. Remove the cake from the pan and let cool completely. Wrap the cake tightly in foil and store in the refrigerator for at least 24 hours before serving.

Yields: 10 servings

Preparation time: 2 hours

ANNA'S CHOCOLATE SAUCE

6 ounces semisweet chocolate
1 cup heavy cream
2 teaspoons instant Espresso coffee

Melt the ingredients together over low heat in a small saucepan, stirring contantly until completely melted and thoroughly blended. Serve on the side as a topping for Chocolate Chip Pound Cake. Vanilla ice cream or whipped cream could also be offered as a topping.

CHOCOLATE CHIP COOKIES

This is our version of our customers' favorite cookie.

1 cup (2 sticks) butter
3/4 cup brown sugar
1/2 cup sugar
2 eggs
1 teaspoon vanilla extract
2 1/4 cups unbleached white flour
1 teaspoon baking soda
12 ounces chocolate chips
1 cup walnuts, coarsely chopped

Preheat the oven to 350°F.

Cream the butter and sugars together with an electric mixer until the mixture becomes light in color. Add the eggs and vanilla. At medium speed, mix very well. Add the flour and baking soda. At low speed, mix until all traces of flour are gone. Fold in the chocolate chips and walnuts.

Drop tablespoonfuls of batter, about 3 inches apart, onto a buttered baking sheet. Press down lightly. Bake for 10 to 12 minutes, or until golden brown.

Yields: 26 large cookies
Preparation time: 20 minutes

PEANUT COOKIES

These good, simple cookies are made everyday at Loaves and Fishes, and placed in an enormous cookie jar in the front. Many people help themselves, feeling quite at home, as they browse around, selecting their dinner.

1/2 cup (1 stick) butter
1/2 cup peanut butter
1/2 cup sugar
1/2 cup dark brown sugar
1 egg
1/2 teaspoon vanilla extract
1 cup unbleached white flour
3/4 teaspoon baking soda
1 cup shelled unsalted peanuts

How do they taste?
They taste like more.
—H. L. Mencken

A plate of cookies and a cup of tea is guaranteed to cheer up any sagging spirit.

Preheat the oven to 350°F.

Cream the butter, peanut butter, and sugars with an electric mixer until light in color. Add the egg and vanilla. Beat until well mixed. Add the flour, baking soda, and peanuts. At low speed, mix until all traces of flour are gone and the batter seems well mixed.

Drop tablespoonfuls of batter, 3 inches apart, onto a buttered baking sheet. Press down lightly. Bake for 12 minutes.

Yields: 18 large cookies

Preparation time: 25 minutes

OATMEAL COOKIES

One of Loaves and Fishes most popular cookies, these are crisp on the outside and chewy on the inside.

1 cup (2 sticks) butter
3/4 cup sugar
3/4 cup dark brown sugar
1 teaspoon vanilla
1 egg
1 1/2 cups unbleached white flour
1 teaspoon baking soda
1 teaspoon ground cinnamon
1/2 teaspoon salt
1 1/2 cups old-fashioned oatmeal (instant oatmeal will not work)
3/4 cup walnuts, coarsely chopped
3/4 cup raisins

Preheat the oven to 375°F.

Cream the butter, sugars, vanilla, and egg until the mixture becomes light in color. In a separate bowl, mix the flour, baking soda, cinnamon, salt, and oatmeal. Add to the butter mixture and blend well. Add the walnuts and raisins, folding them into the batter to distribute them evenly. Drop tablespoonfuls of batter onto a buttered baking sheet 2 inches apart. Flatten slightly. Bake for 10 to 12 minutes.

Yields: 16 large cookies

Preparation time: 20 minutes

LEMON BARS

Lemony, buttery, and moist, these are exceptional, and worth every minute it takes to make them.

CRUST

3½ cups unbleached white flour
¾ cup plus 2 tablespoons confectioners' sugar
1 cup (2 sticks) butter, chilled and cut into small pieces
¾ cup (1½ sticks) margarine, cut into small pieces

FILLING

7 eggs
3½ cups sugar
½ cup plus 1 tablespoon lemon juice
⅔ cups flour
1 teaspoon baking soda

Confectioners' sugar (for topping)

Preheat the oven to 350°F.

To make the crust, place the flour, confectioners' sugar, butter, and margarine in the bowl of an electric mixer. Mix until crumbly. Press the dough into the bottom of a 17-by-12-inch baking sheet with a 1-inch rim. Bake for 15 minutes, or until the crust is just baked but not yet browned.

To make the filling, beat together the eggs, sugar, and lemon juice. Add the flour mixed with the baking soda. Beat to blend. Pour over the baked crust. Bake for 25 minutes. Let cool. Sprinkle with confectioners' sugar. Cut into bars.

Yields: 20 bars

Preparation time: 50 minutes

MADELEINES

Delicate, spongy cookies, flavored with orange, these are a perfect complement to ice cream, mousse, or pudding.

2 eggs, at room temperature
¼ cup sugar
¼ teaspoon vanilla extract
Rind of ½ orange, grated
½ cup unbleached white flour, sifted
¼ teaspoon baking powder
6 tablespoons (¾ stick) butter, melted and cooled
Confectioners' sugar (for topping)

Preheat the oven to 375°F.

Combine the eggs, sugar, and vanilla in the bowl of an electric mixer and beat until light in color. Add the orange rind, flour, baking powder, and butter. Fold the flour mixture into the egg mixture gently by hand, a little at a time. Spoon the batter into buttered and floured madeleine molds, filling each three-quarters full with batter.

Bake for 14 to 15 minutes, or until golden but not yet browned. Remove the madeleines immediately from the molds, being very careful not to break them. Let cool. To serve, dust with confectioners' sugar.

Yields: 18 madeleines

Preparation time: 30 minutes

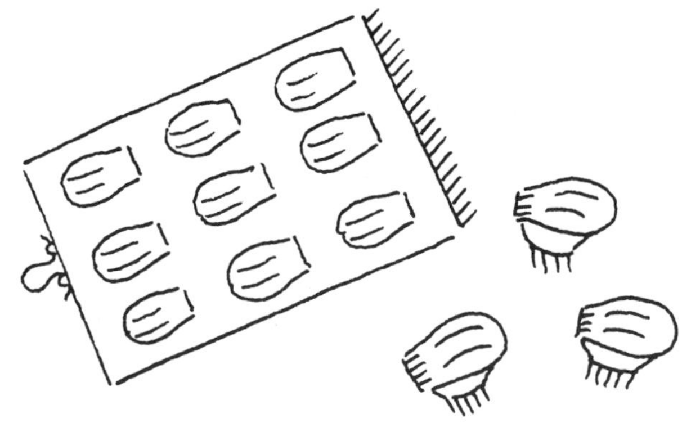

To produce the greatest volume, allow the eggs, whole or separated, to come to room temperature before beating. If you don't have time to wait for the eggs to warm, lay them in warm water for 5 minutes. The result is the same, room-temperature eggs.

She sent for one of those squat, plump little cakes called 'petite madeleines,' which look as though they had been moulded in the fluted valve of a scallop shell. . . . I raised to my lips a spoonful of the tea in which I had soaked a morsel of the cake. No sooner had the warm liquid mixed with the crumbs touched my palate than a shudder ran through me and I stopped, intent upon the extraordinary thing that was happening to me. An exquisite pleasure had invaded my senses. . . .
—Marcel Proust

DESSERTS

The setting sun, and
music at the close
As the last taste of
sweets, is sweetest last,
Writ in remembrance
more than things
long past.
—Shakespeare

At dinner one evening a novelist friend of ours was explaining how some writers construct mystery stories by starting with the last chapter first. Once they know how the story is going to end, the rest of the book is geared to keeping the reader interested, tantalized, and entertained until the surprise ending.

After everyone had gone home, I thought to myself, "That's how I sometimes plan a dinner." A really delicious idea for a dessert comes into my mind, and I begin to plan a meal around it, leading slowly up to the surprise finale. With something like Frozen Espresso Mousse, I don't prepare creamy sauces with the main course or the first course. If it's Raspberry–Walnut Pie, I try to construct the meal so that the various tastes and textures build to a point toward the finish of the meal, when a sweet pie with crunchy walnuts is exactly what the palate yearns for.

Every dinner should have a dessert. It doesn't have to be rich or heavy or terribly sweet: fresh fruit with Crème Anglaise, a scoop of Praline Mousse, or a thin slice of warm, fresh Blueberry Pie with a tablespoon of vanilla ice cream melting over the top. When they were small, my children would sometimes say, "I'm saving the best for last." I'm sure what they meant was that the memory of the last taste would linger the longest.

Once in a young lifetime one should be allowed to have as much sweetness as one could possibly want or hold.
—Judith Olney

STRAWBERRY–TRUFFLE TART

This was for one of my customers who is passionate about truffles and strawberries and asked me to find a way to combine his two favorites into a tart.

CRUST

2 cups unbleached white flour
6 tablespoons (3/4 stick) margarine, cut into small pieces
6 tablespoons (3/4 stick) butter, cut into small pieces
1 egg yolk
2 teaspoons lemon juice
1/4 cup cold water

FILLING

1/3 Truffles recipe
1 pint fresh strawberries, hulled

TOPPING

1 ounce Belgian or Swiss semisweet chocolate
2 tablespoons heavy cream

To make the crust, place the flour into the bowl of a food processor fitted with the metal blade. Add the margarine and butter. Process with an on-off motion 5 times. Add the egg yolk, lemon juice, and water all at once. Process until the dough just holds together. Scrape the dough out onto a flat surface, sprinkle with flour, and work it quickly into a ball. Wrap in plastic warp and chill for 30 minutes.

Preheat the oven to 375°F.

Roll out the dough and line a 9-inch tart pan with it. Place a 14-inch round piece of parchment paper on the tart shell and fill it with white beans. These beans can be reused for blind baking of other pastry. Bake for 30 minutes.

Remove the paper and beans and bake the tart shell for 5 minutes more. Set aside for 30 minutes.

To make the filling, spread the truffle mixture evenly over the tart shell. Arrange the fresh strawberries on top of the truffle layer.

To make the topping, melt the chocolate in a small saucepan. Add the cream and drizzle over the strawberries. This should be served at room temperature.

Yields: 6 to 8 servings

Preparation time: 1 hour 45 minutes (including refrigeration time)

CHOCOLATE RUM CAKE

A rich and moist chocolate cake with a dash of dark rum. Baked chocolate cake such as this one should always be served at room temperature.

We use a Belgian chocolate, which may not be available everywhere. You can substitute any of the following, which are all very good. You should taste each one to find your favorite. Using semisweet, very sweet, or unsweetened chocolate won't make any difference in the texture of your cake:

Baker's Unsweetened Chocolate
Baker's Semisweet Chocolate
Droste Semisweet Chocolate
Lindt Extra Bittersweet Chocolate
Maillard Eagle Sweet Chocolate

3 ounces unsweetened chocolate, broken into pieces
½ cup boiling water
1⅔ cups sugar
1½ tablespoons cocoa powder
3 eggs
1 cup (2 sticks) butter, at room temperature, cut into eight pieces
⅔ cup sour cream
2½ tablespoons dark rum
1 cup unbleached white flour
¼ cup cornstarch
1½ teaspoons baking powder
½ teaspoon baking soda

GLAZE

6 ounces semisweet chocolate
5 tablespoons heavy cream
1 tablespoon dark rum

Preheat the oven to 350°F.

Place the chocolate and boiling water in the bowl of an electric mixer and let stand for 5 minutes to soften. Add the sugar, cocoa, eggs, and butter. Cream for about 5 minutes at medium speed. Add the sour cream and rum and mix well. Add the flour, cornstarch, baking powder, and baking soda. At low speed, mix until all traces of the flour have disappeared. The mixture will be thin.

Pour the batter into a buttered 9½-inch springform pan. Bake for 50 to 60 minutes. The cake is done when there is a slight resistance in the center when pressed with a fingertip. When the cake is cool, transfer it to a serving platter.

This can be made up to 2 weeks in advance and frozen, without the top glaze. Just bring it to room temperature, glaze it, and serve. It will last for 1 week in the refrigerator.

To make the glaze, in a small, heavy saucepan, melt the semisweet chocolate over very low heat. Add the cream and rum. Stir until smooth. Pour the glaze over the cake.

Yields: 8 to 10 servings

Preparation time: 1 hour 30 minutes (excluding cooling time)

FROZEN CHOCOLATE PIE

We had to invent an irresistible dessert pie that could keep for several weeks in the freezer. The Frozen Chocolate Pie turned out to be such a popular dessert that we now have a hard time keeping the orders filled.

1 cup hazelnuts
8 ounces Belgian sweet chocolate
¼ cup unbleached white flour
¾ cup sugar
¼ cup hot water
4 eggs
¾ cup (1½ sticks) butter, at room temperature, cut into six pieces
1 tablespoon Kahlua
2 teaspoons vanilla extract

TOPPING

1 cup heavy cream
2 tablespoons sugar
1 teaspoon Kahlua

This keeps for up to 6 weeks in the freezer if well wrapped in foil. Let set for 30 minutes at room temperature before serving.

Preheat the oven to 350°F.

Process the hazelnuts and 3 ounces of the chocolate in a food processor fitted with a metal blade until coarsely chopped. Transfer to a small bowl, add the flour, and mix well.

Process the remaining 5 ounces chocolate and the sugar in the same bowl until fine. With the motor running, add the hot water. Continue processing until the chocolate has melted.

Add the eggs, butter, Kahlua, and vanilla. Process until creamy, about 30 seconds. Add the hazelnuts mixture. Process until just blended.

Pour the batter into a buttered 9-inch pie pan. Bake for 30 minutes. Let cool. Wrap the pie in foil and freeze for at least 4 hours.

Remove from freezer 30 minutes before serving.

To make the topping, whip all the ingredients until soft peaks hold. Serve with the pie.

Yields: 8 servings

Preparation time: 1 hour (excluding freezing time)

Lemon leaves are available at any florist shop.

LEMON ROLL WITH LEMON CURD FILLING

I love Lemon Roll, particularly with this filling, which is based on the traditional lemon curd in England. It is so light and lemony and looks so beautiful served on a plate blanketed with fresh, green lemon leaves.

SPONGE CAKE

6 eggs
1 cup sugar
Grated rind of ½ lemon
½ teaspoon vanilla extract
1 cup unbleached white flour
1 teaspoon baking powder
½ cup confectioners' sugar

FILLING

2 eggs
2 egg yolks
1 cup sugar
Grated rind and juice of 2 lemons
½ cup (1 stick) butter

Confectioners' sugar and lemon leaves (for garnish)

Preheat the oven to 350°F.

Butter a 7-by-12-inch baking sheet, line it with buttered parchment paper, and set it aside.

To make the sponge cake, place the eggs, sugar, lemon rind, and vanilla in the bowl of an electric mixer and beat at high speed until the mixture is light and has tripled in volume. Mix the flour with the baking powder. Using a rubber spatula, fold this in, being careful not to deflate the egg mixture too much. Pour the batter onto the prepared baking sheet with a 1-inch rim. Bake for 18 to 20 minutes, or until the sponge is very lightly browned. Let cool for 5 minutes. Then invert onto a damp kitchen towel sprinkled with the confectioners' sugar. Gently peel off the parchment paper. Carefully roll the cake lengthwise in the towel. Wrap in foil and let cool at room temperature.

To make the filling, whisk together the eggs, egg yolks, sugar, and lemon rind and juice in a heavy saucepan. Add the butter and, over low heat, cook

A LAYER CAKE

Bake sponge cake in 2 buttered 9-inch round springform pans. Fill with your favorite frosting or fruit and whipped cream.

A CHOCOLATE ROLL

Use the same basic recipe, only instead of using 1 cup flour, use ½ cup flour and ½ cup cocoa powder. To finish, sprinkle the unrolled cake with Framboise, spread it with whipped cream, reroll it, and dust the top with cocoa powder.

the lemon curd until it starts to thicken, whisking constantly. Let cool.

Unroll the cake. Cover with the lemon curd. Carefully roll the cake again, this time without the towel. Transfer to a serving platter. Dust with confectioners' sugar and garnish with lemon leaves. Chill 1 hour or longer.

Yields: 10 servings

Preparation time: 1 hour (excluding cooling times)

CHOCOLATE ESPRESSO CREAM

All you coffee and chocolate lovers out there, this is for you. For those of you who feel especially daring, heat this and pour some of it over the Lemon Roll with Lemon Curd Filling. Otherwise, it's an excellent finale to an elegant meal.

12 ounces imported semisweet chocolate
½ cup sugar
5 cups brewed espresso
1 teaspoon ground cinnamon
½ teaspoon vanilla extract
1¼ cups heavy cream

According to old tradition, coffee was discovered by a goatherd, who perceived a strange restlessness and hilarity in his flock whenever they had browsed on coffee beans.
—Brillat-Savarin

Melt the chocolate, sugar, espresso, and cinnamon together in a heavy saucepan over low heat, stirring constantly to make sure it doesn't stick. Remove from the heat. Add the vanilla, stir again, then chill for 4 hours or more.

To serve, pour into 6 large dessert glasses. Whip the heavy cream until soft peaks hold. Spoon some on top of each glass.

Yields: 6 servings

Preparation time: 15 minutes (excluding refrigeration time)

For inveterate chocolate lovers: Try pouring a trickle of hot chocolate over the mousse.

FROZEN ESPRESSO MOUSSE

This combination of espresso, chocolate, and Kahlua makes an unbeatable dessert.

3 ounces unsweetened chocolate
3 tablespoons Kahlua
3 tablespoons water
6 eggs, separated
¾ cup sugar
2 tablespoons instant espresso
1 teaspoon vanilla extract
2 cups heavy cream, whipped
2 ounces bittersweet chocolate, grated
½ teaspoon instant espresso (for garnish)

Melt the unsweetened chocolate, Kahlua, and water in a saucepan over very low heat. Cover the saucepan tightly.

Cream together the egg yolks, sugar, espresso, and vanilla until light. Add the melted chocolate and mix well. Pour into a large bowl.

Beat the egg whites separately until firm but not dry. Using a rubber spatula, gently fold the chocolate–egg mixture, egg whites, whipped cream, and grated chocolate together until no trace of white is left. Pour the mousse into one 8-cup soufflé dish, or 8 individual 1-cup ramekins. Sprinkle a little espresso on top. Freeze the soufflé dish for 4 hours, the ramekins for 3½ hours.

Yields: 8 servings

Preparation time: 30 minutes (excluding freezing time)

TRUFFLES

A holiday treat or a beautiful gift for some loving friend.

12 ounces Belgian or Swiss semisweet chocolate
½ cup (1 stick) sweet butter, cut into 8 pieces
4 egg yolks
1 tablespoon Kahlua or Framboise
½ cup cocoa powder

Preheat oven to 300°F.

Melt the chocolate in a large metal bowl set inside the preheated oven. While the chocolate is warm, add the butter, egg yolks, and liqueur. Stir vigorously until the mixture is firm enough to hold a definite shape. Using your hands, form 36 mounds and place on wax paper. Refrigerate for about 20 minutes. Then roll each truffle in cocoa powder.

Yields: 36 pieces

Preparation time: 45 minutes

These truffles can keep for up to 2 weeks in the refrigerator.

APRICOT MOUSSE

This recipe is the pleasant result of trying to find a wonderful dessert using apricots. It was an instant success. Our job was made easier by the fact that the mousse can be prepared and frozen for up to two weeks before needed.

When shopping for dried apricots, buy the lightest color you can find. They are the sweetest and best, and haven't been treated with preservatives.

1 pound dried apricots
1 cup sugar
¼ cup lemon juice
1 tablespoon Grand Marnier
5 egg whites
2 cups heavy cream

Reserving 3 apricots for garnish, place all of the rest in a saucepan, cover with water, and simmer for 30 minutes. Drain the apricots and place them in the bowl of a food processor fitted with a metal blade. Add the sugar, lemon juice, and Grand Marnier. Puree until smooth, about 15 seconds, and scrape into a large bowl.

Beat the egg whites separately until soft peaks hold. Fold the egg whites into the apricot puree. Without washing the bowl or beater, pour in the cream and whip until firm. Fold that into the apricot mixture.

Spoon the mousse into individual glasses or ramekins or into a large glass bowl. Freeze for at least 2 hours. Cut the reserved apricots into thin slivers and garnish.

Yields: 8 servings

Preparation time: 45 minutes (excluding freezing time)

This is a pie that can be prepared throughout the year. Serve slightly warmed, topped with a scoop of creamy vanilla ice cream.

RASPBERRY–WALNUT PIE

CRUST

2 cups unbleached white flour
½ cup (1 stick) butter, cut into small pieces
4 tablespoons (½ stick) margarine, cut into small pieces
1 teaspoon sugar
¼ cup cold water

FILLING

Three 10-ounce packages frozen raspberries, thawed
½ cup sugar
2 tablespoons cornstarch
1 cup walnut halves and pieces
Grated rind and juice of ½ lemon

TOPPING

1 egg yolk, mixed with 1 tablespoon heavy cream
2 tablespoons sugar

To make the crust, place the flour, butter, margarine, and sugar in the bowl of a food processor fitted with a metal blade. Pulse 5 to 6 times. With the motor running, add the water. Process until the dough starts to stick together. Scrape the mixture onto a floured surface. Quickly gather the dough and form it into a ball. Cover with plastic wrap and refrigerate for 30 minutes.

Preheat the oven to 375°F.

To make the filling, place the raspberries with their juices in a bowl and drain off 1 cup of the juice to save for another use. Combine the sugar with the cornstarch and add that to the raspberries along with the walnuts, lemon rind, and juice. Stir to blend.

To assemble the pie, roll half the pie dough into a ¼-inch-thick round disk and line a 9-inch buttered pie dish with it. Cut off the overhanging edges. Pour the filling into the shell. Roll out the remaining dough and cover the pie with it. Cut off the excess dough and crimp the edges. Brush the top with the egg yolk mixture and sprinkle with the sugar. Cut a few slits in the pie top. Bake for 50 to 60 minutes, or until evenly browned.

Yields: 8 servings

Preparation time: 2 hours (including refrigeration time)

PECAN–CRANBERRY PIE

Eggs, dark syrup, cranberries, butter, pecans, and rum—it's a fabulous holiday dessert for those who like an unusual combination of sweet, tart, and crunchy.

CRUST

1¼ cups unbleached white flour
1 tablespoon sugar
1 teaspoon baking powder
½ cup (1 stick) butter, chilled and cut into small pieces
1 egg yolk
2 tablespoons heavy cream

FILLING

6 ounces pecans
1 cup fresh or frozen cranberries
1¼ cups dark corn syrup
1 cup sugar
½ cup (1 stick) butter
4 eggs
2 tablespoons unbleached white flour
¼ cup rum

Since the cranberry season is so short, I have had to use frozen cranberries on occasion and found them to be excellent.

To make the crust, place the flour, sugar, and baking powder in a large bowl or on a floured surface. Make a well in the center. Add the butter and work it into the flour with your hands, until it has the consistency of small peas. Add the egg yolk and the cream, working quickly to form it into a smooth ball. Wrap in wax paper and chill for 30 minutes.

Preheat the oven to 350°F.

On a lightly floured surface, roll the dough into a circle about ⅛-inch thick. Wrap it around the rolling pin and unroll it over a buttered 9-inch deep-dish pie pan. Fit loosely into the pan, molding it with your hands. Cut off the overhanging dough and flute the edges.

To make the filling, cover the bottom of the crust with the pecans and the cranberries. Place the syrup and sugar in a saucepan and bring to a full rolling boil. Remove from the heat. Add the butter and stir until it is melted.

Beat the eggs, flour, and rum with an electric mixer in a mixing bowl. With the motor still running, add a little of the syrup–sugar mixture and beat for

10 seconds. Slowly add the rest of the syrup mixture, mixing constantly. Pour the liquid over the pecans and cranberries in the crust. Bake for 45 minutes, or until set.

Yields: 8 servings

Preparation time: 1 hour 45 minutes (including refrigeration time)

PRALINE MOUSSE

This is simply sublime. It takes only twenty minutes to prepare, not including freezing time. When you take it out of the freezer and present it for dessert, you will become an instant star.

1½ cups Praline Powder (see sidebar)
4 egg whites, at room temperature
½ cup sugar
2 cups heavy cream
Seeds from 1 vanilla bean
1 tablespoon Praline Powder (for garnish)

Place the 1½ cups praline powder in a medium mixing bowl and set aside.

Beat the egg whites, adding the sugar slowly until soft peaks hold. Fold the egg whites into the praline powder.

Don't wash the bowl or whisk, just pour the cream in and whip. Add the vanilla and beat until soft peaks hold. Fold the cream into the praline mixture. Pour into a 1-quart freezerproof bowl. Sprinkle with the tablespoon praline powder. Freeze for at least 4 hours before serving.

Yields: 6 to 8 servings

Preparation time: 20 minutes (excluding freezing time)

PRALINE POWDER

1¼ cups sugar
1 cup hazelnuts

Place the sugar in a medium skillet over a low heat. Stir constantly until the sugar is melted, amber colored, and liquefied. Add the hazelnuts and quickly pour the mixture onto a buttered sheet of wax paper to harden. It'll take about 15 minutes. Break up the brittle, and pulverize small amounts at a time in a blender.

Yields: 2½ to 3 cups

Preparation time: 25 minutes

If you would like to make praline candy, follow the instructions, and after it sets, break it up into bite-sized pieces. Keep stored inside an airtight container. It is crunchy and delicious.

CREAMY PUDDING WITH FRESH BLUEBERRIES

This is Sybille's recipe. She is the "pudding expert" at Loaves and Fishes and decided one day to try a variation on the basic Crème Brûlée recipe. Adding blueberries was an inspiration, and a great success. For those who enjoy crusted sugar coating, sprinkle the top with brown sugar and place the dish under the broiler until the sugar melts.

1 pint fresh blueberries, stemmed
1 tablespoon Framboise
½ cup sugar
8 egg yolks, at room temperature
2 teaspoons vanilla extract
4 cups heavy cream

Sprinkle the fresh blueberries with Framboise and set aside. Combine the sugar, egg yolks, and vanilla in a bowl. Whisk until lighter in color and set aside.

In a saucepan, bring the cream to a boil and remove from the heat. Stir in the egg mixture. Over medium heat, continue stirring until the pudding thickens, but don't let it boil. Remove from the heat and continue stirring for a few minutes.

Place the blueberries in a glass heat-resistant serving bowl or in individual dessert glasses. Pour the creamy pudding over the fruit. Chill until set, at least 4 hours.

Yields: 6 to 8 servings

Preparation time: 20 minutes (excluding refrigeration time)

BLUEBERRY PIE

CRUST

2 cups unbleached white flour
6 tablespoons (3/4 stick) butter, cut into small pieces
6 tablespoons (3/4 stick) margarine, cut into small pieces
6 tablespoons cold water

FILLING

4½ cups fresh blueberries
½ cup sugar
3½ tablespoons unbleached white flour
1½ tablespoons lemon juice
½ teaspoon ground cinnamon

TOPPING

1 egg yolk
1 tablespoon heavy cream
2 tablespoons sugar

Preheat the oven to 375°F.

To make the crust, place the flour in the bowl of a food processor fitted with a metal blade. Add the butter and margarine. Pulse 5 times. With the motor running, add the water. Process for about 5 seconds, just until the dough starts to stick together. Turn out onto a floured surface and work quickly into a ball. Cover with plastic wrap and chill for 30 minutes.

To make the filling, mix the blueberries, sugar, flour, lemon juice, and cinnamon thoroughly and set aside.

Roll two-thirds of the dough to ⅛-inch thickness, line a 10-inch buttered pie pan with it, and trim the edges. Fill the pastry shell with the blueberry mixture. Roll the remaining dough, using the leftover trimmings, into a 10-inch circle. Cover the pie with it. Flute the edges. With a sharp knife, cut a few slits in the top crust.

To make the topping, beat the egg yolk and cream together. Gently brush the top of the pie with the mixture. Sprinkle with the sugar. Bake for 45 minutes. Let cool for 30 minutes before serving.

Yields: 6 to 8 servings

Preparation time: 2 hours (including refrigeration time)

Any leftovers can be reheated for 15 minutes in a 350°F oven the next day.

COVERED APPLE TART

On one of my yearly trips to Europe, I stopped for lunch at a small town in Dijon. Lunch was lovely, but the apple tart for dessert was extraordinary. Here is my version of it; serve it with Crème Chantilly.

CRUST

2 cups unbleached white flour
1 tablespoon sugar
¼ teaspoon salt
½ cup (1 stick) margarine, cut into small pieces
4 tablespoons (½ stick) butter, cut into small pieces
1 egg yolk
6 tablespoons cold water

FILLING

6 cups tart apples, peeled, cored, and thinly sliced
⅓ cup sugar
Juice of 1 lime
1 teaspoon ground cinnamon
⅓ cup raisins
½ cup walnuts
1 tablespoon unbleached white flour

¼ cup Vanilla Sugar

To make the crust, place the flour, sugar, salt, margarine, and butter in the bowl of a food processor fitted with a metal blade. Pulse 5 times. Add the egg yolk. With the motor running, add the water. Process until the dough sticks together; this will take only 5 to 6 seconds. Remove the dough from the bowl, cover with plastic wrap, and refrigerate for 30 minutes.

To make the filling, place all the filling ingredients in a bowl, mix well, and set aside.

Cut the dough in half. Roll one piece into a circle ¼ inch thick and fit that into the bottom of a buttered 9-inch springform pan, curling the dough around the sides. Spread the apple filling evenly over the crust.

Roll out the remaining dough to a ¼-inch thickness and cover the apple mixture with it, tucking the sides of the dough into the pan with a thin spatula. Cut a few slits in the top crust. Bake for 35 to 40 minutes, or until the tart is golden brown. Let cool to room temperature before serving.

CRÈME CHANTILLY

A lightly beaten cream to serve with fresh or baked fruit tarts, or as a dessert sauce. Place 1 cup heavy cream with 1 teaspoon sugar and 1 teaspoon real vanilla extract in your electric mixer bowl. Beat at medium speed until the beater leaves light traces on the surface of the cream.

Dust the tart with Vanilla Sugar, cut into wedges, and serve.

Yields: 6 to 8 servings

Preparation time: 1 hour 30 minutes (including refrigeration time)

APPLE SHORTBREAD TART

This is an easy, buttery shortbread crust for people who don't like to make crusts. It is an old family recipe that never fails, and the cinnamon–butter topping on the tart becomes slightly crisped when baked. Try serving the pie warmed with a pitcher of chilled Crème Anglaise on the side.

CRUST

1¼ cups unbleached white flour
1 teaspoon sugar
1 teaspoon baking powder
½ cup (1 stick) butter, at room temperature, cut into eight pieces
1 egg yolk
1 tablespoon heavy cream

FILLING

7 medium tart apples, peeled, cored, and quartered
½ cup sugar
2 tablespoons butter, softened
1½ tablespoons unbleached white flour
½ teaspoon ground cinnamon

Preheat the oven to 375°F.

To make the crust, place the flour, sugar, and baking powder in a large bowl and blend. Make a well in the center and add the butter, egg yolk, and cream. Using your hands, quickly work it together until the mixture is crumbly. Press the dough into the bottom of a 9-inch springform pan.

To make the filling, arrange the apples in a circular pattern over the dough. Mix the sugar, softened butter, flour, and cinnamon in a small bowl until crumbly. Sprinkle this over the apples. Bake for about 40 minutes, or until the apples, pricked with a fork, feel done.

Yields: 6 to 8 servings

Preparation time: 1 hour

The friendly cow all red 'n white,
I love with all my heart;
She gives me cream with all her might,
To eat with apple tart.
—Robert Louis Stevenson, *A Child's Garden of Verses*

CRÈME ANGLAISE

Crème Anglaise is a wonderfully refreshing sweet custard to pour over fresh fruit, lemon pound cake, or plain white cake, and to sprinkle with berries.

This may take you a couple of tries. If the eggs curdle, throw it away and start over again. You will be eternally grateful for getting this down to a fine science. Crème Anglaise lasts for up to 4 days in the refrigerator.

4 egg yolks
1/3 cup sugar
1 3/4 cups milk
1 teaspoon vanilla extract

Place the egg yolks and sugar in a heavy saucepan and whisk until light. This should take about 2 minutes. Add the milk and whisk to blend. Set the saucepan over medium heat and, stirring constantly with a wooden spoon, heat the custard until it starts to thicken. Don't let it come to a boil, or the eggs will curdle. Remove from the heat. Add the vanilla or any flavoring you prefer. Pour the custard into a glass pitcher and let cool.

Yields: 6 servings

Preparation time: 10 minutes (excluding cooling time)

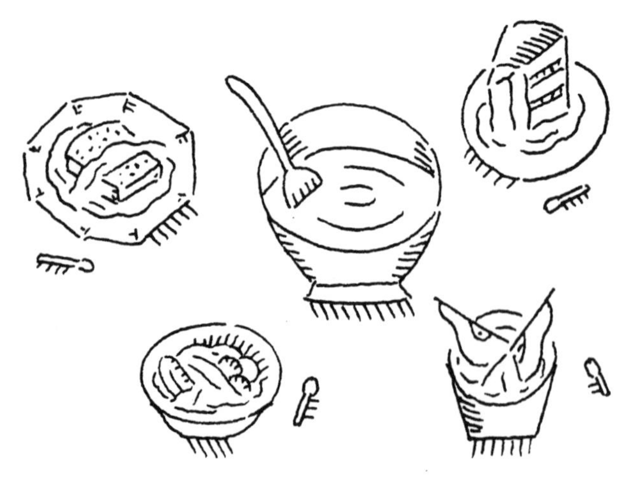

ORANGE PUDDING

A creamy custard with a distinct orange flavor, this is something you can whip up in the morning and present in the evening for dessert.

2 eggs
10 egg yolks
½ cup sugar
2 cups orange juice
4 tablespoons (½ stick) butter
Rind of 2 oranges, grated
¾ cup heavy cream, whipped with 1 tablespoon sugar

Using a wire whisk, beat the eggs, egg yolks, and sugar in a heavy saucepan for about 2 minutes, or until it is light in color. Add the orange juice. Place the saucepan over medium heat and stir constantly, using a wooden spoon, until the pudding starts to thicken. Don't let it boil, or the eggs will curdle. Remove from the heat and add the butter. Stir until the butter has melted. Stir in most of the orange rind, reserving a little for garnish.

Pour the pudding into dessert glasses. Let it set in the refrigerator for at least 45 minutes, or for up to 2 days. Top with whipped cream and garnish with the reserved orange rind.

Yields: 6 to 8 servings

Preparation time: 20 minutes (excluding refrigeration time)

Whenever you're making any kind of egg custard, as in this case with orange juice, don't leave the stove. Keep stirring the custard, and when the sides begin to develop tiny bubbles and the custard is starting to thicken, remove the pan from the stove and keep stirring for another 2 minutes to cool it down.

FRESH CRÈME WITH STRAWBERRIES AND RASPBERRY SAUCE

A special variation of Coeur de Crème. Rich and creamy, garnished with strawberries and blanketed with sweet raspberries trickling over its sides, it's a beautiful dish.

12 ounces cream cheese, at room temperature
1¼ cups confectioners' sugar
Seeds of ½ vanilla bean
2½ cups heavy cream, chilled
1 pint fresh strawberries, hulled
Two 10-ounce packages frozen raspberries in light syrup, thawed
2 tablespoons Framboise

Place the cream cheese, ¾ cup of the sugar, and the vanilla seeds in the bowl of an electric mixer and beat at medium speed until light and fluffy. Add the heavy cream and beat until the mixture holds its shape. Spoon the crème into a small wicker basket lined with 3 layers of cheesecloth. Place the basket in a pie dish and refrigerate overnight.

Puree the raspberries and remaining sugar until smooth. Stir the sauce through a strainer and discard the seeds. Add the Framboise to the raspberry sauce.

When ready to serve, unmold the crème onto a serving plate that has a ½-inch rim. Carefully remove the cheesecloth. Pour the raspberry sauce around the crème, garnish with strawberries, and serve.

Yields: 8 servings

Preparation time: 30 minutes (excluding refrigeration time)

CHOCOLATE-DIPPED STRAWBERRIES

Melt 3 ounces good semisweet chocolate along with ¼ cup heavy cream in a small ovenproof glass dish in a 200°F oven. Dip stemmed strawberries into the chocolate, placing them on a dessert dish lined with clean fresh strawberry leaves, and let set 20 minutes at room temperature. This makes a beautiful centerpiece for dessert. This amount of chocolate will cover about a pint of strawberries.

STRAWBERRIES WITH ORANGE SAUCE

When strawberries are in season, they are simply the best dessert you can serve, either with Crème Fraîche, ice cream, or by themselves. Here is an unusually delicious suggestion.

2 pints fresh strawberries
2 tablespoons Framboise
3 egg yolks
¼ cup sugar
1 cup fresh orange juice
¼ cup heavy cream
Rind of 1 orange, grated

Hull the strawberries and place them in a serving bowl. Sprinkle with 1 tablespoon of the Framboise and chill.

Place the egg yolks and sugar in a heavy saucepan and beat with a wire whisk until light in color. Add the orange juice. Place over low heat. Stirring constantly, heat the sauce until it starts to thicken; don't let it come to a boil, or the eggs will curdle. Remove from the heat. Add the cream, orange rind, and remaining Framboise. Chill the orange sauce for at least 2 hours and serve with the strawberries.

Yields: 6 servings

Preparation time: 15 minutes (excluding refrigeration time)

One must ask Children and Birds how cherries and strawberries taste.
—Johann Wolfgang von Goethe

MERINGUE SHELLS

We had to include this recipe because although the preparation time reads over two hours, only fifteen minutes are actually needed to make the meringues—the rest is baking time.

8 egg whites
2 teaspoons lemon juice
2¼ cups sugar

Preheat the oven to 225°F.

Beat the egg whites with an electric mixer until frothy. Add the lemon juice. Beating at high speed, gradually add the sugar until the meringue is glossy and stands in a peak. Spoon 10 mounds onto a baking sheet lined with parchment paper. Then, using a spoon, shape each mound into little cups. Bake for 1 hour. Leave the shells in the turned-off oven for 1 hour more to dry. Let cool. Store in an airtight container or in the freezer.

Yields: 10 shells

Preparation time: 2 hours 15 minutes (cooling time: 1 hour)

Meringue shells are delicious containers for fresh strawberries and whipped cream, or a scoop of Raspberry Ice Cream covered with hot chocolate sauce; the possibilities are limitless. What about butter pecan ice cream, hot Butterscotch Sauce, whipped cream, and a sprinkling of Praline Powder?

This is an excellent way to use your leftover egg whites.

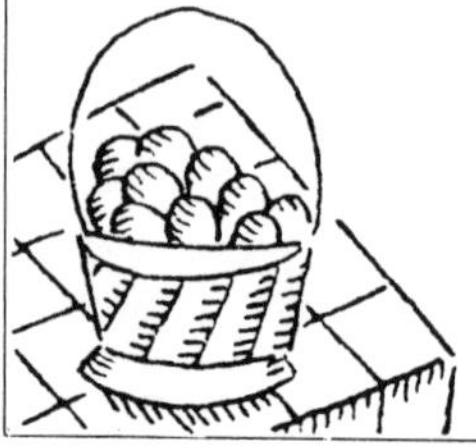

BUTTERSCOTCH SAUCE

My mother's recipe. Needless to say, warmed up, this Butterscotch Sauce is divine over vanilla Swiss almond ice cream. It is so simple to make that I doubt you'll ever buy store-bought sauce again. It also makes a beautiful gift.

¾ cup light brown sugar
½ cup light corn syrup
4 tablespoons (½ stick) sweet butter
½ cup heavy cream
½ teaspoon vanilla extract

Combine all the ingredients except for the vanilla in a heavy saucepan. Stirring constantly, bring the sauce to a boil over high heat. Boil for 5 minutes from the time it starts to bubble at a full rolling boil. Remove from the heat. Add the vanilla. Let cool slightly and serve, or pour it into a container and store in your pantry.

It will keep for 1 week. Reheat before serving, or serve cold if you like.

Yields: 1½ cups sauce

Preparation time: 10 minutes

CARAMEL CANDY

Follow the same directions, only let the sauce boil longer, maybe 10 minutes, until the consistency becomes syrupy. Pour onto parchment paper, let it set, then break it into pieces. Store in an airtight can or glass jar with a lid.

RASPBERRY ICE CREAM

2½ cups fresh raspberries or strawberries
¾ cup sugar
2 tablespoons Framboise brandy
1½ cups heavy cream

Place the fresh fruit, sugar, and Framboise in the bowl of a food processor bowl fitted with a metal blade. With the motor running, pour the cream in through the feed tube. Puree until smooth. Pour the ice cream into individual freezerproof dessert glasses or into one glass bowl. Store in the freezer until needed. If you use glasses, the ice cream will be ready in 30 minutes. A bowl of ice cream takes about 1 hour to set.

Yields: 6 servings

Preparation time: 45 minutes (including freezing time)

If fresh berries are not in season, substitute two 10-ounce packages frozen (not thawed) berries. Decrease sugar to ½ cup and proceed with recipe.

This ice cream, which can be easily made in a blender or food processor, should be eaten within 2 days. In the unlikely event you have any left over, store it in the freezer, making sure that it is covered with plastic wrap.

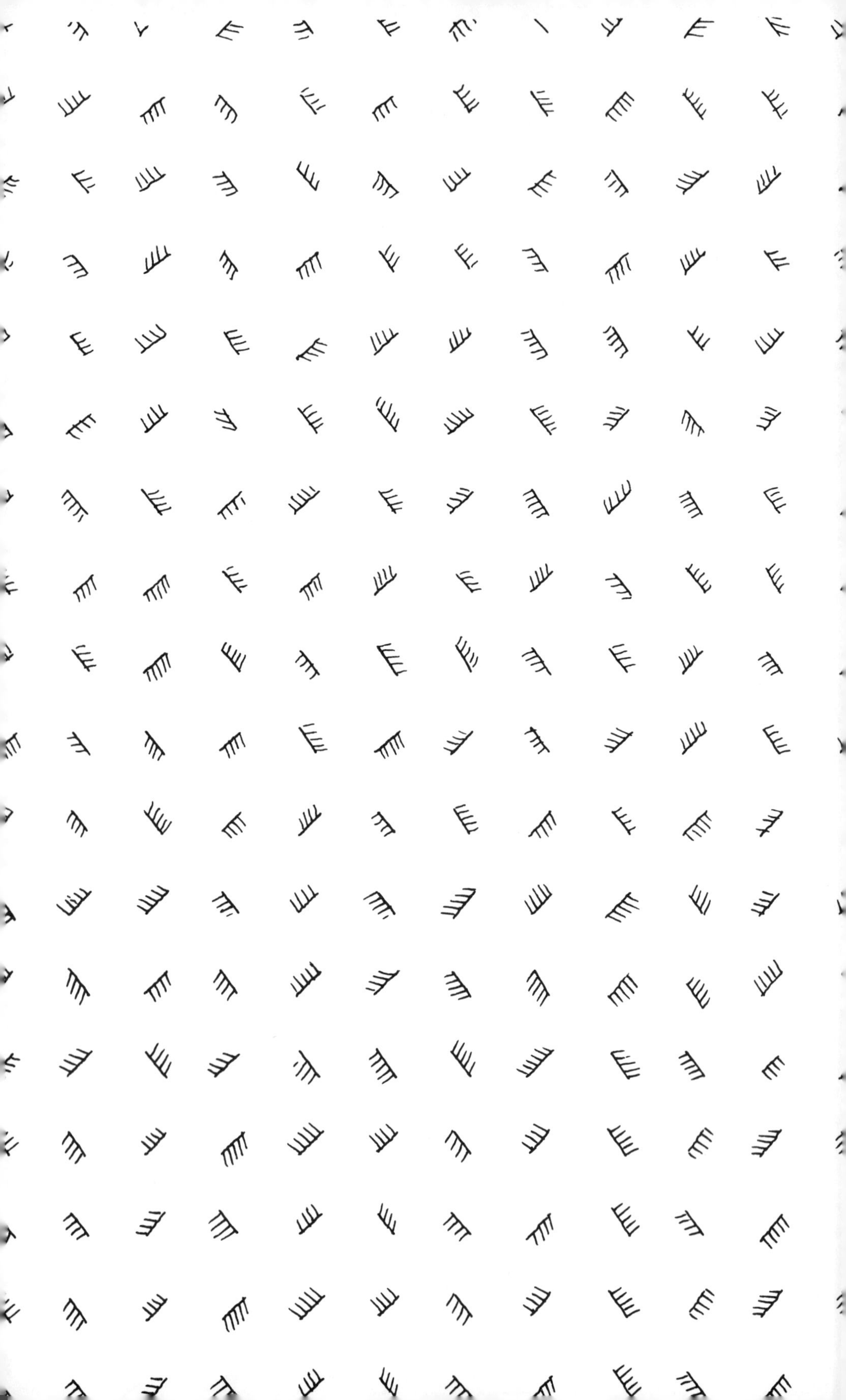

INDEX